The Social Order
of Postconflict
Transformation
in Cambodia

Modern Southeast Asia

Series Editor:
Sunil Kukreja, University of Puget Sound

Advisory Board:
Amy L. Freedman, Rachel Harrison,
Ravichandran Moorthy, and Farish A. Noor

The increased visibility and prominence of Southeast Asia and the societies therein on the global stage during the early years of the twenty-first century have attracted a deservedly rich and vibrant interest among academics, policy-makers, and social commentators. Southeast Asia collectively constitutes one of the most diverse, dynamic, and globally critical regions. This series provides a compelling platform for a diverse range of scholars to engage in discourses on the multitude of critical and timely intra-regional, trans-regional, and societal-specific analyses pertaining to Southeast Asia. The series welcomes proposals and manuscripts from the various social sciences and humanities, including contributions that profile interdisciplinary scholarship which makes a distinctive contribution to the understanding of Southeast Asia.

Recent Titles in Series

The Social Order of Postconflict Transformation in Cambodia: Insurgent Pathways to Peace by Daniel Bultmann

The Social Order of Postconflict Transformation in Cambodia

Insurgent Pathways to Peace

Daniel Bultmann

LEXINGTON BOOKS
Lanham • Boulder • New York • London

Published by Lexington Books
An imprint of The Rowman & Littlefield Publishing Group, Inc.
4501 Forbes Boulevard, Suite 200, Lanham, Maryland 20706
www.rowman.com

6 Tinworth Street, London SE11 5AL, United Kingdom

British Library Cataloguing in Publication Information Available

Library of Congress Cataloging-in-Publication Data Available

ISBN 978-1-4985-8054-0 (cloth : alk. paper)
ISBN 978-1-4985-8055-7 (electronic)

∞™ The paper used in this publication meets the minimum requirements of American National Standard for Information Sciences—Permanence of Paper for Printed Library Materials, ANSI/NISO Z39.48-1992.

Printed in the United States of America

Contents

Acknowledgments

While conducting research on the social structure and transition to peace of the three Cambodian insurgent groups over the years, I was able to talk to countless individuals who shared with me their life stories and their knowledge of the field of study, its history and the inner workings of the armed groups. Many of these people also helped me access people, institutions, and materials in their networks. I am deeply grateful for their support, which forms the very basis of this book. For reasons of anonymity and confidentiality, many of these enablers, friends, and guides will have to remain nameless. I would also like to thank the German Research Foundation (DFG) for their generous funds within the research project "Strategies of Conversion" (reference BU 3104/1–1) without which this project would not have been possible, and the publisher Lexington Books for their trust in this project and editorial support, which came especially from Brian Hill and Julia Torres as editors of the Asian studies list. Lexington also managed to find a very helpful reviewer for the book manuscript. This anonymous reviewer provided tremendously thoughtful, constructive, and comprehensive comments on an earlier version of this book. Reviews are not always pleasant affairs, but this one certainly was.

I would also like to thank Kem Sos, who secretly and effectively guided me through various Cambodian communities; Rik Chor for going on long journeys with me and sharing his comprehensive knowledge and networks; Teng Koy-Try, Sirey Muny, Khun Ratanak, and Kai-Uwe "Otto" Kolar for their assistance in the field and in transcribing, translating, and analyzing the material; Deth Sok Udom and Eng Sothy for their support as scientists and even more as friends; Boike Rehbein for his patient guidance, patronage, and support; and last but not least, an—unfortunately—anonymous language editor, who was not only of great help improving my clumsy English but who herself proved to be highly knowledgeable in the field of study, turning out to be an indispensable interlocutor and commentator on my work.

Two institutions were also vital to the project by providing information and materials. Jennifer Huntley from the Special Collections of the Academy Library at the UNSW Canberra, Australia, provided guidance and materials from the John Sanderson Collection. The Documentation Center of Cambodia (DC-Cam) under Chhang Youk shared documents, background knowledge, and access routes to respondents formerly with the Khmer Rouge.

Writing my fourth book in four years was only possible through the support of my family: my wife Johanna and my children Mathilda and Jonathan. They accompanied me to the field, served as my beloved refuge (not only in times of heightened distress), and provided a deeper meaning for this work.

Parts of this book, notably the chapter on the strongmen, are slightly amended and updated versions of my article "Insurgent Groups During Post-Conflict Transformation: The Case of Military Strongmen in Cambodia," *Civil Wars* 20, no. 1 (2018): 24–44. Some interview quotations are reproduced and adapted from my book *Inside Cambodian Insurgency. A Sociological Perspective on Civil Wars and Conflict.* Burlington, MA/Farnham, UK: Ashgate, 2015. Reproduced with permission of the Licensor through PLSclear.

Introduction

The first Cambodian "strongman" (*boroh khlang* in Khmer) I met asked me to come to his villa in central Phnom Penh, the Cambodian capital. After entering the heavily secured compound, with a villa consisting of two separate buildings behind high fences and barbed wire, I sat down in a spacious office packed with lavish furniture made of luxury wood and large flat-screen TVs. Before I was allowed to talk to the respondent, I had to talk with some of his watchdogs: a row of armed bodyguards and, finally, his personal assistant, who engaged in small talk with me for an hour to glean information about my intentions and personal background. Without this initial screening, which oscillated between chatting about Cambodia and its beauties and my personal life in Germany, the interview would almost certainly not have been allowed to proceed. Two hours after our scheduled meeting time, the strongman arrived in a one-year-old Mercedes Benz GLK, only to leave again to another room on the compound for another hour for "refreshment." It took four hours, countless rounds of small talk, dozens of snacks and fruits, and two bottles of expensive Fiji water until the strongman finally entered the room. Throughout the interview, he spoke in high praise of the current government—his former enemy. Six years later, he, like many other strongmen, was arrested on charges of drug trafficking.

The second strongman I met was very similar in physical appearance, with a body completely covered in tattoos for magical protection and countless battle scars. We met, however, at his poorly cobbled together wooden house in the so-called "camp village" (*phum djumrum* in Khmer), a small settlement near the city of Battambang where inhabitants from the refugee camps along the border had been resettled during the early 1990s.[1] Here he worked as a knife sharpener and lived as a devout born-again Christian. Throughout the interview, which he started off by testing my knowledge of the weaponry used during the Cambodian civil war, he clasped a Bible in his hands and offered water from a purification device. When talking about the government, however, he engaged in anti-Vietnamese conspiracies and slurs. When talking about the insurgent movement, he likewise spoke with hatred for his former brothers-in-arms.

Both of these strongmen had a very similar social background and life course. They came from poor families but made a steep career ascent during the civil war as hardened warriors, ultimately controlling hundreds of men within highly independent units that presided over refugee camps and cross border trade. Both were feared for their violent and aggressive behavior and claimed to be unwoundable in combat. Their rise in status was built upon their warrior charisma, a symbolic resource that lost value drastically during the transition to peace.

The pathway to peace was very different for these two respondents. While one was able to make use of his wartime resources and served in a high position in the government for a long time, at the time of the interview—and as later developments suggest rightly so—he appeared to feel unsafe even in his heavily secure villa compound. The other was not able to transfer his wartime status and resources to the peacetime milieu, and became impoverished during integration, failing to glean any support from his former allies within the insurgent movement along the Thai border.

Stories and differences in pathways like this led to the central research question of this study. While examining the inner structure and functioning of Cambodian guerrilla factions for an earlier project, the current whereabouts and living conditions of the former soldiers and commanders increasingly sparked my interest. While some are impoverished, others make a decent living or even became rich, meeting me for interviews in luxurious hotel restaurants in the capital. But these riches and high positions also came with risks, as is evidenced by the first strongman's fate.

The post-conflict transformation of armed groups and the trajectories for the individuals who fought in them are impossible to explain by sole reference to Disarmament, Demobilization and Reintegration (DDR) efforts, especially in Cambodia, where DDR was halted during the peace mission known as the UN Transitional Authority in Cambodia (UNTAC). Instead of focusing on programs and their failures and successes, this book aims to examine the social logic behind a largely endogenous process that lies at the base of peace-building as a social engineering project (Chandler 2017). The book treats armed groups as social fields consisting of multiple milieus and social groups and asks how these fields, as entities with varying hierarchies in command and social status, transition into a society at peace. On a sociological level, it asks how social fields, which provide resources and valuations to their members, dissolve. Only a small margin of the transition, at best, is affected by DDR programs—in Cambodia and in general.

By making use of the theory and concepts of Pierre Bourdieu, the main thesis of the book is that the trajectories and transition strategies pursued by individuals within the field of insurgency are shaped by their habitus and the economic, social, cultural, and symbolic resources at their disposal. Depending on their habitus, social status, and resources, groups within the field have different levels of preparation to handle the transition and establish a post-war status of their choosing. Their pathways are heavily predisposed by their social milieus of origin and their positions within the insurgent group's social structure, while the process is based upon and guided by social hierarchies and inequalities between the agents. The respondent's social position, habitus, and the resources at his disposal led to a high level of path dependency during transition. Each "habitus group" followed its own pathways to peace. By theorizing these social mechanisms during transition, the book offers a sociological theory of post-conflict transformation that distinguishes between different social groups and the trajectories emanating from their respective social positions.

Empirically, this study deals with three Cambodian insurgent groups that formed a troubled Coalition Government of Democratic Kampuchea (CGDK) throughout the 1980s and continued to cooperate during the 1990s: the Khmer People's National Liberation Front (KPNLF) and its military wing, the Khmer People's National Liberation Armed Forces (KPNLAF); the royalist Front Uni National pour un Cambodge Indépendant, Neutre, Pacifique, et Coopératif (FUNCINPEC) and its military wing, the Armée Nationale Sihanoukiste (ANS), which was later renamed the National Army of Independent Kampuchea (ANKI); and lastly, the Party of Democratic Kampuchea (PDK), better known as the Khmer Rouge, and its military wing, the National Army of Democratic Kampuchea (NADK).

The book dissects and analyzes the trajectories and underlying social mechanisms guiding the strategies of different "habitus groups" within the field of conflict in Cambodia. It shows that even during massive changes, such as the transformation to peace, social inequalities were still reproduced. Yet each group faced different challenges in securing a position in a society at peace. Accordingly, each habitus group had different motives, potentials, and trajectories for a relapse into armed conflict. To put it simply, the desire to take up weapons again returns when agents do not receive the positions they believe they are entitled to in view of their milieu of origin and social status within the field of insurgency. This dynamic during reintegration can be understood through the lens of the theory of relative deprivation, most famously described by Ted Gurr in a classic study on reasons "why men rebel" in the first place (Gurr 1970).

Respondents for whom civil war meant a loss in status (the political elite, for instance) tried to secure a return to a pre-war social status. And those for whom civil war meant a rise in status (the strongmen, for instance) tried to maintain their war-related gains. The social status that these commanders and soldiers feel entitled to can only be understood by taking their whole life courses into account, along with their symbolic universes. Therefore, an analysis of social status needs to account for its diachronic developments through the respondent's life course and how these are interpreted. In the end, the decisive element seems to be what the respondents saw as a fitting position for themselves in an arbitrary but naturalized social order. While symbolic violence—in complicity with a naturalized order—explains why many accepted their post-war fates, a break with this symbolic universe that allocates and naturalizes positions within society leads to open or lingering resistance against the peace process.

Hence, during transition, all habitus groups either tried to return to the pre-war status that they lost or to secure the gains they achieved during war. While most were able to do exactly that, some experienced status losses that triggered at least the articulation of a wish to fight on, or heavy and at times racist anti-government sentiments depicting the ruling elite as "Vietnamese" and anti-Khmer. Their social background, their pathways into a society at peace, and their behavior during transition help us better understand potential motivations for "spoiling" the peace process (Stedman 1997). Most decisive for the post-conflict trajectory and behavior of different groups within the ranks of these armed organizations are their habitus, their social status, and the quality and strength of their vertical and horizontal social resources.

The book claims that the transformation to peace and its obstacles cannot be understood without taking the whole social field into account: its internal structure, its symbolic hierarchies, and the composition of its networks. Cambodia is a particularly good example through which to study the differing pathways to peace since demobilization efforts during the UNTAC peace mission largely failed, which is why very different modes of "reintegration" can be found, stretching over the course of roughly eight years. The Cambodian peace process saw a peace agreement, the formal demobilization of two non-state armed groups, their formal merger into a state military, ongoing resistance by the Khmer Rouge, and lingering conflicts within the newly formed state military erupting in factional clashes in mid-1997 followed by back-door deals between the victorious Cambodian People's Party (CPP) and the defeated commanders of the opposition. Certain social groups, such as the strongmen, fought until the very end; some eventually made deals, while others, for specific reasons, did not. Other groups, such as members of the military elite of several predecessor governments, who viewed guerrilla warfare as a loss in status in the first place, quickly reintegrated at the first possible opportunity and did not participate in the subsequent factional clashes. Taking a holistic look at the post-conflict pathways of the whole field of insurgency provides a new perspective on the extensive literature on the (re)integration of non-state armed groups and the process of conflict transformation.

BRINGING THE SOCIAL BACK IN: TOWARDS A SOCIOLOGY OF POST-WAR TRANSITIONS

Much of the literature on the (re)integration of armed groups focuses on DDR as a collection of projects that come relatively early in international interventions and exist to dismantle insurgent and/or incumbent militaries, to collect their weaponry and reduce small arms circulation, and to assist ex-combatants in their short- and long-term efforts to start new lives as civilians. There has been a wide range of well-considered research shedding light on the successes and failures of such programs (e.g., de Vries and Wiegink 2011, Shibuya 2012, Podder 2012, Özerdem 2012). However, while many studies doubt that DDR processes will yield any statistically measurable successes (Muggah 2010, Pugel 2009), others are often heavily geared toward upgrading specific programming efforts, and therefore focus on project management improvements. But as Stina Torjesen argues, instead of focusing on the narrow program perspective, reintegration should be treated as a holistic process:

> It is a mistake, however, to use the actual project initiatives designed to help some combatants as a starting point for research on reintegration. Such an approach directs scholarly attention away from larger social, political and economic processes associated with combatants exiting from armed groups, and towards short-term and narrow project activities. In order to best increase our knowledge of how ex-combatants come to take part in the social, political and economic structures of conflict-ridden societies we need to move away from technical and narrow assessments of project activities. Instead we need to start with the ex-combatants themselves and their encounters with social, political and economic challenges. (Torjesen 2013, 2)

Torjesen also points to the fact that, in most cases, "reintegration" is a misnomer, as it implies that armed groups are cut off from social relations during war, which they clearly are not, even if they are operating from geographically remote areas (this study is also a case in point, showing how social differences are reproduced during the inception and transformation of armed groups). I would add that it also implies a clear political order and hierarchy in which certain groups are declared external and insurgent, even though they might view themselves as the rightfully incumbent military. In the Cambodian case, the "insurgent" groups could also be considered "incumbent" since they retained the UN seat as the legitimate Cambodian government until 1991. Accordingly, many respondents, especially those from the old military elite that was deposed by the Khmer Rouge in 1975, viewed themselves as the rightful government, which during the peace process and eventual UN peace mission "received" the insurgent structures of the Hun Sen "faction." This shows that the term "reintegration" carries many problematic political connotations, of which we should at least be aware.

Yet while much of the literature referenced above is bound to the perspective of drafting and managing DDR programs, thereby losing theoretical depth, other work focuses heavily on individuals, thereby losing a sense of embeddedness in the field. This type of work also tends to focus only on ex-*combatants*, the fighting rank and file of a military. However, commanders from the top and mid-range of a military organization are decisive in the politics of conflict transformation and should receive attention as potential "spoilers" (Bhatia and Muggah 2009). They are also key in understanding the behavior of armed networks as a whole. Especially early DDR research placed a heavy focus on economic reintegration and the "proper" use of monetary incentives to convince soldiers to pursue civilian goals (Willibald 2006, Gilligan, Mvukiyehe, and Samii 2013). Focusing solely on the rank and file of an movement in order to understand potential factors spoiling peace efforts can be viewed as an act of "symbolic violence" in which frontline soldiers alone are made responsible for the eventual fate of a peace process (Bultmann 2018b).

Many authors have already criticized the vast number of studies trying to upgrade the relatively static program modules and measurements of effectiveness in DDR efforts and the Integrated DDR Standards of the UN (UNDDR 2017), which do not do justice to the complexities of social and military relations and identities in armed groups (cf. Marriage 2010). They point to the narrowness of a "one-size-fits-all" template and the "provider perspective," in which the proper allocation of goods and incentives is the most intense focus of academic interest (Özerdem and Knight 2004, Perrazone 2017, Berdal and Ucko 2010). The provider perspective becomes most obvious when studies are constructed based upon the binary distinction between demobilized combatants who took part in demobilization programs and those who did not (for a critique see Söderstrom 2011).

Many statistical studies yield important insights in understanding the short- and long-term perspective of peace processes, but limit their analysis to examining the necessary socio-political and economic conditions for successful reintegration by the "receiving" society, or the structure and sequencing of interventions using large N-data to detect characteristics of countries with successful or failed reintegration processes, respectively (e.g., Doyle and Sambanis 2000, Glassmayer and Sambanis 2008, Fortna 2004). Social differences between soldiers and commanders are rarely discussed (a notable exception being Humphreys and Weinstein 2007). The overall social structure of these groups, their internal organization and functioning, their ideological differences, and their power relations are also frequently ignored.

In most studies, armed groups are treated either as "loose molecules," disregarding organizational structures and relations, or as unitary strategic entities whose internal differences are irrelevant to reintegration. The first approach focuses entirely on the micro-level, while the second type has a clear macro perspective, but both lack an intermediate level of analysis (Bultmann 2018a). Only few studies take the meso-foundations of reintegration into account—looking at, for example, the impact of network structures on the success of DDR processes (Cardenas, Gleditsch, and Guevara 2018) or the spatiality of post-conflict violence (Zukerman Daly 2016).

Very few studies work with qualitative research methods trying to understand the motives of ex-combatants (e.g., Uvin 2007). This becomes most obvious in the discussion of "spoilers" that goes back to Stephen Stedman, who developed a typology of motivation for potential spoilers and a corresponding set of possible responses: 1) "limited" motives of belligerents, whose resistance might be met by minor changes in the peace process to trigger their willingness to cooperate (response: inducement), 2) "greedy" motives of those who try to secure their war sinecures, which can be addressed by adjusting aspects of peace dividends and acceding to their financial demands (response: socialization), and 3) "total" motives, whose aims are unalterable and can only be met by force (response: coercion) (Stedman 1997, Alden, Thakur, and Arnold 2011, 21).

The motives that lead ex-combatants to return to fighting or avoid peace processes in the first place are often not developed by in-depth study, but by mere speculation ("they must be greedy") that neatly fits into the argument that has long been prevalent in the literature that economic benefits are the origin of warfare in general (Collier 2000, Collier and Hoeffler 2004, Collier and Sambanis 2005) due to the opportunism of so-called warlords turning warfare into a lucrative business they do not wish to lose (MacKinley 2007, Robinson 2001, Vinci 2007, for a critique compare, Perrazone 2017). While the effectiveness of peace missions, their programs and single modules, and the prerequisites of effective program planning have been tested several times, very few studies have tried to systematically examine the motives of belligerents and their pathways to peace (an exception combining aggregate data and in-depth interviews can be found in Fortna 2008).

The following study reflects and furthers a stronger focus in current DDR research and program planning focusing on sustainable and long-term development of reintegration—a focus on the R-phase of DDR. The UN currently defines reintegration as "the process by which ex-combatants acquire civilian status and gain sustainable employment and income. [It] is [. . .] a social and economic process with an open timeframe, [. . .] taking place [. . .] at the local level. It is part of the general development of a country and a national responsibility, and often necessitates long-term external assistance" (UNDDR 2017, section 4.30, 2). While DDR packages were initially mere support instruments embracing short-term security goals within the clearly defined time frame of an intervention, project planning and research within the so-called "second generation" currently entails a strong long-term perspective on reintegration and development:

> Nested within a 'peacebuilding' paradigm, DDR evolved from pursuing spoiler management strategies to occupying a central place in ensuring sustainable peace through military, humanitarian and development activities. Yet, after three decades of practice and institutional development, DDR—and its 'R-phase' in particular—is still prone to programmatic and implementation weaknesses. (Perrazone 2017, 255)

By showing how the habitus and the different resources possessed by groups within the wider subset of armed combatants (different ranks) leads them to pursue divergent strategies during post-conflict transition, this book shows how inequalities and hierarchies among these groups of belligerents are transmitted from pre-conflict society, through the conflict, to be reproduced within a post-conflict setting. The current literature on post-conflict transitions tends to come from an individualist methodological standpoint, looking at combatants as economic agents abstracted from social relations, and leading to an emphasis on "providers" of "incentives." However, this study adds to a literature focusing on the political order (Porto, Alden, and Parsons 2007, Barma 2017) and state-building processes (Giustozzi 2012) by bringing the social back into the conceptualization of post-conflict transformations. It also adds to an emerging literature making use of Bourdieu's theory and methodology for the analysis of conflicts (Münch 2018, Bultmann 2015, Metelits 2018), peacekeeping forces (Goetze 2017), and post-conflict politics (Hensell and Gerdes 2017).

METHODOLOGY AND ACCESS TO THE FIELD

The study is based upon 168 qualitative interviews with commanders and soldiers from each rank of the three insurgent militaries: the KPNLAF, the ANS/

ANKI, and the NADK (105 of these interviews are cited in the book). Data for each "habitus group" consists of at least fourteen to eighteen interviews supported by additional documentary material (such as field notes, photographs of the living conditions, or archival documents from the UNTAC period). However, this study deals with the military wings of these groups only. Its research design excludes all members who had solely political functions. This distinction was not always as clear-cut as one might expect, leaving the exact line to the researcher to draw. Within the Khmer Rouge, in particular, the line between politics and influence on warfare strategies and tactics was very blurry. Members of the military directorate, for example, were also members of the Central Committee. And people like Pol Pot and Nuon Chea were not just political figures but had direct or indirect command of the forces.

Depending on the respondents' wishes, the interviews were conducted either in Khmer or English. Before starting the interviews, all respondents were informed that the gathered information would be treated confidentially and that they would remain anonymous using the coding system applied in this book. Even though most did not actually care much about confidentiality and anonymity, it was important to some (especially within the higher ranks). All gave their formal consent to be interviewed on tape (since many were illiterate). The Cambodian Ministry of Defense issued a research permit but did not extend it during the second research trip (most likely due to changes in the political climate at that time). However, very few respondents—all from the upper ranks of the Khmer Rouge—actually wanted to see the permit. Meetings took place during seven field trips from 2011 to 2017. Due to the diaspora's important role as a space for refuge for military leaders and political support, research also included field trips to communities in the United States (Washington D.C., Lowell, Long Beach, Fresno, and Oakland), Thailand (Bangkok and Sukhothai) and France (Paris). Most interviews, however, were conducted in the cities of Phnom Penh, Battambang, Pailin, Anlong Veng, Samraong, and Svay Sisophon, and in small villages in the countryside, usually in provinces along the Thai border.[2] As mentioned before, some data was gathered from 2011 until 2014 for an earlier project on habitus and disciplinary practice within the three insurgent groups (Bultmann 2015, 2014).

The interviews followed the method of habitus hermeneutics and included open questions on different stages of the respondents' life courses (cf. Bremer 2005, Vester-Lange 2007, Jodhka, Rehbein, and Souza 2017). Among others, the study builds upon Ralf Bohnsack's "documentary method" in the interpretation of these life course interviews, attempting to operationalize Pierre Bourdieu's concept of habitus and construct habitus types in an inductive way (cf. Bohnsack 2013). The life course interviews comprised questions on family background, childhood, parenting style, education, recruitment into armed groups, professional career in the military, and most decisive experiences during the Khmer Rouge regime and the civil war, with more extensive questions on the pathway to peace and the respondents' movement out of insurgency, as well as their current living conditions. All interviews were transcribed in their original language and then—if necessary—translated line by line into English.

Interviews with respondents were facilitated through several access routes. First, contacts from the US State Department (a Cambodian who served as an intermediary between the guerrilla groups and the US government during the 1980s) and UN officials who had been working along the border brokered access to respondents. Second, a former monk and member of a Buddhist organization within the refugee camps, who had many contacts through the religious counselling and guidance he provided to combatants and commanders, made many interviews possible and helped to build trust during initial talks over the project, its aims and purpose, and its terms of confidentiality and anonymity. Third, a research permit (at least at the beginning) allowed the researcher to access leading commanders who had defected to the government.

Fourth, after gaining insight and trust into the research project and the researcher as a person, former respondents brokered interviews with their superiors or underlings (the "snowball" principle). And last but not least, the researcher traveled to several "strongholds" of the guerrilla factions: Anlong Veng, Pailin, Samlaut and Veal Veng for the Khmer Rouge; and Samraong, several villages close to Battambang and along the border, and the so-called "camp villages" for FUNCINPEC and KPLNF. Local authorities were asked for permission to talk with respondents. This facilitated contacts through networks of local authorities (usually themselves former members of these groups) as well as the opportunity to go door-to-door talking to people without being directly referred to them.

Since interview data could not always be trusted in assessing the income and economic resources of the respondents, assessments through interviews were supported by observation methods, field notebooks, and photographs. When a respondent, for instance, claims to earn "a few hundred dollars," but invites the researcher to one of the most expensive hotel restaurants in Phnom Penh and appears in an expensive Lexus SUV, the claim of poverty seems to reflect not so much the truth as a picture he wants to paint to a foreign academic familiar with negative discourses on corruption surrounding the Cambodian political establishment.

Still, this qualitative methodology is neither comprehensive nor without limits and pitfalls, especially when it comes to the study of armed groups and their modes of post-conflict transformation. One serious limitation is a lack of access to certain groups. In this study, some groups could not be interviewed fully enough to create a complete picture, leaving their depiction sketchy. This was the case with Khmer Rouge leaders, many of whom are either dead or in prison. This was also the case for female Khmer Rouge combatants. Many respondents from the upper ranks of the Khmer Rouge were afraid of being implicated in the investigations of the ongoing tribunal to try international crimes committed during the Khmer Rouge era, the Extraordinary Chambers in the Courts of Cambodia (ECCC). They also feared saying something about colleagues and former superiors that might get them in trouble. Judicial investigators showing up in villages to read out indictments without official backing, and rumors about investigators disguising themselves as researchers, made things considerably worse (cf. Hennings 2017, 9).

On top of that, some deal-makers with lucrative positions in the post-conflict elite were not willing to be included in life course interviews about their pathways into the government or the state military. But surprisingly, others did not worry about my intentions and after only minor assurances of anonymity and confidentiality, they were willing to share their life histories and even openly criticize the ruling party. This also tells us a lot about the current state of affairs in Cambodian politics, in which loyalties seem clear on the surface, but become more complicated as soon as one takes a closer look. In the end, there are certainly more habitus groups within the field of insurgency than accounted for in this study. The ones discussed here are the ones the author could access, gather sufficient data on and whose habitus formation and resources seemed to help explain the post-conflict trajectory of their lives.

The book is divided into eight chapters. The first chapter provides a short overview of the history of the Cambodian conflict and the transition to peace. It aims at explaining specific conflict lines, the hierarchies and histories of the different warring factions, and the different opportunities for these groups for a transition to peace. Each group and different subsections within these groups had different windows of opportunity to reintegrate into Cambodian society, the military or the state apparatus. These different stages and opportunities are essential for an understanding of the pathways to peace for the "habitus groups" analyzed in this study in the following chapters. The second chapter explains the social structure of the insurgent military and the theoretical instruments used here to study habitus, different types of resources, and group formation. It explains central concepts taken from Pierre Bourdieu, how these concepts help to understand peace and conflict dynamics, and how, in turn, the studied dynamics might shed light on Bourdieu's concepts and methodology. The study of a social field in transition, however, necessitated several amendments to Bourdieu's approach and methodological tools.

The third, fourth, and fifth chapters deal with the strategies of the habitus groups during "reintegration" and the mechanisms guiding their post-conflict transition into other social fields. Chapter 3 deals with leadership groups, chapter 4 with the mid-range in command, and chapter 5 with the rank-and-file soldiers respectively. Chapter 6 turns to the symbolic reconstruction of Khmer Rouge combatants and mid-range commanders, so-called "blank pages," who tried to construct a narrative of religious conversion in order to mark a transition to completely new and peaceful selves, or to stake their place in ongoing struggle for democracy and national unity. Chapter 7 turns to female combatants of the Khmer Rouge. The Khmer Rouge proclaimed equality between men and women and had many female cadres, combatants (with one unit of entirely female combatants), and even some commanders in the mid-range of their military. However, their gains in social status during war were limited in time and scope.

The last chapter of the book, chapter 8, closes the analysis of the field of insurgency by discussing the role of the diaspora as a support base and a refuge for some higher-ranking commanders. The insurgency has been a transnational field from the beginning, not only because of how many refugees resided on Thai soil, but also because of leaders who commuted between the diaspora and the border, and the organizational and political support the insurgencies received from communities in the US and France. This official as well as unofficial support was also relevant to the pathways to peace; some insurgents, for instance, returned to the diaspora, while others received financial support to live in post-conflict Cambodia.

NOTES

1. Another small "camp village" is located near the city of Pursat.

2. These interviews were conducted either in Khmer or English—in Cambodia with the assistance of Koytry Teng and Sirey Muny and in Thailand with the assistance of Kai-Uwe "Otto" Kolar. All interviews were transcribed and translated into English with the further assistance of Ratanak Khun in Berlin. Material gathered during 2011 and 2012 was also used in part for an earlier project on the social structure of the CGDK and its power practices (Bultmann 2014, 2015).

Chapter One

A Short History of the Cambodian Conflict and Peace Process

After a parliamentary coup against the head of state and former king, Prince Norodom Sihanouk, by General Lon Nol and Prince Sirik Matak in 1970, Cambodia devolved into chaos (Kiernan 2004, Chandler 2008). A five-year civil war ensued, pitting the US-backed Khmer Republic, led by Lon Nol, against the Communist Party of Kampuchea (CPK), better known as the Khmer Rouge, which was strengthened by the support of its new ally, Norodom Sihanouk, and the backing of China, as well as US carpet bombings in the country's east and the infiltration of North and South Vietnamese troops. The Khmer Rouge, under the leadership of Saloth Sar (better known by his *nom de guerre,* Pol Pot), finally seized power on April 17, 1975, and immediately started a program of rapid socioeconomic transformation (Kiernan 2002). The attempt to create a purely Socialist utopia, in which each individual—in theory at least—was to be considered an equal in a modern largely agrarian-based collectivist order, resulted in the immediate expulsion of all city dwellers into forced labor in the countryside, and the eventual deaths of 1.6 to 2.2 million people due to executions, starvation, overwork, and illness (Tabeau and Kheam 2009).[1]

What is less known is that resistance against the communist regime began from day one (Corfield 1991). Small units of the toppled Lon Nol regime, for instance, escaped to the Thai-Cambodian border to fight the newly established Khmer Rouge state, known as Democratic Kampuchea (DK). However, like most Cambodians living under the communist regime within the interior, these units had to fight for their own survival and could not mount any sort of attempt to topple the regime.[2] While some members of the old military managed to flee abroad (to France or the US), others lived along the Thai-Cambodian border or on Thai soil during the years of Pol Pot's reign. But famines, mass executions in an extensive prison system, and harsh living

1

conditions weakened the power base of the communist government, even as
the Khmer Rouge provoked a war with neighboring Vietnam. The communist
brother state started a large-scale offensive on Christmas Eve of 1978, which
put an end to the Khmer Rouge state and resulted in a decade-long occupation
of Cambodia by the Vietnamese, forming the People's Republic of Kampuchea (PRK) (Slocomb 2004, Gottesman 2004).

At this time, the Khmer Rouge joined their former enemies along the
Thai-Cambodian border to organize a resistance. The remnants of three
regimes—Sihanouk's Sangkum Reastr Niyum, Lon Nol's Khmer Republic,
and Pol Pot's Democratic Kampuchea—fought for their own survival and
tried to lobby for international support against the Vietnamese occupiers and
the new communist "puppet government" under the nominal leadership of
Heng Samrin as head of state, as well as Pen Sovann (1981) and Chan Sy
(1982–1985) and Hun Sen (1985 until today) as successive premiers. Cold
War logic led the US and the UN to support the insurgency along the border, while refusing to acknowledge the newly established Soviet-backed and
Vietnamese-controlled regime in Phnom Penh.

Three insurgent movements were established in refugee encampments
along the border: the Khmer Rouge under their new official name, the Party
of Democratic Kampuchea (PDK); the remnants of the Lon Nol regime under the name Khmer People's National Liberation Front (KPNLF), which
formed in 1979; and a group under Norodom Sihanouk's leadership, the
*Front Uni National pour un Cambodge Indépendant, Neutre, Pacifique, et
Coopératif* (FUNCINPEC), founded in 1981 (Conboy 2013). These three
former archenemies from the country's political elite all established separate
armed organizations, thereby reproducing old hierarchies and conflicts. Eventually, however, all joined forces to form the troubled Coalition Government
of Democratic Kampuchea (CGDK) in mid-1982. Through this coalition
government, the Khmer Rouge were—in an almost "Faustian pact" (Haas
1991)—even able to keep their seat in the UN as the legitimate government of
Cambodia until 1991 (from 1982 onwards under the umbrella of the CGDK).
This "government," however, barely managed to control aid flows and refugee camps in the borderlands; they eventually ended up pushed back entirely
onto Thai territory after a large-scale offensive by the Vietnamese military
in 1985 and a four-year long attempt to seal off virtually the entire Thai-
Cambodian border with wire fences secured by a wide strip of minefields, a
project known by the code name K-5 (Slocomb 2001).

The peace process came about through several steps (Brown and Zasloff
1998). The first resulted from the impending breakdown of the Soviet Union.
From 1987 onwards, small-scale peace talks between former King Sihanouk and the new prime minister of the PRK, former Khmer Rouge deputy

regiment commander Hun Sen (himself in power since 1985), were made possible by the announcement that the Vietnamese planned to pull out their 150,000 troops from Cambodia. Heightened international diplomatic involvement and several rounds of small- and large-scale negotiation resulted in the Paris Peace Agreements of 1991, setting the stage for a two-phase peacekeeping mission. From October 1991 until March 1992, the UN Advance Mission in Cambodia (UNAMIC) arrived to prepare a much larger and ambitious mission known as the UN Transitional Authority in Cambodia (UNTAC). From February 1992 to September 1993, the incoming UNTAC forces had a mandate to disarm all four warring factions by 70 percent, monitor peace and human rights issues, take control of state administration, and assist in democratic reforms and the staging of elections (Widyono 2008, Heininger 1994, Findlay 1995, Doyle 1995).

Despite losing these elections to FUNCINPEC under the leadership of Norodom Ranariddh (Sihanouk's son), the incumbent Hun Sen government was not willing to hand over power or state administration, resulting—after a short period of political turmoil and even a brief secession led by the CPP General Sin Song and Norodom Chakrapong (Ranariddh's brother)—in a two-headed government with two co-prime ministers, Norodom Ranariddh and Hun Sen, head of the newly-established Cambodian People's Party (CPP)—a direct successor to the partly that led the PRK. The motive for the secession is still clouded in mystery. Most believe it was a ploy by Hun Sen to pressure Ranariddh into a power sharing deal; others point to Ranariddh's and Chakrapong's father, Sihanouk, and some even suspect an intraparty attack on Hun Sen that backfired and left him with more power than before (Strangio 2014, 74).[3]

After a short period of calm and cooperation, mistrust led both parties to make efforts to strengthen their security forces. The inevitable result was a two-day skirmish in the capital from July 5–6, 1997, in which Hun Sen's forces attacked the FUNCINPEC military barracks, claiming that they had built up a substantial military force out of the remnants of the Khmer Rouge and tried to import weapons illegally. FUNCINPEC forces tried to resist, but eventually had to flee back to the borderlands, where they fought on for almost a year until the elections of 1998, which they lost to the CPP (the elections were widely believed to be fraudulent). The military remnants of FUNCINPEC had only two choices: to fight on without much hope for success, or to make a deal with the victorious Hun Sen government. FUNCINPEC then joined the government as a virtually powerless junior partner.

The "second life" of the Khmer Rouge also came to an end around this time (Rowley 2005). Although they were restricted to "liberated zones" along the border, the Khmer Rouge's breakdown was intimately linked to rising tensions between Ranariddh and Hun Sen. At first, after the Paris Peace Agreement was signed, it seemed as if the Khmer Rouge were willing to comply with it and take part in the 1993 elections (Heder 1996). But already during UNAMIC, their attitude began to change as they started to realize that the Hun Sen government was unwilling to concede its control over the state apparatus. The Khmer Rouge constantly complained that the SNC held no real power and that the UN should take control over the state from "top to bottom." The UN, however, declared that this was not part of their mandate and would render state control as such impossible (Heininger 1994, 18–19). One incident made the Hun Sen government's unwillingness to cede control and the low chances for success in the poll particularly clear to the Khmer Rouge leadership. At the end of 1991, Khieu Samphan moved into a villa in Phnom Penh to prepare his party for the upcoming election under UNTAC administration. However, after a short stay, he was attacked in front of his mansion by an "angry crowd." Among that crowd was a group carrying walkie-talkies and people filming the incident for state TV. Samphan fled the capital and the Khmer Rouge increasingly alleged a continued Vietnamese presence in the country and again demanded that the SNC be given full control over the state.

On May 30, 1992, two months after his arrival, the head of UNTAC, the Japanese diplomat Yasushi Akashi, travelled to an area controlled by the Khmer Rouge in Pailin at the Thai border. However, he was barred from access by cadres at a small barrier made of bamboo. Instead of demanding access and thereby marking the authority of UNTAC, Akashi's entourage backed down and returned to the capital. Akashi explained what became known as "the bamboo pole incident" by saying he did not want to escalate tensions, and pointed to the fact that the mission had no mandate to enforce peace, but it became clear that the Khmer Rouge regarded the UN administration as a paper tiger. In a letter three days later, they declared that they would no longer take part in the peace process and would not disarm their forces (Heder 1996). Due to the Khmer Rouge's pullout, the CPP under Hun Sen were able to convince UNTAC officials that they also needed to stop disarming and demobilizing their troops to guarantee safety and stability. In the end, only the troops of the KPNLF were completely demobilized. But even many of these troops simply switched sides, with most joining FUNCINPEC's armed network within the newly founded state military, the Royal Cambodian Armed Forces (RCAF), and some joining the ranks of their former enemy, the CPP. As UNTAC commander-in-chief General John Sanderson put it:

> They [those troops that had been put into cantonment] certainly weren't their prime troops they put into the cantonments, and certainly the weapons they put into the cantonments weren't their best weapons. We were confronted with the

idea that they were justified in not disarming because the Khmer Rouge stayed out in the countryside and the Khmer Rouge were justified in not disarming because the Cambodian police and elements of their own military were not compliant with the process. (Sanderson 1998, 22)

All four groups involved in the Cambodian peace process were cheating on disarmament in some way (Wang 1996), adding it to a long list of peace processes that left underground paramilitary structures behind (Giustozzi 2016, 8). Many soldiers showing up at cantonment sites were fresh recruits, or not even soldiers but farmers. Due to the ongoing fighting, UNTAC eventually allowed cantoned soldiers from the state military to go on "agricultural leave," officially to help out during harvest time, but very likely to fight for the state military (Ferry 2014, 139, Findlay 1995).

Since no country contributing troops to UNTAC was willing to send them to combat, some of the weaponry collected within the disarmament process was even given back to the state military to fight the Khmer Rouge (Berdal and Leifer 2007).[4] In the end, demobilization had to be suspended completely. With the Khmer Rouge pulling out, the other factions stopped disarming and even called many of their troops back into service. At the end of the demobilization process in 1993, 36,000 "soldiers" had officially been demobilized, but many names on the list were printed more than once, or were elderly, sick, disabled, or even civilians (Ferry 2014, 135). In order to retain their troops in spite of the agreement to demobilize 70 percent of their forces, each faction from the outset "overstated their effective strengths by about two-thirds in order to retain their effective troops for the new army or for continued struggle, depending on how the [peace] process unfolded" (Bartu and Wilford 2009, 10). With the CPP and FUNCINPEC even restarting their recruitment machinery, UNTAC became an onlooker to resumed warfare. Many feared that UNTAC's central mission, the staging of a free and fair election and the implementation of a formal democratic system, might fail as well.

To the surprise of most observers, however, the election took place without major interference from the Khmer Rouge. A few weeks before election day, Khmer Rouge troops received an order not to attack, most likely due to a lack of capacity. For a brief period after the election, some "moderate" wings of the Khmer Rouge even declared their willingness to join the new government and the other factions in forming a neutral state military. Many units of the Khmer Rouge started to realize that, at least in the long run, they would have to join the patronage network of either Ranariddh or Hun Sen, who forced himself into a power sharing deal after Ranariddh won the elections. King Norodom Sihanouk also spoke out in favor of "national reconciliation," which would mean offering the Khmer Rouge positions in the government. Following his father's path of national reconciliation, Ranariddh was the first to offer the Khmer Rouge roles as "advisors" to the government during informal talks, as early as July 1993 (cf. Anon. 1993b), and later in a public appeal via radio on August 12, reaching out to possible Khmer Rouge defectors (Siv 1993, cf. Im 1993). However, the Khmer Rouge's willingness to join the government seems to have faded after the enforced dual premiership. At this stage, Hun Sen's approach was still to destroy the Khmer Rouge and continue barring them from the government, whether as ministers or advisors. Since their archenemy Hun Sen had managed to keep himself in power despite his electoral loss, all wings of the Khmer Rouge opted for a continuation of warfare.

By May 1994, the amalgamation process of the three factions into a "neutral" state army came to an end, leading to "anarchic promotions," with the RCAF suddenly swelling to include roughly 2,000 officers at the rank of general (Bartu and Wilford 2009, 13). After a failed attempt to destroy the strongholds of the Khmer Rouge in late December 1993 and early January 1994, Sihanouk proposed transferring more power to himself for the sake of "reconciliation" and national "salvation" so that he could unite the Cambodian nation. However, both Ranariddh and Hun Sen, strongly objected to this move, and Sihanouk retreated to Beijing due to "serious illness." From that point on, he limited his role largely to symbolic functions. For the first time, Ranariddh clearly departed from his father's path of reconciliation and agreed to a law—proposed by Hun Sen—to outlaw the Khmer Rouge, mandating punishment for membership in the movement, while granting a short period of amnesty for those who defected. After the end of the amnesty period, the Cambodian government intensified its attacks on the remaining Communist strongholds and in 1995 obtained a closure of the Thai border through diplomatic channels, bringing an end to the lucrative illegal trade between the Khmer Rouge and the Thais. Throughout 1994 and 1995, the Khmer Rouge suffered from high rates of defection and was reduced to an increasingly insignificant force.

After a short period of at least superficial calm and cooperation between the two co-premiers, tensions started to rise again. In part, this was due to both premiers starting to compete over who would be first to integrate the remaining Khmer Rouge forces. Although Khmer Rouge commanders and high-level officials contacted negotiators from both premiers, most seemed to be joining Hun Sen's networks within the state apparatus and the military (most notably Keo Pong and his small community in Oral district, Kompong Speu province, in February 1996 and Ieng Sary and his allies in Pailin, Malai, and parts of Samlaut in September 1996). Most defectors opted for CPP networks in this period due to the CPP's capacity to allocate state and natural resources (timber in particular). Under the auspices of what he called his "win-win policy," Hun Sen offered potential defectors state resources, government positions, and access to natural resources.

This, along with the widely shared belief that Hun Sen would outmaneuver his co-premier ahead of the upcoming elections, persuaded many Khmer Rouge leaders to opt for the seemingly stronger side. One Khmer Rouge commander explained that he defected to the CPP rather than to FUNCINPEC "because the development promises made in August [by Hun Sen] were good. . . . FUNCINPEC cannot provide schools, etc. . . . because its party is poor and FUNCINPEC will lose the elections [scheduled for 1998], so it's better to be with CPP. CPP will give us power, not FUNCINPEC" (Le Billon 2002, 576). Before defecting, they wanted a guarantee that they would be able to return to a society at peace while making only minimal concessions to their inherited political, social and economic status. It was not only about timber, but about receiving the whole package of resources and power that would allow them to transfer their status into Cambodian society.

The brief conflict in early July 1997 that deposed Ranariddh was triggered—or justified—by a deal made between Ranariddh, who felt outmaneuvered in governmental powers and by previous defections, and some segments of the Khmer Rouge leadership in the border town of Anlong Veng (Khieu Samphan in particular). After FUNCINPEC commander Serey Kosal failed to convince defectors in Pailin to join them, Ranariddh's top commander, Nhek Bunchhay, brokered a deal in which the Khmer Rouge, under the formal leadership of Khieu Samphan, would join a pre-election coalition with Ranariddh, his former KPNLF ally Son Sann, and Sam Rainsy, a former FUNCINPEC minister. (The deal would exclude major figures of the Khmer Rouge leadership such as Pol Pot, Son Sen, and Ta Mok, but they were promised safe passage into exile.) Soon after news of the deal was leaked, Hun Sen troops prepared for a final showdown, and a few weeks later attacked FUNCINPEC forces in the capital between July 5 and 6, 1997, removing Ranariddh from power.

After their once and current strategic ally Norodom Ranariddh was ousted, Ta Mok, Khieu Samphan, Son Sen, and Pol Pot were completely isolated, and the remnants of the Communist movement started to devour themselves. Like Hun Sen, Pol Pot was angered by the attempted deal between Khieu Samphan and Ranariddh, which would have sent him into exile, viewing it as a coup against him. He arrested Khieu Samphan and killed Son Sen alongside twelve members of his family and close entourage. However, his attempt to arrest Ta Mok failed, and he in turn had to flee with about three hundred of his last remaining loyalists in doomed effort to avoid being caught by his one-time deputy, with whom he had been feuding since the defection of Ieng Sary and others (Pol Pot blamed Ta Mok for losing Pailin, Samlaut, and other strongholds to the government).

Eventually, Ta Mok was able to catch Pol Pot and set up a "people's tribunal" for the "traitor" along with some members of his entourage (Dy and Dearing 2014, for a detailed conflict history within the Khmer Rouge enclave in Anlong Veng). Pol Pot received a life sentence and remained in Ta Mok's custody until his death on April 15, 1998—officially of a heart attack. At the time, he was reportedly in expectation of a car to pick him up to bring him out of the country to an international tribunal. After his death and the elections in July 1998, thousands of Khmer Rouge joined the victorious Hun Sen government. Ta Mok, who briefly hoped to revive the old coalition with Ranariddh and his commander on the ground, Nhek Bunchhay, went into hiding until he was arrested on Thai soil close to the Cambodian border on March 6, 1999, marking the effective end of the Cambodian civil war. The next chapter will turn to the social structure of these three groups and of non-state armed groups in general. It introduces central theoretical concepts such as habitus, discusses different types of resources, and adds important insights from studies on non-state armed group formation.

NOTES

1. The death toll has been highly contested and the numbers used here are drawn from the most recent estimate by the Khmer Rouge tribunal, the Extraordinary Chambers in the Courts of Cambodia (ECCC). And of course, the Khmer Rouge did not succeed in creating an equal and collectivist society but introduced new principles of hierarchy (e.g., between cadres and non-cadres, "new" and "old" or "base" people) or inverted old ones (e.g., the hierarchy stemming from age) (see Tyner 2017 for an analysis of the Khmer Rouge's ideology and practices). On top of that, a number of groups within the leadership of the Khmer Rouge came from an intellectual elite background. The chapters discussing the Khmer Rouge structure and internal hierarchy will show how old inequalities were reproduced, new ones were created, and others, to a certain degree, were dismantled. This is highlighted by the proposed methodology of this study and will be important for understanding their pathways into peace.

2. Of course, this does not mean that there has been no resistance at all. Besides those units fighting—even though largely fighting for their own survival only—many Cambodians deployed various practices to resist the regime, yet small and local in scale. Many survivor accounts tell stories exemplifying the "weapons of the weak" (Scott 1987) under the Khmer Rouge regime (e.g., Ung 2005, Him 2001, Ysa 2006)

3. Sin Song and Chakrapong made yet another coup attempt in early July 1994, just one year later. This time, Hun Sen sent former FUNCINPEC and KPNLF commanders to end the plot, to arrest Sin Song and Chakrapong (sending the latter into exile in Malaysia) indicating that he did not trust his own forces within the CPP.

4. Most weapons (42,368 out of roughly 50,000) came from the incumbent government anyway (Nhem 2013, 122).

Chapter Two

The Social Structure of the Insurgency

A society at war does not turn social relations and structure upside down, but perpetuates them, transforming them in only some respects. Most of the hierarchies within insurgent groups can be explained by the continuation of social networks that have simply been militarized (Staniland 2012, 2014, Hoffman 2007). The three Cambodian guerrilla groups stationed in refugee camps along the border are no exception and—as shown in an earlier study—largely reproduced established social hierarchies that existed prior to their inception (Bultmann 2015). The top echelon was recruited from among the political and military elite of three former regimes, while the mid-range members consisted of their patrimonial clients, mid-level civil servants, and former members of the military state apparatus. The rank-and-file soldiers were without exception recruited from the lowest strata of society: a war-displaced peasantry and working class.

However, the field of insurgency also set its own rules and valuations of each agent's resources. For example, some soldiers managed to rise in rank due to the perceived value of combat experience and survival. These combatants were able to claim symbolic, codified superiority through the display of a warrior ethos. In the Cambodian cultural context, these people would be called "strongmen" (*boroh khlang* in Khmer), although they usually receive the less honorific title of "warlords" in English-language academic literature. Following Pierre Bourdieu, society can be conceived as a social space consisting of multiple fields, in which the position of agents is the result of access to different types of "capital" (Bourdieu 1985, 723–25). Agents can acquire four types of "capital"—or "resources," as they will be called in this book to minimize the economistic interpretation—that are relevant for structuring social hierarchies, including during periods of social transition (Bourdieu 1986, 1990, Rehbein 2011).

- *Economic resources* relate to any kind of possession with a monetary or exchange value that can be used for bartering in the field.
- *Social resources* are relevant connections to people holding influential positions in institutions, companies, or political offices. However, the analyses in the upcoming chapters make it necessary to differentiate between, on one hand, social resources in terms of horizontal networks among people with the same status in the field (e.g., among top commanders), and on the other hand, social resources consisting of vertical networks (e.g., the size of an agent's military entourage). These networks may also have different qualities, as they may consist of either weak or strong ties (Granovetter 1973). Some commanders, for instance, interacted heavily and regularly with their entourages, whereas others did not and kept some measure of social distance.
- *Cultural resources*, the third type, consist of all sorts of skills, knowledge, and education, as well as the possession of culturally relevant objects. In the field of insurgency, military socialization (a form of knowledge) was highly valued, as was formal high-school and university education.
- The fourth resource is *symbolic*, represented by codified forms of superiority such as "honor." A symbolic resource can also function like a meta-resource, giving weight to other resources. It defines the value of these resources when claiming a symbolically codified superiority.

Bourdieu himself is not very clear on the nature of a symbolic resource. In the end, the three other resources have a symbolic value related to the specific field in which they are at use, but as soon as this resource can be used to claim a symbolic superiority, it becomes an explicitly symbolic resource. There is a certain double-usage of "symbolic" at play here—most likely because Bourdieu did not delve further into the changing symbolic value of the other three resources, but simply created a separate fourth resource. Each social field, however, has its own rules and values certain resources differently, which is why the social position of an agent can differ according to the rules of the field he is a part of. What is of lower or higher symbolic value in the field may not be valued somewhere else, thereby altering the status of the agents between different fields. Field positions are quite often, but not necessarily homologous with positions in other fields and society at large (Bourdieu 1996).

Leaving a social field, therefore, means putting certain resources at risk of devaluation, with some being more at risk than others. In the situation discussed in this book, it is the existence of a field of organized violence that primarily determines special rules of valuation. War introduces new classifications, valuations, resources, and practices of its own, while simultaneously perpetuating and disrupting existing categories. For example, economic resources lose value while social resources tend to rise in importance (Schlichte 2003). And, most importantly, certain agents can rise in the ranks of their respective field positions depending on the stock of battles they have fought, which function as a symbolic resource that is of value almost exclusively in the field of insurgency.

Having fighting skills might be viewed as a cultural resource, but within the context of the warrior ethos it marks a symbolic superiority, framing battle survival and fighting skills as a sign of being chosen to survive and destined to lead. This is how Cambodian military strongmen frame their claim to leadership (e.g., Nhek 1998). During war, some agents may experience a significant rise in status within certain fields, but also risk significant losses in their status due to the unstable and field-bound valuation of particular skills—in this case, the aggressive and fear-instilling behavior, battle experience, and combat survival skills that make up a warrior ethos. A symbolic resource like this is in every sense of the word short-lived. Its unstable valuation during and after conflict stands in stark contrast with the resources of other groups, which are comparatively stable across different fields and over longer periods of time, such as the cultural resources of the old military elite or the intellectuals within the leadership of the insurgent movement (Bultmann 2014). This has major consequences in terms of how these groups behave during transition. Other belligerents managed to rise in rank by making a career in military training institutions (members of the old military elite within the Cambodian insurgency set up military schools, e.g., in the Boeung Ampil refugee camp). Having at least some "formal" military education separates these individuals from those building their career solely upon a warrior ethos of strength and invulnerability. The careerists' cultural resource is also easier to transfer—at least if they stay in the military.

An agent's *habitus*, as the term is used in this book, refers to the totality of behavioral dispositions that have the tendency to reproduce behavioral patterns learned during the agent's socialization process in certain social milieus, not restricted to but especially linked to that of their family of origin. It encompasses schemes producing a "family resemblance"—as Wittgenstein described it—among an agent's thoughts and behaviors in ever-changing situations (Wittgenstein 2001). The habitus, hence, has the tendency to reproduce the conditions of its own formation. In Pierre Bourdieu's own classic formulation, these schemes are able to structure practice and "organize the totality of an agent's thoughts, perceptions, and actions by means of a few generative principles" (Bourdieu 1990, 110). Each group sharing a similar life course, upbringing, set of resources, position in the military hierarchy, and habitus constitutes a "habitus group," although it should be kept in mind that this is a scientific construct by the observer, not a conscious sense of group belonging on the part of the respondents (much to the contrary, there is often a certain level of misrecognition of this).

The study adapts certain theoretical elements and methods used by Bourdieu. The main difference is that it focuses on the diachronic aspect of habitus formation and emphasizes that positions of agents are not homologous (the same) across fields. For Bourdieu, positions within the social space of a society are homologs; that is, the social distance between agents in all fields remains the same. Therefore, while in theory acknowledging that "[t]he social world is accumulated history" (Bourdieu 1986, 241), Bourdieu in the end argues that it is a nation's current social space that matters most for the formation of the habitus, not participation in different fields during an individual's lifecourse (see Bultmann 2015, 166). Lifecourse, in Bourdieu's view, is just a mechanism of what he calls "social aging," an agent's self-adjustment to a preset life trajectory inherent to his or his parents' social position. For him, "social aging" describes a process in which people "become what they are and make do with what they have" (Bourdieu 2010, 105).

While Bourdieu has a strong tendency to derive habitus and "capital" (resources) from a synchronic perspective, in which both seem to emanate from a social space in which each person has a certain clearly defined stock of resources and a clearly defined spot in the social structure of a society (France in his case), this study emphasizes the more dynamic aspects of habitus formation and resource accumulation. Habitus is the result of a primary socialization process within the family of origin and its social milieu. It is also the result of a secondary socialization process within different social fields throughout an agent's lifecourse. Although the primary socialization process lays important foundations, aspects of the secondary socialization process might be decisive as well (for instance, when commanders define themselves through their battle experience as adults).

This is why a "habitus hermeneutics" and qualitative research methods focusing on the lifecourse of the respondents were employed instead of a statistical synchronic snapshot (as used by Bourdieu employing correspondence analysis). Lifecourse events (such as experience of war and displacement) are formative for the habitus and—as will be shown in the subsequent chapter—explain much of the behavior of the belligerents, not only, but especially during the transition to peace. Lifecourse differences may explain behavior, and they are not easily detected using quantitative measures. What makes a difference in habitus formation, however, can be detected inductively by what makes a difference to the respondents themselves.

On the other hand, much of the behavior also hinges upon the fact that the value of resources changes over time, particularly during certain moments of history and field development. The value of combat experience, of money, of social contacts, of education may change according to the symbolic universe giving weight to these resources in different fields and moments of transition. Both aspects (lifecourse differences and their impact on habitus formation as well as ever-changing resource valuations) led the author to the decision to use a methodological tool that is more sensitive to these things and may be used to focus on diachronic developments. These tools are not at odds with Pierre Bourdieu's theory, but slightly change its focus and appear less reductive (in terms of the view, not held by Bourdieu himself but one that emanates from subsequent analysis of his work, that the exact stock of capital at a given point in time creates a fixed position in a social space that may be used to deduce all sets of behavior and tastes of agents).

The social structure of the military wing of the insurgency, which will be discussed in depth in the following chapters' analyses of the strategies of these habitus groups during post-conflict transition, was laid out in an earlier study (Bultmann 2015), but was elaborated and further refined for the purposes of this project using additional information from new rounds of interviews. Taken together, the structure of the insurgency may be summarized as follows:

Table 2.1.   Habitus groups within the Cambodian insurgent movement, 1979–1999

Leadership	Old Military Elite		Intellectual Commanders	Anti-Intellectual Intellectuals	Strongmen
Mid-range Operators	Patrimonial Network	Military Careerists	Warrior Monks	Blank-Page Leaders	
Rank-and-file Soldiers	Displaced Peasantry and Workers		Children of War		Blank Pages

Respondents were considered part of the rank and file when they held the rank of a section commander (commanding eight to twelve people) or lower. The mid-range went up to battalion commanders (commanding three hundred people at most). Mid-range commanders were those who had to implement plans from the top command, but still did not engage in combat themselves and usually did not know all of their subordinates personally. In theory at least, the highest rank was a division commander (commanding a maximum of 1,500 soldiers). However, based on their actual number of followers, many should be rather categorized as brigade or even regiment commanders. Decisive here is not the number of their followers or their formal rank, but whether they had to implement the commands of someone else. If not, they were considered part of the leadership, no matter how small their followership actually was.

As a rule, therefore, brigade and regiment commanders are treated as members of the leadership as long as they had no one above themselves they had to answer to. Some of the strongmen discussed in the chapter on the leadership had a very low number of followers, but were nevertheless independent in their command. For instance, they might have been company commanders in rank, but did not listen to the commands of others and constantly quarreled with the high command of the CGDK. In an earlier study, I treated them as a different habitus group, as "battle-hardened roughnecks" (Bultmann 2015). This time, however, I chose to treat them as "strongmen" since they tend to share a similar habitus and social background to other strongmen. The difference in the size of their followership is important, however, and makes a difference during transition to peace. Judging by these artificial ranks and by the size of their units, strongmen are simultaneously part of the leadership and the mid-range, even though they all acted independently and share the same habitus. Although there is a strong correlation between habitus group and rank, formal rank is not decisive for habitus formation or the degree of independence in command, as the case of the strongmen makes clear.

Old military commanders within the non-communist groups in particular often tried to formalize the units and establish classical military rankings. Again and again, they complained that people were not sticking to their proper ranks and responsibilities. But in the end, if there was a powerful commander who led a few hundred soldiers along an important strategic route, he still claimed to be an "independent" company or battalion commander; some regiment commanders in theory commanded more people but were subordinates of a brigade commander and followed his command. Labels did not fit, and many ignored them, especially when they controlled a camp with a sufficient number of soldiers to keep them afloat. In a similar vein, a company or even a battalion commander might be treated as a rank-and-file soldier in this book if, for instance, he was promoted to this rank very late. Within the Khmer Rouge in particular, promotions to higher ranks were used as rewards in a desperate attempt to keep people in the movement during the final stage before organizational breakdown. This is why it was important to know at which stage of the conflict, the respondents had been promoted. Treating all Khmer Rouge who had been promoted during the last few years—if not months or weeks—to higher ranks as mid-range commanders would be an analytical mistake and blurr the realities in the field.

Chapter Three

Leadership

This book maintains that the resource composition and habitus of these groups predispose certain pathways to peace. Each habitus group within the insurgency's inner structure is differently prepared to handle the transition to peace, and therefore employs different strategies of adaptation during the transition into to peace. All try to secure a position after war that is similar or better than their position in the insurgency, or to restore a lost pre-war status. Depending on their main resources in peace-relevant fields and on the degree of the restriction of their value to the specific field, some groups find it easier than others to transfer their position, and may therefore end their military affiliation earlier—some respondents even almost eclipsing their membership to military units throughout their interviews with the author (e.g., RC-KPNLF -1).[1]

The composition of resources, together with their habitus formation, will be used in the upcoming chapters to explain the tendency to favor or suspend warfare and the strategies employed during transition. These strategies do not necessarily relate to membership in a specific formal organization, as they may differ between belligerents active in the same organization and can be similar for former combatants and commanders active in different organizations. Membership, however, may explain certain aspects of the transition, such as different degrees of "symbolic blood" associated with these groups, necessitating different types and intensities of symbolic conversion or in-group solidarities, especially in the case of the Khmer Rouge.

The following chapters will outline the social structure underpinning almost all of the habitus groups' pathways, starting with the leadership. Some groups could not be interviewed for several reasons: most of their members are in prison today, they were afraid of being interviewed in the current political climate, and/or most of their members are dead. This was especially the case for various groups within the upper Khmer Rouge leadership (among these its anti-intellectual intellectual elite, former Khmer Vietminh as well as anti-colonial veteran commanders) and for members of the royal family who were active in the military. Since royalist commanders within the insurgency were sparse, their anonymity would not be guaranteed if details from their interviews were used. Hence, they also needed to be left aside for ethical reasons. Systematic interviews with habitus groups within the Khmer Rouge start at the level of upper mid-range commanders, the "blank-page leaders." This, of course, means that certain segments of the insurgency are over-represented. The upper ranks of the Khmer Rouge will be discussed in a comparatively brief manner, using mostly secondary sources on the logic of their transition to peace.

As shown in the historical overview (chapter 1), the military leadership of the CGDK was a reconstruction of the political and military elite of three predecessor regimes. The former elites of the respective state apparatuses each created an organizational entity into which the decades-old political and military networks were transferred: FUNCINPEC as a successor of the Sangkum under Norodom Sihanouk, the KPNLF as a successor to Lon Nol's Khmer Republic, which toppled Sihanouk in 1970, and the PDK as a successor of Democratic Kampuchea, which toppled the Lon Nol regime in 1975.[2] As always, sympathies and allegiances were not always clear-cut, and many people held loyalties within several political networks, called *khsai* ("strings") in Khmer. Many within the KPNLF, for example, already during the civil war favored a merger with FUNCINPEC as the groups' networks and interests overlapped. This instigated an inner-party conflict that resulted in a virtual split of the KPNLF from 1985 onwards and the formation of two KPNLF political parties under the UNTAC administration, one loyal to Son Sann and one to General Sak Sutsakhan.[3] Even the anti-feudalist and anti-intellectual Khmer Rouge incorporated a number of members of the royal family, the old intellectual elite, and the democratic opposition. During "reintegration," these *khsai* cross-connections allowed for clandestine negotiations between seemingly conflicting political parties. Network politics across organizational umbrellas are therefore essential in understanding not only conflict lines during the civil war, but also pathways and complexities during transition.

NETWORK POLITICS

During UNAMIC and UNTAC, the political and military elite within the leadership circle of the CGDK tried to secure its network access to state resources, as well as to the newly emerging civil society and thousands of nongovernmental organizations (NGOs) popping up all over the country. Like new political parties and state institutions, civil society absorbed a considerable portion of the movement's networks, creating an alternative political opposition and a space for the old elites. Civil society provided a much-needed job market and political space, not only for lower and mid-range members of the insurgency, but also for its elite, transferring entire political and military networks to newly formed NGOs.

Initially, however, the main sources of income for the old insurgent network were state institutions that granted access to revenues, state and party positions, and concessions for natural resources. After the power sharing agreement, revenues from state positions and economic concessions (for timber in particular) were used for political accommodation and feeding the followers of both CPP and FUNCINPEC loyalists: "Parallel revenues were [. . .] used to consolidate [Hun Sen's and Ranariddh's] position by financing personal security forces, buying off political alliances, or personalizing public welfare programs through direct donations. Funcinpec, in particular, needed to build up its capacity as it lagged well behind the CPP in terms of financing its political activities" (Le Billon 2002, 568–69).

The effect was that all state institutions and formal command of military regions ended up divided, at least in theory, to enable a political and financial balance (cf. Ashley 1998). However, FUNCINPEC loyalists became increasingly frustrated with the fact that, despite a formally equitable division, they were barred from exercising real power or taking up the most lucrative positions (Widyono 2008, 231–51). Despite contestation from former CGDK members, the UN, and internal party rivals (Chea Sim and Sar Kheng), Hun Sen managed to maintain and even increase his control over the central pillars of the state, its resources, and its military institutions.

The problem for the political and military leadership of the insurgency was that, due to Hun Sen's presence in all spheres, their access not only to state institutions, but also to civil society and private businesses, was profoundly insecure. Especially in state and military institutions, former members of the CGDK were left powerless, as people did not listen to their commands. As a former mid-range FUNCINPEC commander, who asked to be transferred to the customs department due to his weak position in the new state military, put it: "A hen could not lead ducks. Everyone was eager to protect his own forces" (BAC-FUNCINPEC -1). Members of different political networks simply ignored each other and went on with their jobs as if nobody else was present. In order to heighten their chances of reconstituting their former elite status and power, the old leaders had to position their networks within as many institutions and formal organizations as possible and to find source of income for them. However, due to the inherited control of the CPP networks over the state apparatus, the newcomers from FUNCINPEC and KPNLF were much less able to consolidate control over meaningful spheres of power or lucrative flows of revenue.

A constant theme within the interviews was how patrimonial networks spread in order to secure access to various sorts of institutions. Under a formal agreement, many units were simply transferred to the "neutral" Royal Cambodian Armed Forces (RCAF), mostly still stationed in the same area in which they were operating during the civil war (e.g., BC-KPNLF -1, BAC-FUNCINPEC -2, BC-KPNLF -2). Many commanders were able to keep their former units with only minor defections; these commanders provided not only military jobs for their followers, but also farmland and other business opportunities, both legal and illegal (e.g., BC-KPNLF -2, BAC-NADK -1, RF-NADK -1).

A second major absorber within the state was the police:

> Back then, [former KPNLF commander-in-chief] Sak Sutsakhan asked [his former deputy] Dien Del to set up a police section by recruiting people from the border. My former commander [name omitted] was appointed as the head of that police section. And since I could speak some English, he chose me as his deputy [literacy and language proficiency in either French or English had been decisive skills during UNTAC; D.B.]. We then recruited ordinary people to join our unit. Since, at that time, in 1991, all political prisoners, including those from the KPNLF, were released, I invited them all to join the police. There were five police stations, and we divided our people across all of these. (BAC-KPNLF -1)

The KPNLF's securing control over sections of the national police meant that many respondents were able to forge a career path from political prisoner to law enforcement officer. Today most of these respondents still serve as policemen or are recently retired from police service. However, all respondents from the police reported that they were effectively barred from exercising any meaningful control over the national police's operations, from the time of the factional clashes in 1997 if not earlier.

The insurgent network poured not only into state institutions via quota agreements, but also into civil society. It was especially common for members of the political leadership and intellectual commanders to become heads of NGOs, especially those who obtained government positions at first, but had to leave them after the factional clashes (e.g., RC-KPNLF -1, -2, BC-KPNLF -4, -5). Here, as well, these former commanders provided jobs for their clients in the lower ranks of these NGOs. Many of these organizations were under constant pressure from the government, not necessarily because of their political work in a narrow sense (some for example working in the—at least on the first sight non-political—demining sector, BC-KPNLF -3), but because their staff predominantly comprised former CGDK members. The current government—to a certain degree, correctly—still views civil society as an oppositional force that is not politically independent (cf. Coventry 2017). Sometimes, the only reason these organizations survived was pressure from donor states on the government to leave them intact: "I was able to keep my position here because the United States, Australia, and Canada wanted us to answer to them directly" (BC-KPNLF -3). Because of the weakened presence of the US government under President Trump, Hun Sen is currently trying to grab the opportunity to totally dismantle what is left of this civil society, which in his view is still "foreign."

Due to the constant political threat after returning to the interior under UNAMIC and UNTAC, the old leadership of the CGDK tried to use all possible pathways to reconstruct its status as an oppositional political elite. Membership in FUNCINPEC and the successor parties of the KPNLF—Son Sann's Buddhist Liberal Democratic Party (BLDP) and General Sak Sutsakhan's short-lived Liberal Democratic Party (LDP)—were used almost interchangeably as vehicles for a return to the political field. Often decisive was not membership in an official political party, but membership in an informal political network trying to secure access to as many organizations and institutions as possible:

WE had that idea; why I stayed with KPNLF [meaning with BLDP during UNTAC]? I have—I have a FRIEND and I call him Mister BROTHER (laughs). He is my brother and we-we DISCUSS. I discuss with him. "Bong [name omitted], NOW we have these two factions. So—to preserve our FUTURE—PLEASE: you-you join with the FUNCINPEC, the Sihanouk faction [hm]; ME, I have to stay with Son Sann. ONE day—one day, if one of faction failed, we still have another one [hm] [interviewer: if one loses the OTHER one is still there]. YEAH. So IF-IF KPNLF fail [hm], I go to join with you at the Sihanouk faction. IF Sihanouk faction fail, you come to join me (both laugh) [interviewer: very strategic]. YEAH (laughing). That really why I stay with KPNLF (laughing). (BC-KPNLF -5)[4]

After the weak performance of Son Sann's BLDP in the elections administered by UNTAC in 1993 (securing only ten seats in parliament) and the death of Sak Sutsakhan in 1994, the respondent "preserved his future" by joining FUNCINPEC via his "brother," taking up a position in the divided governance of a military region in the country's northeastern province of Ratanakkiri. In a similar vein, working with the former enemy was also possible due to personal networks and previous relationships: "I was born in Svay Rieng province. And most of the TOP officers in the CPP army, they are from Svay Rieng [OK]. YEAH, PERSONAL RELATION, RIGHT? We know each other since EARLY childhood. PERSONALLY. We trust we know each other" (BC-KPNLF -5). During transition, personal patrimonial networks counted more than organizational umbrellas, which were often used only as vehicles for access to resources and positions.

After the elections, many from the political and military leadership of the KPNLF (which split into Son Sann's BLDP and Sak Sutsakhan's LDP) changed sides to FUNCINPEC or even to the CPP, thereby creating an apparatus with competing patrimonial networks that were, from the outside, obscure. As the UNTAC commander-in-chief, General John Sanderson, put it in an interview:

> Let me say that a lot of the forces came from a different policy base into Cambodia. That was one of the revelations to me, coming from a country where there is a single policy base for the employment of its military forces outside the country, to find that there were military forces there that were operating on different strands of policy that came from different parts of their executive. For example, you could have a part of a military force which is responding to a strand of policy that came from the Defense, a part of it which was responding to a strand of policy which came from the Presidential Palace, and a part of it which was responding to a strand of policy which came from the Department of Foreign Affairs, and it was quite difficult to determine which of these was influencing their reaction to the situations in the countryside and indeed their reaction to the standard operating procedures. This made it all the more important that I appealed to their military pride, in the uniform, and in their professionalism, to overcome those things. Some were able to overcome it more easily than others because they were a little bit more remote from their country, and the hand of their own operational commanders did not lie as heavily on them. (Sanderson 1998, 38)

These networks within state institutions and even political parties remained largely incomprehensible to observers and the UNTAC administration, making control over the state, in the words of one UNTAC official, the "mission's myth" (Widyono 2008, 41–54).

The UN had to rely on an already existing administration as an intermediary for its rule, thereby—unwittingly—bolstering the position of the CPP administration (similar to the Congo mission, cf. Veit 2010). Underneath the UN's struggle for control, political networks originating from four different regimes scrambled to (re)establish and secure control over political institutions and the security sector. In this situation, affiliation with institutions and political parties was not the guiding principle of politics. While the two-headed government from 1993 onwards afforded the political opposition access to a wide range of state institutions and their revenues, FUNCINPEC's ouster by Hun Sen with military force in 1997 meant that ongoing access depended on the goodwill of Hun Sen's CPP and on keeping a low profile while at least officially acknowledging the supremacy of the CPP. Many respondents reported having to go to Hun Sen or other CPP officials to provide assurances that they acknowledged the supremacy of the CPP after the "coup" of 1997. As will be shown in the forthcoming chapters, diverse forms of accommodation in political talk and action were the only chance of preventing a stark downturn in status during this stage, even for those who managed to hold on to higher positions within civil society.

The following chapters provide a glimpse into major patterns of how one group within this ongoing scramble, the members of the military wing of the insurgency, tried to secure positions during the process of "reintegration" into Cambodian society over the course of the past two decades. All respondents were members of either the Khmer People's National Liberation Armed Forces (KPNLAF), the National Army of Independent Kampuchea (ANKI, formerly ANS), or the National Army of Democratic Kampuchea (NADK, more widely known as the Khmer Rouge). Over the years, many were members of at least two of these groups, and some even belonged to all three.

INTELLECTUAL COMMANDERS

Most of the intellectuals in the sample who became leading commanders for the non-communist wing of the CGDK (ANS/ANKI and KPNLAF, *not* NADK) came from the political elite. Some were even born into families that had served in the state apparatus or the opposition for at least two generations, reaching back to the colonial state administration (RC-KPNLF -1, DC-FUNCINPEC -1, RC-KPNLF -2). This group of respondents went to schools which back then were largely reserved for the political upper class, mostly the capital's Lycée Sisowath, and had private French tutors at home.

Others came not directly from families within the political elite but from well-off families and managed to rise in rank due to higher education that they received before the Khmer Rouge takeover in 1975. In part, this was due to their high status within the rural administration or to coming from economically prosperous rural families and to the massive expansion of the education sector under Sihanouk's reign from 1954 to 1970, which brought more children than ever before into schools (Ayres 2000). Having at least some higher education—at minimum, a bachelor's degree from a Cambodian university—was a means for these intellectuals to access state institutions under Lon Nol, thereby entering the political elite in the capital early in their careers (BC-FUNCINPEC -1, GS-KPNLF -1, BC-KPNLF -6, -5), or to rise in rank to top commanding positions within the insurgent military, especially when serving in units led by intellectuals from the political elite (RC-KPNLF -4, BC-FUNCINPEC -2, RC-KPNLF -3).

While education is usually stable in value across different fields (it was slightly more valuable during this period due to the destruction of the school system under Democratic Kampuchea), the last group of respondents coming from rural upper classes did not have as strong ties to the political elite as the others due to their slightly lower social milieu of origin. Their vertical social resources were considerably weaker and field-related, as they made connections with the upper political elite during their service in the insurgency and not before the start of the Khmer Rouge era. This would later make a difference during the transition to peace. The intellectuals with an elite heritage, either by birth or by virtue of having worked in the Sihanouk or Lon Nol governments, did not join the insurgency on a lower level, but were "asked to help out at the frontline" or "created" the insurgency "with friends" (E-US -1, RC-KPNLF -2, BC-KPNLF -5, -6, E-US -2).

The intellectuals' main symbolic resource was their high level of education, which, in their words, set them above "ordinary Cambodian people" (RC-KPNLF -2) or "normal refugees" along the border (BC-KPNLF -6). During the Khmer Rouge era, they either fled abroad to the United States or France (some had already been abroad, becoming stateless after the Communists' takeover) or were prime targets for execution within Democratic Kampuchea, where former members of the Lon Nol government were singled out. Concealing their identities, the respondents managed to flee to the border to organize a resistance force. As members of the newly formed insurgent military, they viewed themselves as special: "I was more a theoretician, a teacher, a thinker than a commander leading men in battle" (GS-KPNLF -1). After a couple of years, they found themselves fighting alongside their former arch-enemy, the Khmer Rouge. They reconstructed an old political and intellectual but dispossessed elite along the border striving to reconstitute their social status in the interior by deposing the new rulers installed by the Vietnamese occupiers. All of these intellectual commanders maintained close ties with the political wing of the insurgency.

For them, the military hierarchy within the tripartite CGDK insurgency reflected a quasi-natural order, with normal, war-craving Cambodians within the rank and file and themselves at the top, guiding these natural-born warriors. As a regimental commander described it:

> During my five years of military soldier I never killed anyone. Even though I was commander of the operation. I got a pistol in my pocket but never used it. I used it just to exercise, to shoot, you know, just in case. But I had my bodyguard and when there was a bomb exploded my bodyguard are on the foot. READY TO ENGAGE. But I had to STOP them. I said "Try to find out, where does it come from, who shoot that, how far is it from and where are other elements and so on and son on." [I: The training comes back] YEAH. So I approach in a

very LOGICAL sense of way you know. But then—NO—you see THEM: JOY. Whenever there is a fighting, they are ready to fight, but asking questions like fight for who, fight for what, fight where and this and that and so on: It is just the mindset, they turn to that. (cited from Bultmann 2015, 57–58)

This is what Pierre Bourdieu would call "symbolic violence," in which social agents mistakenly perceive an arbitrary social order as natural and unchangeable: "Symbolic violence is misrecognized obedience in that symbolic power is accepted as legitimate rather than as an arbitrary imposition" (Swartz 2013, 83). The notion of a natural and therefore also unchangeable social order as a motive for becoming a soldier or a commander came up in almost all interviews and will be discussed on several occasions throughout this book (see also Bourdieu and Wacquant 1992, Bultmann 2018b). For the ordinary rank-and-file soldier, the intellectual asserts, there is nothing unusual in being a combatant:

> *Respondent*: the PEOPLE—I don't say that the people LOVE to do war. But for THEM—BECAUSE it is wartime—it is NORMAL that they are recruited to be a soldier of the resistance movement [hm]. So there is no problem AT ALL, you know?
>
> *Interviewer*: It is a logical choice.
>
> *Respondent*: logical choice, YEAH. (RC-KPNLF -2)

While, in the intellectual's view, it is simply a logical choice for "ordinary men" to fight, elite commanders' own motive for serving in the military is slightly more complex; typically described as a process of being "willingly manipulated by external factors" (RC-KPNLF -1). It seems like some felt that their military service did not fit their current position in society and that the apparent discrepancy called for an explanation of how they could possibly have ended up as military commanders. A chair of an international NGO, for example, phrased it this way:

> You know political life, you know, its like-its like a CHAIN. You don't decide in advance. You decide only the PRINCIPLE of engagement at the START. But once you ACCEPT the rules of the GAME [hm], the EVENTS draw you— INFLUENCE on you, from one step to another. Sometime you don't have any HOLD on-on the event [hm]. The events was create by external factors, but as long as you believe that its still in the framework of what YOU believe—to SERVE the country—to serve the PEOPLE. You FREELY and consciously accept to be MANIPULATED or-or to be DRAWN INTO the events [hm] itself [hm]. BECAUSE never once I feel that the WAY, the-the WAY I-I was used by the resistance organization was OUTSIDE the framework of people interest. IF I feel THAT [hm] I would leave the-the organization [hm] RIGHT AWAY [hm]

because there-there was no STRING, there was no TIE on my hands. I can-I can QUIT. I can leave [hm] the-the frontline anytime [hm]. This is not a FILM, this is not a novel about CIA, you know [interviewer: laughs]: "If you leave our organization, you would be KILLED or [interviewer: laughs], you know, and this and that. NO, its not like THAT. I-I was very FREE to-to do all those things [hm]. But EACH time I believe that—that I COULD contribute [hm], whatever, however MODEST my contribution was [hm], but I could contribute to that. (RC-KPNLF -1)

External factors did create a chain of events that forced him to be part of the military, but as long as this act *conformed* with his free will and a—rather vague—principle he had set at the very beginning, he accepted being "manipulated." And after the war's end, most intellectuals managed to be "willingly manipulated" into higher positions within the two-headed government and its "neutral" military or civil society. These pathways, together with impoverishment and taking refuge in the diaspora, were the four basic routes taken by the intellectual commanders in this sample.

Pathways of Reintegration and Their Narration

The first pathway is characterized by an intricate balance between critique and accommodation after becoming part of the two-headed government in 1993. Many intellectuals were part of the government for roughly four years, either in a military or a political function, until 1997. After being ousted in 1997, they either had to find new positions (usually within the civil society) or adapt to being sidelined in the new government in 1998. For those intellectuals who joined civil society, this was not necessarily a matter of conflict, benefits, and accommodation, but of being firm in "serving the people" in different capacities and finding a position that fit their "personality." This, at least, is how it was framed by one intellectual who became a consultant for the international community and head of an NGO after 1997:

I joined the government in nineteen ninety three. WHEN-WHEN I see that I can NOT SERVE the country and the people, I would have left [hmhm]. And-and PEOPLE told me that all "Oh, when you join the government and the CPP and so on, you cannot live like that and so on." This is NOT true [hm], you know its depend on WHAT you WANT [hm]. If-if [interviewer: its your CHOICE]— YES, yeah—if you are STILL think in term of BENEFIT, think in term of position or social rank, social status and so on [hm], its very DIFFICULT for you, to LIVE. But IF you are sincere with YOURSELF, with your believe [hm], you know—you can leave ANYTIME and you can RECONVERT it, you can work, you can serve the people from DIFFERENT ANGLE [hm], from different FRAMEWORK. Being in the government is NOT the only framework that you can serve the country, I don't believe so. That's why I-I-I EXPERIENCE the, you know, the freelance life until I find that THIS is the best FIT to my personality, to my FREEDOM of mind and-and so on. (RC-KPNLF -1)

He does not even mention what others in the opposition would call the "coup." For him, it is just a rather sudden change from being in the government to being a "freelancer" in civil society—a "different angle" of being willingly manipulated, of serving the people and of finding a "better fit" for your own "personality" without thinking in terms of benefit, position, or social rank. Even being ousted from the government is still framed as a choice to serve the country from within a different "framework," to "experience freelance life," marking the final end of a journey to "freedom of mind." Over the course of every step imposed on him by external forces, this respondent still claimed to have maintained his principles:

> I was influenced by EXTERNAL factors as well [hm], but nevertheless whatever happened, I have always eh MAINTAINED a TRAJECTORY, a PART that I would like to be. [Back at the border] I was engaged in the noncommunist resistance for eleven years. BUT NOTHING PERSONAL. When I come back here, war was over and I accepted to work with the CPP as advisor to deputy prime minister of interior Sar Kheng [. . .] I didn't see the CPP as ENEMY anymore. I saw CPP as a PARTNER. (RC-KPNLF -1)

The respondent's past and current accommodation with the government as a member of civil society made it complicated for him even to talk about his military service with the insurgency; he mentioned it for the first time more than thirty minutes into the interview. And of course, his military engagement was—as quoted above—"nothing personal," as they—the CPP government—are "partners" now. When talking about the government today, the respondent asserted, it was important to weigh one's words so as not to shake the tottery foundations of peace. Within the intellectuals' discourse, being part of a critical civil society does not conflict with accommodating the government, e.g., when talking about endemic corruption:

> They [the CPP government] are VERY dedicated. BUT because of the Cambodian government system—they have to be CORRUPTED [hm]. (raising his voice) OTHERWISE, YOU KNOW, THEY COULD NOT HAVE ANYTHING, TO SEND THEIR KIDS TO SCHOOL, you know [hm], to-to raise their family, to have car or to have house and this and that and so on. And I think that WHOEVER working in that level would HAVE to be corrupted [hm]. But its not about hundred and hundred hectares of land, you know, its not about CONTRACT on oil and gas or forestry or fishery, its-its not that MULTIMILLION dollars corruption [hm]. ITS what I call—its a SURVIVAL corruption

[hm]. EVEN THOUGH it allows you to have nice VILLA or MERCEDES [hm] or LEXUS [hm] and this and that, you know, because this what the SOCIETY WANT [hm]—its wrong, its COMPLETELY WRONG—BUT I don't BLAME THOSE director in ministry department [hm]. I have learned to RESPECT them and maintain a lot contact with them, many of them becoming now director general and this and that. [They] continue to be very corrupted but continue to be COMPETENT. (RC-KPNLF -1)

While some former commanders entered civil society's elite after being ousted from the government, reconstituting old opposition networks within NGOs, others remained in politics when the remnants of FUNCINPEC (those who were not killed or did not flee the country) under the leadership of the returning Norodom Ranariddh made a deal with the government after their electoral loss in 1998 (the CPP won 64 seats in parliament and FUNCINPEC won 43). Over the years, FUNCINPEC became an increasingly powerless junior partner in the government, with a shrinking share of the popular vote. Ranariddh served as president of the National Assembly until 2006, when he resigned from this position and was ousted as the head of FUNCINPEC.[5] Many former intellectual commanders changed back and forth between several political parties and are nowadays closely associated with the Cambodian National Rescue Party (CNRP), which at the time of writing had just been dissolved by court order.

Those intellectuals who did not make use of their dual citizenship to go to the United States or France after the factional clashes in 1997, and did not find refuge in civil society, became increasingly sidelined as members of FUNCIN-PEC in the government. They had formal titles and positions, but practically no power. They became "non-trustable persons" who retained a comparatively high level of income and an important position within the opposition networks, but were excluded from decision-making processes and governance:

YEAH right, it is a POLITICAL mindset, political mindset influenced by SIDE of the COMMUNIST and SOCIALIST [hm]. They keep separate, yeah, between the Khmer refugee and the Khmer inside. They say that even they NOT show up their APPEARANCE: but inside, the MIND, they keep asking—like when I was working in the general staff—they KEEP asking "Are you from KP—KPNLF? You are from the FUNCINPEC? and you are from?" They RECOGNISE that in the LIST, a LIST they keep. That why they SAY "I cannot LONGER work with you AT ALL." (BC-KPNLF -5)

All intellectual respondents had lost contact with their former subordinates in the military. Already, in their capacity as commanders, they had kept a social and physical distance from the rank and file. The end of the war meant that their relationships within the command structure also ended. When asked about their former combatants and units, the intellectuals usually stated that they had no clue what happened to them, as they did not keep in touch with them after the 1991 peace agreement or the UNTAC period. Some, however, maintained an abstract feeling of responsibility for the "people from the border." One commander, for instance, set up a foundation to help the poor along the border in towns predominantly inhabited by former CGDK members and refugees (BC-KPNLF -6).

Already the commanders who had become sidelined in the government were beginning to indulge in conspiracy theories about the origin of the Hun Sen government as a puppet of the Vietnamese. A common theme was that foreigners were not able to differentiate between the appearance of Vietnamese and Khmer people, so only Cambodians could know the extent to which secret Vietnamese agents were controlling the country. Within the sample, the level of anti-Vietnamese conspiracy theorizing correlated heavily with the respondent's degree of impoverishment and exclusion from the government. Those who were not part of the political elite and lost their positions when resources became scarce after 1997 were particularly prone to believe that this was due to a Vietnamese conspiracy. One even believed that events in Cambodia were at the center of the Third World War:

> The Yuon [the oftentimes derogatory word for Vietnamese], for a long time already, have planned to control our country. You know the people selling lighters or cakes, or who repair shoes on the street? They are Yuon officers. They receive their salaries from the Vietnamese Embassy. They live in Cambodia in order to protect the 10 million Yuon living here. Look! I'll draw a map for you. Here is South Vietnam, here is the North [of Vietnam], there we have Thailand, and here is Phnom Penh, which is called "Nam Yang" in Vietnamese. All these territories formerly belonged to Cambodia. The real map of Cambodia is in Switzerland, and the money that Sihanouk and other corrupt leaders earned for that is at the IMF, but now it is frozen. France ceded Kampuchea Krom to Vietnam without asking for permission from Cambodia. The real map is kept in a golden safe deposit box; if you see it, you can't find Thailand, Laos, or Vietnam on that map. Our land is a golden land[6] that attracts every country around the globe. Has anyone told you about this before? You know, the Third World War is happening now. And it is happening here. (BC-FUNCINPEC -2)

The most decisive events for the post-conflict trajectory of the intellectuals were 1) the peace mission, 2) their participation in the two-headed government after the elections, and 3) the military conflict in 1997, which ousted large portions of these commanders' networks from state institutions and excluded them from obtaining resources. These were critical moments during which all "habitus groups" had to make use of their resources to adapt to new socio-political and economic circumstances. Very few intellectuals faced a stark downturn in status immediately after the war's end. Those who did were not members of the inner circle of the political elite, despite having similarly high levels of education as a central resource and even similar ranks. Perhaps they did not have a particularly elite family heritage or were not part of the upper state apparatus under Sihanouk or the Lon Nol regime. Initially, they managed to rise as "intellectuals" due to the scarcity of education as a resource after the Khmer Rouge regime (most educated Cambodians with had been either killed or resettled in the United States or France after 1979). As Margaret Slocomb pointed out when discussing the similar problems faced by the incumbent government in staffing their administration: "The pool of educated human resources was both small and shallow at the beginning of 1979" (Slocomb 2004, 66–67).

After the "coup" in 1997, however, membership in the traditional upper opposition elite became decisive in securing a role within the small pocket remaining within the state apparatus or in finding an outside position. Options for the network to provide jobs for their military wing were shrinking (cf. Roberts 2002, 104), and non-elite intellectual commanders with only weak ties to the political establishment were among the first to be sacrificed. To stay afloat, group members had to balance political opposition and accommodation with Hun Sen's CPP, be it as official members of the government or as members of civil society. In later years, civil society absorbed a certain share of the military wing of the insurgency, thereby partially stabilizing the political arena as it opened up a field of political participation and contestation for the deposed old elites who were either marginalized or completely excluded from the state apparatus after 1997. Therefore, even though the power of the elite was shrinking, all intellectuals managed to retain a social status similar to their pre-war status, with many finding refuge either in politics or civil society. This group, however, is currently under heavy surveillance by the Hun Sen government, which has started to dismantle any vestiges of opposition in the political field, civil society, and its own state apparatus. Not all, but many intellectuals have reacted by—at least officially—glossing over their membership in the military opposition (even during the interviews it often took a while until they would speak about it) and stressing their "independent" position as "advisors" who had no "personal problem" with anyone from the Hun Sen elite.

OLD MILITARY ELITE

Members of this habitus group came from a displaced military elite apparatus that served both the Lon Nol and Sihanouk governments. Most respondents came from families with a long history of military service, with one even stating that "most of us" had a family ancestry within the state military dating back as far as "the King's grandfather's time" (likely a reference to Sihanouk's grandfather Sisowath Monivong, who ruled from 1927 to 1941) (DC-KPNLF -2). While many found refuge in the diaspora after the Communist Party of Kampuchea seized Phnom Penh in April 1975, some managed to hide their background under the new regime and eventually fled to the border to begin forming a resistance force.

Members of the uppermost echelon of the old military apparatus, such as Dien Del and Sak Sutsakhan, returned from the diaspora in the early 1980s to unify and organize the small and scattered armed groups in control of refugee camps along the border and to establish an armed wing for the newly formed KPNLF, the Khmer People's National Liberation Armed Forces (KPNLAF). Starting in March 1981, some elite commanders also joined the newly formed military wing of FUNCINPEC, which was a merger of several small groups and a larger one, the Movement for the National Liberation of Kampuchea (MOULINAKA), under the command of former Lon Nol colonel Nhem Sophon (preceded by former naval captain Kong Sileah, who died in 1980).[7] The military leadership of both groups had strong roots in the French and US diasporas, which became vital for many during the peace process, as a source of income or a potential destination for asylum. It is a typical pattern for the upper echelon of these insurgent groups and its "first movers" to originate from a deposed state elite, particularly its military (cf. Schlichte 2009, 30–38).

The habitus of these Lon Nol top commanders revolves around military ethics, discipline, and superior knowledge of the principles of strategic leadership. For them, it was their "calling" to be in the military "from birth" (RC-KPNLF -5). They were "raised in military barracks" (DC-KPNLF -2); some attended elite military schools such as the Royal Military Command and Staff College and the Royal Cambodian Officers Academy, or even went to military schools in Paris. In the 1950s and 1960s, the military state apparatus was supported and trained by the French. During the Khmer Republic from 1970 to 1975, the United States took over the provision of military assistance. Therefore, most top commanders are fluent in French (some having even lived in Paris), and many have good connections within the United States as well. However, not everyone was highly educated; for some, just having been born into a family with a long heritage in the military elite was enough to become part of the CGDK military leadership. Like the intellectuals, these commanders with a military heritage view the hierarchies within the insurgency as a quasi-natural order.

Being a leader of a non-state armed group, however, was not something they were particularly proud of. They were disconcerted by the "greedy" and "wild" strongmen within the military apparatus of the CGDK (DC-FUNCIN-PEC -3, DC-KPNLF -1). The state of the new military recruits at the time was also unacceptable to them. They had "long beards," were "undisciplined" and "illiterate" in military tactics, and needed to be "molded" by drills, ranging from "cold to lukewarm to hot methods" (DC-KPNLF -2). Most felt that the Sihanouk and Lon Nol years had been a golden age. They saw their natural social place within the upper echelons of the state military, not in a diaspora or the disordered state along the border. They were very proud that through "high discipline" they were able to "organize the camps well" for the "ordinary refugees" (BC-KPNLF -4) and that they were following "strict military rules," acting as a "hard-working example in military conduct" for their followers (DC-FUNCINPEC -4). Drills, discipline, military ethics, and strategic knowledge were central to their claim to superiority. However, they also kept a distance from the political wing of the insurgency, causing leadership quarrels along the border and a factional split within the KPNLF that led to the creation of two political parties during UNTAC (one under the political head Son Sann and one under General Sak Sutsakhan). Even during the conflict in 1997 that ousted Ranariddh, many elite military commanders kept their distance from politics and did not engage in fighting or resistance of any sort.

Narratives and Status Change during Transition

While General Sak Sutsakhan and the upper level of the KPNLAF broke with the political leadership under Son Sann, forming the LDP, all but one respondent managed a transfer to elite positions, either becoming part of the amalgamated RCAF between 1993 and 1994 or taking up positions at the head of civil society organizations. After the peace deal and the creation of the RCAF, all tried to reconstitute their formerly lost status within the military elite but had to content themselves with high ranks but relatively low power in the military state apparatus beyond their own units. After the coup, in which none of them played a role, they kept to themselves within the military regions they oversaw, within which they had been granted large swaths of land for themselves and their subordinates. Despite their lack of involvement in the coup, they felt its consequences: "I did not expect much [after integration], nothing except for a decent life like others had. But after the events on July 5 and 6, my life became difficult," even though "we got along well with the CPP" (DC-KPNLF -3). Maintaining good relations with the CPP did not forestall being disempowered within the military.

Many former top KPNLAF commanders initially followed General Sak Sutsakhan, as they respected him as a military commander, but after their loss at the polls and his early death in 1994, some quickly joined the CPP in order to reconstitute their position in the state's military elite and were awarded with one or two stars. They did not see this as accommodating Hun Sen, but, much to the contrary, as Hun Sen accommodating the true liberators of the Khmer:

> I have served the nation and brought the country to its current status. Without me, Cambodia would not be what it is today. It's not just me, though, but all the people in the resistance movement. Without Khmer Rouge and other people like me, Cambodia would not be what it is today. Think about it: Without people like me, Cambodia would have been like Laos today. In Laos, even a village chief is controlled by Yuon. Let me be clear here. A country without freedom fighters would lose its essence. Only with fighters like these were we able to receive international attention and assistance. Like Pol Pot once said: "Where there is repression, there is resistance." So why was there resistance? It was because something was not right in our country. So there had to be fighters to bring peace to the country. We are who we are today because there were freedom fighters. We understand that you [the Hun Sen government] liberated us from the Khmer Rouge, but this achievement was also made possible by people in the resistance [fighting along the border before January 1979]. If everything could have been done solely by Hun Sen, he would not have joined the tripartite coalition [meaning: the insurgent CGDK]. Why was that so? It was because the other two were also important. That's why he joined the alliance [through the peace process]. Understand? (BC-KPNLF -1)

Not only does this respondent claim that the armed groups that would later become the KPNLF toppled the Khmer Rouge in the first place—together with the Vietnamese military and the exiled Khmer Rouge of the Kampuchean United Front for National Salvation (KUFNS)—but in his interpretation of history, Hun Sen also needed the old CGDK coalition to finally get rid of the Vietnamese and bring about peace in the country, which is why *Hun Sen joined them*. They construe themselves as the legitimate state military, while Hun Sen is merely the leader of a faction.[8] This logic shows how, despite their seeming accommodation, the old military elite still claims military and political superiority over the Hun Sen government. In their view, their resistance efforts made it possible to diminish the influence of the Vietnamese over Cambodia—and in the end, as noted by almost all military elite members, to prevent the country from vanishing into Vietnam. Due to their success in expelling the Vietnamese and installing the "Second Kingdom," they could finally—as one phrased it—"accept" working with the current government (DC-FUNCINPEC -4).

However, for most, their living conditions did not keep pace with their expectations. While they were able to (re)enter the military state apparatus at a high level, factional conflicts between CPP and the opposition led to a constant diminishment in their status and power. They are still in charge of large chunks of their old units, receive good salaries, and even own large stretches of land along the border or elsewhere, but they have no real power within the military hierarchy even as they see others being promoted on a regular basis. Because of this, many are exasperated with the influence of politics over a military that, in an ideal democracy, would be independent:

[At the beginning,] those who led a division would become a high commander. Those who led a regiment would become a colonel, while those who led a battalion would become a major or a captain. Later on, this arrangement format changed when politics became involved. These days, I notice that people who are already at retirement age are still working and holding their positions. So there is now a huge crowd of people with high positions in the structure, and everyone starts to focus only on their respective political party. What position you get, how long you can stay, what you can do, depends on your degree of allegiance to a political party. (BC-KPNLF -4)

Since integration of the military factions, members of the old military elite have found themselves in a double bind: They must distance themselves from the political opposition to stay afloat in the current state military, and at the same time, as former members of the CGDK military, they face discrimination and distrust from the Hun Sen government. Going to the diaspora, however, is not an option for most of them, as they "would be working as subordinates of others" there, an unacceptable status reversal (DC-KPNLF -1). In their view, those who had flipped sides and joined the CPP were just greedy and, of course, lacking in military discipline:

Before integration people only wanted peace. But afterwards, when money and development set in, they became greedy. When soldiers got wealth and salaries, the behavior of some changed completely. Before, they were so disciplined and good. (DC-FUNCINPEC -4)

The military elite strove to reestablish their lost status in the state apparatus but faced a constant deterioration of their actual power and connection to decision-making bodies. Their status in the CGDK enabled them to be reintegrated at rather high levels through shared military commands and to retain social status in contemporary Cambodia similar to the one they held before. But in terms of military powers, they eventually ended up with control over little more than the remnants of their old units.

Only one of the elite Lon Nol commanders interviewed for this project did not accept integration into the military, citing supposed ongoing Vietnamese control over the Hun Sen party as his central motive for rejecting the offer. As with the intellectuals who became impoverished after the war's end, he came from a lower social milieu, but managed to rise in status due to receiving higher education under the Lon Nol regime. However, he was frequently in conflict with the commanders from elite military backgrounds after they joined the CGDK, which is why he never held a rank higher than battalion commander. These quarrels also meant that they did not support him during and after UNTAC. Cutting off his links with the insurgent elite, he also claims to have declined an offer to join the CPP, stating that he was too "proud" to work for a government under "Vietnamese control" that even "made up the whole Khmer Rouge period":

> Because in my opinion, we should have gone against Vietnam, and not worked for them [the Hun Sen government]. If I had agreed, I certainly would not be poor nowadays. Even though my destiny determined my life already, I don't beg them. (BAC-KPNLF -2)[9]

Among the commanders from the military elite, all of those who came from families with an elite heritage managed to reconstitute their high status within post-conflict society and even stay at the senior command level of the state military, at least in terms of formal rank. However, they did not take part in the factional fighting in 1997 and constantly distanced themselves from these events. Instead, they accommodated with the government and tried to maintain their status, which was the result of the integration of forces under UNTAC. Yet, the conflict between the Hun Sen network and the old network of political elites meant a loss in power within the state military, limiting their sphere of influence to their units, usually still stationed somewhere along the border. Civil war meant a loss in status in the first place. Therefore, emigrating to the diaspora is not an option for them, as it would precipitate a similar loss in status, as would a return to civil war. As long as they are able to maintain a higher status within the military state apparatus, at least on paper, this group does not desire a return to war. Even though their current status in the country's elite does not completely match their expectations, all alternatives would leave them worse off—and they are still able to claim a symbolic superiority over the "Hun Sen faction."

ANTI-INTELLECTUAL INTELLECTUALS AND KHMER ROUGE VETERAN COMMANDERS

The Khmer Rouge leadership was composed of many different groups over the years. It was certainly not a monolithic entity (for a detailed history of the creation and demise of the Democratic Kampuchean leadership compare Kiernan 2004, 2002, Etcheson 1984). However, during the last years of its existence and after decades of internal purges and conflict, the top leadership and military directorate throughout the mid- and late 1990s mainly comprised two habitus groups: anti-intellectual intellectuals and veteran commanders who, in many cases, had been members of the anti-colonial resistance, the Khmer Issarak, during the 1940s and 1950s.

Due to their role within the state apparatus of Democratic Kampuchea, a handful of figures from the regime's senior leadership are currently facing trial at the Extraordinary Chambers in the Courts of Cambodia (ECCC). Several have died of old age, while others fell victim to the purges that convulsed the movement during its last months of existence. Some of the few remaining military figures were afraid of being interviewed for this project due to the activities of the tribunal (with rumors circulating that judicial investigators disguise themselves as researchers). These are the primary reasons why the upper echelons of the NADK could not be interviewed for this project. Due to the special character of the Khmer Rouge leadership, their highly sensitive deals with the central government, their mode of reintegration, their current living conditions, and their comparatively numerous deaths, the empirical method employed in this study would have had limited success with this group. The chapter therefore draws upon rather indirect and mixed evidence, mainly from secondary sources.

Only those anti-intellectual intellectuals who had been near the top of the Khmer Rouge leadership and a few veteran commanders actually managed to reintegrate into Cambodian society. Before turning to a short overview of their life courses and at least the initial reintegration of the veteran commanders, the mode of reintegration of the anti-intellectual intellectuals will be discussed, as this reveals a great deal about the reproduction of social inequalities, even with regard to a group such as the high-ranking Khmer Rouge, who probably rank among the most feared and hated leaders in Cambodian society.

A note on a third group of high-ranking—at least on paper—commanders of the NADK is necessary here. Some commanders rose to high ranks very late, receiving these positions as a symbolic reward during the final stages of the conflict when defections had already decimated the guerrillas. Throughout much of the conflict, they had neither supreme positions at the command level nor the power to lead their units autonomously, which is why they—despite their formal rank during reintegration as, for example, division commanders, and their comparatively high positions within the local governance of post-conflict Cambodia—are discussed as mid-range commanders under the heading "blank-page leaders." This is basically a theoretical decision by the author in view of actual command powers and influence over the wider military apparatus of the NADK. These commanders were, on paper, in charge of "divisions," but these units were usually the size of battalions at best.

Anti-Intellectual Intellectuals

Contrary to their own self-propagated ideal of anti-intellectualism, anti-feudalism, and anti-elitism, an important wing of the NADK leadership—and of the top echelon of the Democratic Kampuchea regime—came from privileged families with deep roots within the country's political, economic, and academic elite (cf. Bultmann 2015, 77–82). This group shared a similar social background and life course, which even at early stages of their lives constantly overlapped. Due to their family backgrounds, all had significant social, cultural, and economic resources to pursue careers in the political field. While they were screening for recruits with "pure revolutionary backgrounds," their own families of origin were well-off farmers owning large tracts of land, wealthy businessmen, members of the royal court reaching back to the colonial administration, members of the educated upper class, or officials within the Sihanoukian state apparatus. Many members of the inner circle of the Communist leadership went to the renowned Lycée Sisowath in Phnom Penh or finished their degrees at other exclusive high schools in the capital (including Pol Pot; Short 2006).

Their family and school connections earned them scholarships—not least by nationalist wings of the Democratic Party—to study in Paris during the late 1940s and early 1950s. The "who's who" of the future Communist party leadership went to Paris during the same period and encountered a European Communist movement on the rise and a highly politicized student body. Many became formal members of the French Communist Party, while a famous reading circle was formed by central figures such as Saloth Sar (Pol Pot), Ieng Sary, Khieu Samphan, Son Sen, Thiounn Mumm, Thiounn Prasith, Hou Youn, and Hu Nim, among others (Becker 1998, 212).

While some had to discontinue their studies for more or less political reasons (e.g., Son Sen, whose scholarship was withdrawn, and Pol Pot, who simply failed out), others returned to Cambodia with a PhD (e.g., Hou Youn and Khieu Samphan). Less than a decade after their return, the Paris-educated intellectuals took over central positions within the Cambodian leftist movement (particularly after the death of the party's chairman, Tou Samouth, in 1963), whose formation can be traced back to the split of the Indochinese Communist Party into three national formations in Cambodia, Laos, and Vietnam in 1954.[10] However, at the time of their return, the Communist party was still highly marginalized and Norodom Sihanouk seemed untouchable.

With at best a few hundred members, it could barely be called a movement (Kiernan 2004, Chandler 2008, Bultmann 2017).

Due to the increasing spillover of the Vietnam War (with North Vietnamese troops using the Ho Chi Minh Trail through Cambodian territory from 1965 onwards), deepening economic problems (partly caused by the war in neighboring Vietnam), an autocratic rule during an escalation of Cold War politics, and, finally, the parliamentary coup against Sihanouk in 1970, Cambodia slid into civil war. The Khmer Rouge found themselves elevated from an extremely marginalized position to controlling the entire country by April 1975. This was due to the support of Norodom Sihanouk, who had in 1970 formed a coalition with them after being ousted in a coup, as well as several other factors: heightened US carpet bombings, the infiltration of North and South Vietnamese troops, and Vietnamese (until 1973 at least) and Chinese backing. The intellectuals occupied central political positions guiding and instructing the military apparatus, with some even directly in charge of matters of defense (Son Sen even assumed the supreme command of the NADK forces after Pol Pot's official retirement in 1985). Throughout the regime, more moderate intellectuals were killed (e.g., Hou Youn and Hu Nim), while other more hard-line intellectuals remained atop the leadership pyramid until the late 1990s.

Veteran Khmer Rouge Commanders

At the upper command level of the NADK forces before major defections set in during the mid-1990s, another important group of Communist leaders had been long-serving veterans: Ta Mok, Meas Muth (Ta Mok's son-in-law), Sou Met, Ke Pauk, and others, of whom many had been part of the anti-colonial resistance, the so-called Khmer Issarak ("Free Khmer"). By the late 1990s, these battle-hardened commanders had been part of the anti-colonial and Communist military for four to five decades already. Ta Mok, for instance, went to a Pali school in Phnom Penh, then dropped out to join the Khmer Issarak in the early 1940s. As a young member of the anti-colonial and, later, the Communist rebellion, he rose fast in the armed forces fighting for a completely equal and independent society and was a central figure in the party purges from 1975 until 1979, earning himself the nickname "the butcher." During the civil war from 1979 to 1999, these anti-colonial veteran commanders were in charge of military regions and important units. After the murder of Son Sen in 1997, Ta Mok even named himself supreme commander of the NADK.

The "Win-Win Policy" and its Influence on the Politics Surrounding the Khmer Rouge Tribunal

There were two main waves of defection from the NADK leadership to the government.[11] The first was in late 1996, when Pailin and Malai (Ieng Sary, Y Chhean, and Sok Pheap) as well as factions in Samlaut (including Meas Muth[12] and Sou Met) followed the government's call to defect. They received the promised land, positions in the government and military, a certain level of political autonomy, and—in case of Ieng Sary, who had been sentenced to death in absentia by the People Revolutionary Tribunal in 1979 under the newly formed People's Republic of Kampuchea (PRK)—immunity through a royal pardon (for a detailed timeline of the defections see Nem 2012, 140–44).

The second wave of defections occurred after Pol Pot's death, the clashes between the co-premiers Hun Sen and Ranariddh, and the FUNCINPEC election loss in 1998. In 1997, FUNCINPEC had secretly negotiated a deal with members of the Khmer Rouge to augment its forces so it could counter the Cambodian People's Party (CPP) under co-premier Hun Sen. Over several weeks, and without the knowledge of Pol Pot, Nhek Bunchhay, Khan Savoeun, Tun Chay and Long Sarin met with Ta Mok, Khieu Samphan, Tep Khunnal, and Long Tem (Dy 2015, 176–77). The negotiations not only increased tensions between the co-premiers, but also between Pol Pot and the "traitors" talking to FUNCINPEC, culminating in the murder of Son Sen and his family, and skirmishes between supporters of both Khmer Rouge factions. Eventually, Pol Pot and his entourage were arrested by Ta Mok's men and put on trial as "traitors to the revolution" (Widyono 2008, Dy and Dearing 2014, 101–28)

However, due to the clashes between Hun Sen and Ranariddh and FUNCINPEC's eventual election loss in mid-1998, the deal-makers surrounding Khieu Samphan had few options but to "defect" to the Hun Sen government (without receiving government positions) and to return to the "national fold." Given the politics and allegiances of reintegration, it looked more like a surrender than a defection. All late defectors and those who negotiated with Ranariddh either ended up in prison at the international tribunal in Phnom Penh (Khieu Samphan, Ta Mok, and Nuon Chea) or still live in constant fear of persecution and revenge reprisals by the Hun Sen government. This became clear over several years of research, during which repeated attempts to talk to the "second-wave defectors" who did not end up at the ECCC failed, as they said they were too afraid to be interviewed given the current political atmosphere.

Reintegration remains tenuous for them, and thus a topic they prefer to avoid. Ta Mok, who remained on Ranariddh's side even after the factional clashes in July 1997, was the only Khmer Rouge leader who neither defected nor surrendered; instead, he went into hiding until being arrested on March 6, 1999. He died in custody seven years later while awaiting trial. By contrast, those who sided with Hun Sen even at the very last moment, attacking Ta Mok's units alongside the Hun Sen troops, and who had not been part of the negotiations with FUNCINPEC, were put in charge of the local government and received land as well as lucrative positions in the state military in the same areas (Anlong Veng and Preah Vihear).

The level of protection from prosecution by the international tribunal follows, among others, these political allegiances stemming from the two waves of defections, with the factions that defected early being the best protected. As of the time of writing, Hun Sen is still blocking cases 003 and 004 at the Extraordinary Chambers in the Courts of Cambodia, which among others would have included Meas Muth and Sou Met, who joined the state military comparatively early, during the "first wave" in 1996.[13] The Hun Sen government was also heavily at odds with the inclusion of Ieng Sary, who received a royal pardon in 1996 in exchange for giving up guerrilla warfare (for a closer discussion of political interferences by the Cambodian government in the proceedings of the tribunal compare Torrens 2016).

The tribunal, however, refused to recognize the pardon and forced the government to drop its protection of Ieng Sary (Heindel and Ciorciari 2014, Selbmann 2016). Although Ieng Sary's inclusion in the tribunal could not be prevented by government interference (mainly due to international pressure and his obviously senior position), his family still controls important positions in the local government and economy of Pailin province (e.g., his son Ieng Vuth is the province's deputy governor). By contrast, Ke Pauk (defecting in 1998) likely would have faced trial if he had not died of a stroke in 2002. While constantly speaking of a possible relapse into civil war if, for instance, Meas Muth was to be included in the proceedings, the prime minister had a strikingly different reaction to the death of Ke Pauk: "Hun Sen refused to mourn him, saying he was a killer" (APTN 2002). As a result of the politics of defection and the different stages of reintegration, as well as complex network allegiances, many inhabitants of Anlong Veng who fought until the very end are still strikingly more skeptical of outsiders than the communities in Pailin, Malai, or Samlaut (cf. Hennings 2017).

Not-So-Happy "Winners"

Although every Khmer Rouge leader except for Ta Mok defected to the government and abandoned guerrilla warfare, and most also took up positions in the "win-win framework," not all former Khmer Rouge feel safe or happy with the government. Chan Youran, for instance, now lives withdrawn from politics in a pagoda in Phnom Penh, claiming to strive for "peace and quiet" after a "life of pain" (Chan 2009). Several former Khmer Rouge commanders interviewed for this project who fought until the end took refuge in pagodas. In interviews, many told of their theories that the country is still in the midst of a Vietnamese occupation that should be resisted.

Other intellectuals returned to civilian jobs. The Paris-educated Tep Khunnal, for instance, who married Pol Pot's second wife, Meas Son, and adopted their daughter, Sar Patchata, after his death, became head of the ruling CPP in Malai district and, on the side, returned to his academic roots and is currently working at a university in Battambang City teaching strategic management courses, with a special focus on the business theories of Peter Drucker. He also manages an investment firm "promoting capitalism" (Willemyns and Hul 2014). While most former Khmer Rouge cadres publicly praise Hun Sen's leadership, especially the defectors of the "second wave" and former allies of FUNCINPEC, most of the time they try to keep a low profile and claim that they have "nothing to do with politics" anymore (Chan 2009). When visiting them at their homes in Anlong Veng, Samlaut, Battambang, or Pailin, or in pagodas across the country, it becomes clear that by no means all of them got rich in backroom deals. The decisive factors were the period during which they defected, and whether they had been close to FUNCINPEC and other opposition networks.

At first glance, and again with the exception of those who ended up at the tribunal, most former upper-level commanders of the Khmer Rouge armed forces returned to high positions in the government, the military, or education, thereby appearing to reproduce social inequalities in transition. However, not only are the members of the "second wave" of defectors now struggling to remain underneath the political and juridical radar, but the impression of lucrative deals and new-found loyalty to Hun Sen fades quickly when taking a closer look at their current lives. For example, an intellectual who was interviewed for this project in Samraong, Oddar Meanchey province, was granted the honorific title "Advisor to the Ministry of Defense" and given a high-ranking position in a provincial government after reintegration. However, he claims that he never attended a single meeting at the ministry and did not receive a pension after retirement, a statement supported by the fact that he now lives in a cobbled-together wooden shack without electricity or clean water. When talking about the government, he said that he was still "very concerned" about its intentions, but "at least there are now some human rights organizations who take care of that, so I am a bit less concerned"

(BC-NADK -1). Thus, these high positions did not automatically yield riches; money had to be earned by early and ongoing loyalty. The benefits of the "win-win policy" were clearly not equally distributed; not everyone "won" the same amount of money, opportunity, and security.

For this respondent, the breakdown of the Khmer Rouge during its last three years of existence was highly regrettable. In his view, internal conflicts among the ranks of the Communist movement arose due to the "political situation" and—of course—"Yuon interference," which led to rifts within the leadership. All he could do then was "to make myself survive" (BC-NADK -1). Since he opted "for the wrong side" during the factional clashes in mid-1997, he was "on the run" for a longer period of time before defecting. In the end, he "joined" the government because Pol Pot's death meant an end to all resistance to him—without Pol Pot the armed struggle lost its purpose and he surrendered. He compared the final days of the Khmer Rouge movement to those of Nazi Germany: "It was like with Adolf Hitler. Without him, Germany collapsed" (BC-NADK -1).

In his view, it was Germany that collapsed, not just the Nazi movement. In a similar vein, many of the defectors still imagine Cambodia on the verge of destruction by Vietnamese plots. This continuing discourse of a life-and-death resistance against Vietnamese aggression was evident among almost all ranks of the Khmer Rouge, but particularly among the "second wave" defectors, and will be discussed in a later chapter on the symbolic conversion of the former NADK combatants and commanders. For many, defection was a necessary tactical move of aging rebels in an ongoing struggle against the Yuon and their colonialist aims. Even for the Khmer Rouge top command, social inequalities were reproduced during transition, although national and international politics have interfered more heavily in their case. However, the importance of inherited social status—or lack thereof—is particularly visible in the case of the guerrilla strongmen discussed in the next chapter.

STRONGMEN

ឃ្លូ មិន ខ្លាច ទៅ ខ្លាច ខ្លា។

—A Cambodian aphorism: "You do not fear the *kleh* (cockspur thorn), yet you fear the *klah* (tiger)."

While most in the field of insurgency—even the Khmer Rouge top command—were able to claim leadership through a largely inherited social, cultural, or economic status (along with the requisite resources), strongmen came from rather low strata of society, almost without any resources at their disposal. All came from distant villages in the countryside and found it difficult to obtain schooling due to their families' poor living conditions. Many could not finish school and viewed themselves as illiterate. For instance, one strongman said, "I was born into a poor family, and did not reach a high level of education. [. . .] I know nothing; I am very stupid. I can't even spell out the alphabet properly" (CC-FUNCINPEC -1). The strongmen thus had highly field-bound resources, which makes their case especially interesting for studying mechanisms of transition.

When young, very few managed to finish schooling (at least up to Bac I in the Cambodian system).[14] Almost all, however, managed to become local policemen, Lon Nol rank-and-file soldiers, or low-ranking civil servants within the countryside. This explains why all of the interviewed strongmen said they had feared being executed as "enemies of the people" under the Khmer Rouge regime due to their relations with the besieged Lon Nol government and its state apparatus and military. They did not actually "join" the insurgency, but instead formed small armed groups, mostly out of fear of being executed by the Communists. These groups consisted of little more than a handful of people and even fewer weapons, if any. During the Khmer Rouge reign, they fought for their own survival, not only against the Communists, but also against the Thai forces in the borderlands.

Being part of these first insurgent formations brought a steep rise in status when the Vietnamese arrived to dismantle the Pol Pot regime in early 1979. Suddenly, these armed bands were among the few forces with which it was possible to create an insurgency against the Soviet-backed Vietnamese. The returning political and military elite from the diasporas in the United States and France were badly in need of a fighting force, and the strongmen, who managed to take control of the early refugee encampments even with the limited power of their small weaponry, were among the few available "military" formations to appropriate and expand upon. Most of the strongmen rose in rank during these early years, in which superiority was derived from a warrior ethos of being fatefully unwoundable and battle-hardened as well as the simple fact that there were few fighting forces around to rely on. Others started off as child soldiers, with some even having been part of the Khmer Rouge military and then joining the non-Communists during the early 1980s. Many of their colleagues died over the years, leaving behind only those who—in their own view—"were meant to survive" (DC-FUNCINPEC -2).

The habitus of the strongmen revolves around a warrior ethos. In their interviews, and often even within the whole setting in which these interviews took place, all of the strongmen tried to portray themselves as fearless roughnecks. Combat had been their main strength and symbolic resource. In the words of one strongman, "I was not like all the other commanders, wait-ing at the back and commanding from hundreds of kilometers away" (RC-FUNCINPEC -1). This strongman received comparatively little education, but was well-taught by the school of combat, stating, "I received only little education, but I have been proficient in fighting. I am only saying that I got involved in countless battles, and this makes me know all the necessary tech-niques" (RC-FUNCINPEC -1). They seemed to know no fear. According to another, "I would never lower myself during combat" (CC-FUNCINPEC -1). They also led their people by being models of heroic soldiers, always walking in front. For instance, "When there was a mine, I would tell [my people] to stand still, and I would walk past it for them" (CC-FUNCINPEC -1). During the interviews, one respondent even mocked the researcher, constantly asking whether he was afraid of him at that time (BC-KPNLF -7). Bravery and an aura of fear were central to their symbolic claims for leadership. As one aptly noted, "I am brave. And I always made sure that people were afraid of me" (CC-FUNCINPEC -1).

Being strong and fearless was described as a function of being chosen by fate to survive and to lead. Especially for those who remain in high posi-tions today, it was important to constantly claim that they were "meant to be a commander" and that this was their "fate." All played upon a notion of being spiritually protected, and all had magical tattoos covering their bodies and possessed countless amulets and powerful cloth talismans. They claimed this was why they could walk upright through battles with no need to duck or crawl, without being hit by a single bullet or piece of shrapnel.[15] In their own view, it was not a matter of mere luck that enabled them to rise in rank but a matter of being chosen by fate to lead. All explained their rise to leadership roles in the KPNLF and FUNCINPEC as a matter of being commanders by an inborn character:

> Everyone who knows me knows that I have a high leadership potential. When I was still at school, I was a leader throughout all the classes I attended. After finishing school, I became a soldier. After finishing six months of military school, I was chosen to lead a company of 100 men against the incoming Khmer Rouge. After I fled the Khmer Rouge, I was able to organize my own forces. You see, I have always been a commander. And soldiers were always safe with me. (BC-KPNLF -8)

However, they also stressed that they had little tolerance for dissent in the ranks, and disobedient soldiers were treated violently (e.g., by hitting them with sticks), scolded for misconduct, or even killed. As one strongman em-phasized, "As a commander, if we speak nicely to our soldiers, they would not follow. We have to use violent means to command them. Using morality would fail" (RC-FUNCINPEC -1). A commander had to be feared not only by competing factions along the border, but by his own followers as well. Commanders, as one strongman explained, had to be a *kleh*, the plant known in English as a cockspur thorn: "If we compare soldiers to tigers, the commander has to be *kleh*" (RC-FUNCINPEC -1). This metaphor is drawn from a traditional Cambodian fable in which a blind man and a disabled man are walking together through a forest. As they move along, the blind man says that he is in the woods because he is afraid tigers would spot them out in the open. The disabled man then starts to mock him, as he thinks that the *kleh*, the cockspur thorn, would be much more dangerous than a tiger (*klah* in Khmer), since it is a more concrete threat to them at that moment. Overhearing the conversation, a nearby tiger starts to believe that a *kleh* is an even mightier and more frightening animal than himself. The tiger, the most feared animal in nature, suddenly gets scared of the power which for him is unknown: the *kleh*.

Although they may be frightening thorns—or maybe "unknowns"—to their tigers, strongmen also picture themselves as caretakers. One even described how fiercely he protected his family and the people under his command:

> One day they [other leaders from the insurgency in cooperation with the Thais] plotted to murder me. [After a Vietnamese attack], the Thais demanded to hand over all the weapons in the camp, and then started to take them. My wife said I would certainly die if I gave them my weapon. But I had no choice, because they would have killed her first. Later that night, the Thais came in to manhandle our people. However, I still had a small knife, which I could use to protect my people. They did not dare to come close to me as I would have chopped all of them into pieces. (CC-FUNCINPEC -1)

The strongmen were rough and violent, but also viewed themselves as protectors and patronized their followers. According to one, "Commanders need to know their subordinates' needs and sufferings. Education has no function here. Some are highly educated, but still cannot lead" (BC-FUNCINPEC -3). The strongman was to take care of his followers as if they were members of his family.[16] All strongmen amassed a large network which they took great pains to provide for using various sources of income, from the diversion of aid to profits from cross-border trade. These economic activities did not just serve their own enrichment, but first and foremost secured obedience within their entourages. The use of economic profits was pre-eminently political, in the sense of securing loyalty to the ruler. They also kept very close to their soldiers by eating with them, going into combat together, constantly monitoring their loyalty to their patrons, and violently punishing disobedience to their own command, while misconduct against civilians went largely unpunished.[17]

Steve Heder identified three pillars of political legitimacy in postcolonial Cambodia: *sdech*, the royal legitimacy of kings and princes keeping order within a universe governed by *dharma*; *neak cheh doeng*, people of higher education and knowledge (the symbolic resource that fits the intellectual commanders best); and more in correspondence with the strongmen's bid for legitimacy, *neak tâsou*, people who successfully took part in armed struggle against social injustices (Heder 1995).[18] However, while the first two claims for political rule in Cambodia are rather stable, it was difficult for the strongmen to maintain the wartime value of their symbolic resource as a *neak tâsou* in times of peace (the same problem also affected the Khmer Rouge veteran commanders).

Status Change and Resource Valuation during Transition

All strongmen stressed that they served as role models for ordinary soldiers. They were perfectly brave, violent, solicitous, and obedient soldiers. However, during the transition to peace this emerged as a problem for them: Symbolically, they were nothing more than perfect soldiers. The strongman's main symbolic resource evolves within the field of insurgency and is very much bound to its existence. Peace threatened their status through a potential relapse into a low social milieu. The perpetuation of conflict, therefore, was in their best interest, which is most likely why all of the strongmen interviewed fought until the very last day of the Cambodian conflict. They did not leave the guerrilla factions after the Vietnamese withdrew in 1989, the main political motive of the warring factions. They did not even leave after the Paris Peace Agreement in 1991. They also did not leave after the election in 1993 but remained active within the military networks inbetween often preparing for an eventual relapse into civil war.[19] And even after the "coup"—in which all played major parts—they fought on until the elections in 1998.

However, these former strongmen faced very different fates after 1998. While one group lost all its wartime-related resources and social status, another group brokered very good deals with the incumbent Hun Sen government, but was neutralized militarily, with some facing persecution after a decade or even sitting in jail, showing that their status remains insecure until today. The main resource for brokering a deal with the government was the size of their military entourages. The strongmen with higher ranks, such as brigade or even division commanders, and those who had larger entourages with at least 1,000 people under their command, were able to make deals and join the ranks of the government in lucrative and formally senior positions, either in the military or the political domain. After joining, however, they were all given positions without direct control over a specific unit in order to contain their military strength (Levy 1999). All maintained small military entourages of bodyguards, but that seemed to be the limit of their personal authority (although the informal reach of the network is almost impossible to assess). These guards served as watchdogs and lived at their home compounds. During the interviews, it was striking to discover how their homes resembled small military barracks even more than a decade after the end of the war. This stood in stark contrast to their official positions in the top echelons of the government and their reputations among the populace as opportunistic politicians who were only interested in personal gain.

Why did they broker deals with the government, and not with their losing but still existing opposition network? The answer lies in the quality of their networks within the insurgency. All strongmen had somewhat negative reputations due to their warrior habitus, and their origin in lower social milieus. Commanders from the long-standing opposition elite always stressed that they were "not really high-ranking" and "not important," "illiterate," and rather "wild" (DC-FUNCINPEC -3, DC-KPNLF -1). Even though these commanders had an extensive network within the resistance, they were simply dropped afterwards and did not participate in the reconstitution of the group as a *political* network. Therefore, each commander was forced to make deals with the government on his own. They constantly likened this to being a child in conflict with his father, a situation in which "we had to be able to understand how opportunities could be sought, what we should do, how to be flexible under changing societal circumstances and so on" (BC-KPNLF -9). The government's newly adopted children simply had to adapt to the new conditions:

> I also did not know what to do [after the war's end]. The most important thing was just to adapt ourselves and to get into a position granted by an elected and lawful government. Regardless of whether we are happy with the government, there is nothing we can do. After all, however, we cannot have a government which everybody likes anyways. In a family, when the father makes mistakes sometimes, there is nothing we can say. We see that the government's leadership has both good and bad points, but we have to adapt to it for the sake of our personal happiness as well as that of the whole society. Everyone claims that they love their country. They also love it, and so do we. We are not jealous of them as long as they lead the country forward. I managed to survive during the ten years [of civil war] fighting countless battles, and I also managed survive [politics] during the past ten years. So we all will just try to maintain our happiness. (BC-FUNCINPEC -4)

However, despite this deflated optimism, one respondent even faced legal action some months after the interview. He was imprisoned under on charges of owning weapons and dealing drugs. Three top commanders from very similar social backgrounds who fought with him during the confrontation with Hun Sen from 1997 to 1998 were also arrested under the same charges. The rest remain tightly secure in their home compounds.

Those who did not have big enough bargaining chips for deal-making during the transition lost almost everything. Not only were their reputations as strong warriors worthless, but they actually hampered (re)integration due to the blood on their hands (especially for those who had been part of the Khmer Rouge before joining the non-Communist factions, serving in the dreaded "Black Eagle Unit").[20] Besides losing their symbolic value, they also lost support from the network within the opposition elite. Even when they were still part of the insurgency, they were constantly getting into trouble with their own people, with one strongman admitting, "People in FUNCINPEC did not trust me" (RC-FUNCINPEC -2). Recalling an argument with the commander-in-chief of FUNCINPEC, one strongman vividly described his own brash style of confrontation: "Then I pointed my finger at his head and said, 'You fucking dog, who the hell do you think you are?' At that moment, he was shaking all over his body. I threatened to kill all these guys [standing by] with my bullets" (RC-FUNCINPEC -1).

Their strongman, roughneck habitus made it difficult for them to stay with their old network. The horizontal network consisted not only of weak ties, but even in terms of support in different fields, negative associations as well. A deal with the government, with the estranged "family," was their last chance for survival in the new world. Those who could not make a deal due to low ranks and small entourages compared themselves to dead people due to the loss of their horizontal networks. According to one such strongman, "I can be compared to a dead person because no one wants to be friend[s] with me anymore" (CC-FUNCINPEC -1). They constantly stressed how bad their lives had become after reintegration. As another strongman put it, "Every time I talk about the history of my life, I cannot hold back my tears" (RC-FUNCINPEC -2). At first they were happy, as they expected a good life after the war's end ("We were all very happy with the end of the war as we expected to receive positions of power and money, among others" (RC-FUNCINPEC -1)). But this did not work out, as they were soon dropped by their old networks and were seen as not worth dealing with by the incumbent government. As one strongman stated, "So I lost everything. [. . .] Although I tried my best along the border and had a tough life, in the end I got nothing from it. I was cheated by the King [as former head of FUNCINPEC]. I really regret [my loyalty to him]" (CC-FUNCINPEC -1).

Nowadays, these former mid-range strongmen (in control of a regiment at best) are poor farmers who are highly dependent on support by development organizations and family members (their own children in particular). Some even live in villages that were set up by international relief organizations during UNTAC in order to relocate the border camp population into the interior. Even today, these villages are called "camp villages" (*phum djum-rum*) among residents and neighboring communities, and people living there are stigmatized within the broader local populace. One respondent said he would prefer death over his current life; after the war he had hoped to at least receive some farmland, but instead got a tiny worthless plot near the "camp village": "I always tell my relatives that I was a protector of our nation's land but ended up having no land for myself. Every time I talk about this, I cry. Those who died during the war are luckier than me, because they do not have to endure these hardships like I have in these days" (RC-FUNCINPEC -2). For one strongman, the only hope was a return to war, a chance to fight for the old cause to liberate the Mekong Delta in South Vietnam, an area called "Lower Cambodia" (*Kampuchea Krom* in Khmer) by Cambodian nationalists that was "lost" to the Vietnamese in the seventeenth century. In his view, "If there [was] anybody supporting me, I would return to live for my dream to fight to get Kampuchea Krom back from the Vietnamese" (RC-FUNCINPEC -2). Fighting in itself seemed to be the main point of interest for him, largely because it would allow him to revert to his status as a respected warrior.

Whether or not they were successful after (re)integration, all strongmen faced a steep devaluation of their social, cultural, and symbolic resources, which were what had brought them into certain leadership circles in the first place. Their relations to the leaders of the insurgency had remained fragile throughout the war, and these rather opportunistic alliances quickly broke down during the transition. As their weak horizontal networks began to disintegrate, the strongmen did their best to maintain their vertical networks, essentially consisting of their military entourages, who even today may serve as guards in the strongmen's residential compounds. Strongmen, unlike elite commanders in the field, took great pains to position themselves as caring father figures to their entourages.

As a result, these soldiers within their entourage to this day speak of their strongman commanders as benevolent caretakers. In the words of one, "My commander loves me; he never left me. He still likes me and I like him as well. If we do something good for him, we receive a lot, such as money" (GBC-KPNLF -1). All of these guards come from rather low social milieus, just like their commanders. One of the guards interviewed in a strongman's compound stressed that he was treated like a family member, although at the same time he unintentionally betrayed the underlying fear of the others in his unit, stating, "If there is some fruit on the table, he would share some with us. If there was a case of beer, he would give us half of it. He ate what we ate. He didn't mind me sitting at his table. Although, besides me, none of his staff dared to sit next to him" (GBC-KPNLF -1). Even though the strongmen were not present during the interviews with their followers, these answers of course do not necessarily reflect actual affection, but rather the nature of an asymmetric relationship in which "love" (expressed through money, jobs, and other resources) flows down in exchange for loyalty.

Still, in addition to this support, the strongmen needed extensive financial input or government positions and resources to sustain their patrimonial entourages. While those who were able to make deals had the power to keep their entourages afloat, others could not afford to sustain internal cohesion and had to break away from their followers. They lost not only the symbolic value of being powerful warriors, but also their essential social resources: both their horizontal and vertical networks. Even harder for them was that everything that had enabled them to rise in the field of the insurgency changed diametrically. During war, they were feared and respected for their fierce behavior; when peace arrived, they were disrespected for having been so fierce.

Religious Conversion

This symbolic loss had to be compensated for through a symbolic conversion into a narrative of a "new personality." Until today, the strongmen have struggled with the stigma—as Erving Goffman would call it—of having their virtual social identity fail to fit their actual social identity (Goffman 1963). This creates a mismatch that they try to bridge—or, in Goffman's terms, a "spoiled identity" they try to get rid of by creating a new (positive) virtual social identity which their current actual social status will fit into and which will lift them up in status (again). The strongmen who believed that they had lost everything had to find a way to reconstruct their social status within the community, and either looked for a chance to be part of an insurgency again or turned to Christianity. One example of a conversion narrative by a strongman is particularly striking. Over the course of the interview, he stressed how nasty he was as a commander and how badly he treated people, particularly his own followers: "I always scolded them. I could not stop myself from that habit. I could speak nicely only if I was not angry. As soon as I turned angry, I wouldn't talk more than three words. I would punch if I needed to. I never cared about committing a sin at all. I did not believe in things like god or sin. Although I used to be a monk, I found no hope in religion. I never believed in it" (RC-FUNCINPEC -2).

Buddhism did not inspire him either. He read about Buddha's teachings only to be disappointed. According to his own understanding, Buddha said that "religion could not help us, but it could lead us to god. That god is called

Preah Se Ah Metrey. He would come in the near future, but very few people would accept him. This teaching disappointed me because Buddha says religion could not help us. He simply told us to do good things so that we can live long enough to witness this god" (RC-FUNCINPEC -2). Interestingly, *Preah Se Ah Metrey* is a god in Cambodian Buddhist mythology, but one who did *not* reach enlightenment. According to the strongman's narrative, life during war was misguided by Buddhist teachings, which were of no help to understanding sin or to witnessing god. He did not yet understand the powers of *Preah Se Ah Metrey*. But then, after the war's end, a woman came to his house on a regular basis, annoying him by telling him he should read the Bible. He always refused, sending her away each time. Sometimes, he even picked a fight with his wife or his kids just to get her away. This did not help, since "she kept on coming to my house, again and again. As I got frustrated with her, I started talking to her. I asked her to stop coming to my house after giving me the book. She then gave me a Bible" (RC-FUNCINPEC -2).

Over the course of the interview, he kept his Bible firmly in his hands. He went on to talk about how reading the Bible had pushed him through a period that changed his life:

> When I got the Bible, I started to read it. Life as a soldier was not joyful. Even at those times when we did not fight, we were sleeping in our hammocks or cooking our meals. I read the Bible a lot, and I sometimes even fell asleep with it on my chest. When I woke up, I went on reading right away. I then started to think about what the Bible says. God says that he is the alpha and the omega, the first and the last. [The Apostle] Thomas, who did not believe in Christ's resurrection, said he was merely a ghost. Then, Christ asked him to touch his ribs, which had been stabbed, and his palm, which had been nailed. The Bible also told us to talk to God if we wanted to understand more about Christianity. At that time, I talked to Christ, saying, "Christ, if you are really the promised *Preah Se Ah Metrey*, please introduce yourself to me, so I can accept you." (RC-FUNCINPEC -2)

Reading the Bible made him realize how everyone on earth is plagued by an original sin. He started to believe that he himself was sinful, aggressive, and abusive as a warrior due to his neglect of Christ. In his view, "After I gained faith in Christ, I thought I became such a bad person because all people in this world are full of sin" (RC-FUNCINPEC -2). However, true faith made him a better person, since he said, "As a soldier, I had been a very aggressive person. But when I started believing in God and his teachings, I became a much better person. Afterwards, I could finally live my life happily. I have a small house now. I am patient, and I strive. What I have achieved today is actually the result of God's assistance, and not of my own making" (RC-FUNCINPEC -2).

Conversion to Christianity allowed him to realize the true powers of the promised *Preah Se Ah Metrey*. On a symbolic level and more importantly maybe, it also allowed him to get rid of his former personality, becoming patient and calm instead of aggressive, respected instead of disrespected, and part of a larger community of believers instead of being abandoned by his former colleagues in the insurgency. The loss of the powerful identity of a strongman was compensated by a new set of symbolic and peaceful gains. The description of his conversion to Christianity resembles a *rite de passage* (rite of passage), as described by the cultural anthropologist Victor Turner, in which a person goes through a period of conversion and crisis detached from others (in the strongman's case: reading and studying the Bible, and realizing the sinfulness of his old self) until he becomes a new and symbolically cleansed self (cf. Turner 1969). In a world where his old self did not fit anymore, this strongman developed a narrative of change to construct a new self—at least in the eye of others.

Due to the high value of battle and weaponry experience during the early years of internal warfare and of a warrior ethos in the field of insurgency, the strongmen were able to rise rapidly in status. They positioned themselves as anti-elitist, or as model soldiers, who joined the frontline, taking all the risks necessary to prove their strength and show they were chosen by fate to lead. Part of their habitus was also to scold and threaten people, including their "colleagues" within the leadership. However, their symbolic and social resources came under heavy duress during the conversion to peace and the dissolution of their former field. Their value was highly field-bound, and therefore almost non-transferable into a society at peace. This explains why: (1) they fought for so long; (2) some may have even preferred a relapse into conflict; (3) they desperately needed to make deals with the incumbent governments to secure positions, especially after being dropped by their own networks; (4) vertical networks were strategically so important to them during the transition and beyond; and (5) symbolic conversion was needed to reintegrate into the new society if they were not able to make good deals, thus restoring their social recognition through other means.

While the civil war made higher levels of social mobility possible, all faced the risk of a status reversal during the transition to peace. Only those who were able to make a deal with the ruling party due to their control of strong vertical networks retained a high socio-political status within the new state. However, it is questionable whether this would last long (as already indicated through imprisonment and loss of powers over the years) and over generations to come. All members of the insurgency's top command with an elite family heritage were able to make use of pathways to retain their high social status; only those coming from lower social milieus and climbing steeply in status within the insurgency, like the strongmen, risked a return to their pre-war status. All respondents who made a career within the insurgency and had no elite heritage—the strongmen in particular—struggled to transfer their wartime social status into modern Cambodia and its political field.

While some strongmen had very few followers, which meant that they were mid-range commanders in rank and made it impossible for them to secure a position in the government, they were treated as members of the leadership in this chapter since all acted as leaders of independent units. The following chapter, by contrast, deals with those commanders who had to implement the command of others.

NOTES

1. The first two letters of the coding system for the interviews relate to the position or military rank of the respondents before reintegration. Within the second part, I chose to refer to the formal membership of respondents *before* the start of the UNAMIC and UNTAC peace missions. The main reason for this decision is the fact that, after the elections in 1993 at the latest, most members of the KPNLF military wing joined the more powerful winner of the elections, FUNCINPEC. This meant that, at the end of the conflict, the majority of respondents officially belonged to FUNCINPEC. Formal membership, as will be outlined more in detail later, is not very important anyway. Respondents who have changed their allegiances more than twice are referred to as "MF": Multiple Factions (changing sides between the three insurgent factions or sometimes even the incumbent government).

2. The network of the KPNLF, however, reaches much further back, with many members even having declared their allegiance to the Democratic Party under Sihanouk's Sangkum, which was officially dissolved in 1957 (e.g., RC-KPNLF -2, PL-KPNLF -1).

3. There seems to have been a generational divide between an old military elite and military "newcomers" as well. Some respondents believed that this was the actual cause for the divide. However, it seems that they did not mean newcomers as of the 1980s during which the split took place but refer to a divide caused by new commanders entering the apparatus during the Lon Nol regime—coming into conflict with commanders from the Sangkum period. Most likely, old animosities within the military establishment caused by the coup in 1970 against Sihanouk came up while forming a "united front" against the Vietnamese during the 1980s—at least, adding fuel to the split between Son Sann and Sak Sutsakhan, who had been a Minister of Defence during the Sangkum period in 1957.

4. Interviews that were conducted in English are cited word-for-word, with capitals indicating accentuations.

5. Many former CGDK members also joined the Sam Rainsy Party (SRP) or Kem Sokha's Human Rights Party (HRP), which merged into the Cambodia National Rescue Party (CNRP) in 2012. Due to FUNCINPEC's current lack of power and ef-

fectiveness, and infighting within the party, countless former CGDK politicians and intellectuals have switched to the CNRP over the last several years.

6. In the Khmer original, the respondent used the term *suvannaphum* here, which translates as "golden land" and is the Khmer version of the Sanskrit *suvarnabhumi*. This mythical kingdom was mentioned in several classic Buddhist sources and has spawned competing claims in South and Southeast Asia over its exact location.

7. Kong Sileah reportedly died of malaria. In an interview, however, one commander close to him claimed that he was poisoned due to a dispute over whether to join the KPNLF (DC-FUNCINPEC -2).

8. In a way, they are right to claim the status of commanders within the state military before the Paris Peace Agreement, because the international community allocated the seat at the UN to the CGDK as the "legitimate" Cambodian government. Hence, viewed exclusively from the perspective of formal status at the UN, they had been the *state* military until 1991, while the Hun Sen government was an illegitimate insurgent faction. Cold War politics said so. However, this point also hints at a deeper problem in civil war research: Since many armed groups are not clearly attributable to the state or its adversaries, the line between state and non-state actors is often blurred, as with criminal networks (cf. Schneckener 2017).

9. He claimed—as did many others, mostly those who are impoverished and dealing with heavy status losses—that the Khmer Rouge were actually secretly under the control of the Vietnamese, and that tales of Khmer Rouge killings of Vietnamese were invented to delegitimize and weaken Khmer people.

10. Only Nuon Chea, who was an ally of Tou Samouth and studied in Thailand rather than Paris, was able to retain his high position after the chairman's death (Murashima 2009).

11. UNTAC and the immediate post-UNTAC period also saw a high rate of defections, but these were largely limited to lower mid-ranking commanders, foot soldiers, and mercenaries.

12. For a short period, however, Meas Muth was convinced by his father-in-law Ta Mok to return to fighting during the clashes of 1997.

13. A draft US bill in July last year stipulated that the US pressure the Cambodian government to lift its protective umbrella due to Meas Muth's alleged involvement in the capture of the S.S. Mayaguez in the Gulf of Thailand in 1975, which sparked a deadly rescue mission. According to the bill, the United States would provide further funds to the Khmer Rouge tribunal only if it pushed ahead with Meas Muth's case. Sou Met, however, died in 2013, evading arrest and prosecution.

14. Cambodia adopted the French Baccalaureate with Bac I for general knowledge and Bac II for specialized subjects and graduation after twelve years.

15. Walking upright but unwounded through a battlefield as a sign of being selected by fate was mentioned by all six respondents serving in higher government positions today.

16. Every strongman interviewed for the project likened their followers to a family that needed to be taken care of, even comparing some of them to "troublesome children." Even though it is a common theme in Cambodian politics in which leaders

liken themselves to heads of families, no other respondent from the leadership in the sample did so.

17. Asked about abuse of civilians such as rape or looting, most strongmen stressed that they told their soldiers to "stop it." In contrast, however, disobedience to command was punished severely, mostly by death. This would be in line with earlier studies, in which misconduct—such as rape and looting—may both hamper and facilitate internal cohesion (Winslow 1998).

18. A thick analysis of political legitimacy in post-conflict Cambodia can be found in Astrid Norén-Nilsson's article about Hun Sen's attempt to claim to qualify as a *sdech*, specifically his claim that he is a (re)incarnation of the sixteenth-century king Sdech Kân, who rose to his position through his merits as a *neak mean bon* and military successes as a *neak tâsou* fighting an unjust king (Norén-Nilsson 2013). However, *neak tâsou* has a wide semantic range, and while it has strong military overtones, it may also relate to purely political struggles. The opposition politician, Sam Rainsy, for instance, also constantly refers to himself as being a *neak tâsou*.

19. Some strongmen created bases for ultimate military retreats and kept them active over the years. UNTAC files show how they stored food and weaponry along the border and how they planned to mobilize thousands of soldiers in these strongholds (Military Information Branch 1993).

20. The "Black Eagle Unit" was a FUNCINPEC unit that consisted of former Khmer Rouge defectors only.

Chapter Four

Mid-Ranking Operators

Strongmen from both high- and mid-ranking positions were the ones organizing hide-outs and storing food, building materials, and weaponry along the border during UNTAC, in case of a relapse into armed conflict (cf. Anon. 1993a). The network was always prepared for a return to warfare and the remilitarization of large chunks of their demilitarized followership. At lower levels of the insurgency, a constant ebb and flow of engagement and disengagement was normal, and even after UNTAC the network kept mid-ranking and rank-and-file soldiers as a reserve: "In case of our country relapsing into war, we would have been able to remobilize our troops quite easily" (BAC-KPNLF -3). In fact, many had been called back into service for a brief period during Hun Sen and Ranariddh's troop build-ups from March 1996 to early July 1997. Others had already been part of the newly formed Royal Cambodian Armed Forces (RCAF), holding their old networks together and keeping them armed. The continuously changing cycles of de- and remilitarization were most obvious within the lowest ranks (chapter 4).

While many from the lower ranks of the Khmer Rouge, especially those who had been short-term recruits and not veterans, defected during and immediately after UNTAC, the mid-range command remained largely intact, as it without exception consisted of long-serving veterans who had been recruited into the movement as juveniles or children, which created a strong allegiance to the Khmer Rouge military apparatus. Only those who had served the movement for a long time were entrusted with mid-ranking leadership positions. Accordingly, their habitus was a product of decades of indoctrination and seclusion from social spheres beyond their military units. All resources were bound to this sphere, which is why they opted to remain within it as long as possible—until the very end of the conflict and, in most cases, until today.

Much of what is written in the following chapters about the network politics of non-Communist mid-ranking commanders also holds true for the Khmer Rouge. However, their heavy dependence on the social sphere of their military units and the symbolic blood on their hands from their positions in the Democratic Kampuchea regime makes the (re)integration of Khmer Rouge veterans different in many ways. Therefore, the following chapters tell us something about all mid-ranking commanders, but they deal explicitly only with the non-Communists. The special nature of the conversion of Khmer Rouge veterans, who will be called "blank-page leaders," will be discussed separately in the last chapter on the mid-range command.

PATRIMONIAL NETWORKS

For large parts of the non-Communist mid-ranking leadership, social status after reintegration hinged on the post-war trajectory of their superiors—often just one superior to whom they had been closely connected as part of a patrimonial network. With mediocre education at best and virtually no economic resources, their main resource was social, in terms of vertical loyalty to a superior, which is why their fates were intimately linked to those of their network patrons. As for many others within the insurgent movement, social resources were decisive during transition for these mid-range commanders. Some simply took jobs within the state administration and the police that were allocated to them by their superiors, but most—partly due to the conflict in 1997—remained excluded from lucrative positions and became increasingly sidelined within the state institutions as former "para" (a term often used to refer to paramilitary fighters). Many could not rely on their salary only but tried to find additional sources of income or relied on family support.

Most respondents from this group came from relatively well-off rural families with connections to the local administration; when they were young, they often became low-level civil servants, rural teachers, or mid-ranking members of the Lon Nol military. During the Khmer Rouge regime, they were considered "new people," and could easily turn into "enemies of the people" due to their class background. All respondents eventually had to flee to the border to avoid imprisonment, torture, and execution. After a period of disorientation and fighting for survival along the Thai border, they got in touch with their former colleagues, school friends, and superiors from the Lon Nol government. Most said that they joined the insurgency simply to survive, and that they had been given their positions as mid-ranking commanders because they were "very well-liked by all the top commanders" (BAC-KPNLF -1), because they were part of a group following a top commander who "brought them in" (CC-KPNLF -1), or because they had known certain members of the insurgent elite "for a long time already" (BAC-KPNLF -4).

Their habitus revolves around patrimonial loyalty to their superiors framed as (military) discipline and a superior intellectual capacity to draft tactics for combat. Those who did not already have a military background within the entourage of a former Lon Nol general went through a stint of military training at the schooling facility in the Ampil camp. Asking the patrimonial loyalists about their leadership style or what military techniques they used to plan combat or discipline their soldiers did not make much sense to them; they emphasized that they simply followed the guidelines dictated by their superiors: "We learnt the techniques from our senior commanders at Ampil, so we simply followed their commands" (BAC-KPNLF -4). All respondents from this group entered the insurgency at the same rank (as a Company or Battalion commander), which they also held for the remainder of the conflict, for more than ten years. While others constantly switched roles and rose in rank, the patrimonial loyalists are the only ones—with the exception of some rank-and-file soldiers—who did not receive nor even strive for job changes or any sort of upward mobility within the military organization.

For them, being a good commander meant possessing loyalty and discipline (not just appeasing their superiors) in implementing the strategy of the top command in drafting tactics on the ground, and in supporting their work as "advisers" or "consultants" (cf. Bultmann 2015, 101–12). All had a mediocre level of schooling and military training, but at the time any training at all was quite scarce, and therefore valuable. In their view, this therefore put them at a level above the "illiterate" rank-and-file soldiers, making it seem natural and obvious that they would become commanders. Still, to them it remained a mystery why exactly their soldiers followed their commands: "I have no idea why the soldiers followed our commands—they just did" (BAC-KPNLF -4). Maintaining command and discipline was not a matter of conscious power techniques, but of a naturalized order derived from symbolic violence. They saw their place in the hierarchy as normal, just as it was natural that displaced and illiterate peasants and manual workers were on the bottom doing the "dirty work."

Status Change and Resource Valuation during Transition

It is a risk for demobilization programs to treat mid-ranking commanders as mere soldiers and lump them together with their subordinates, often sparking resistance to reintegration because of a lack of "respect" (cf. Özerdem and Knight 2004). However, most of the mid-ranking commanders in Cambodia did not take part in any formal reintegration process anyway—not just because it had to be stopped due to the Khmer Rouge pull-out, but because they were part of a network securing access to positions in state and non-state institutions. Reintegration programs as a pathway to peace did not matter for most.

Almost all respondents from this group found positions in either state administration (e.g., in a ministry or in customs departments) or the police force. When asked why and how they were able to secure their positions, almost all answered that they were simply given them by their former commanders and the upper echelon of their faction. Some simply stated that the job came to them "due to reintegration" (BAC-FUNCINPEC -1). None of these newly fledged civil servants or police had previous experience—let alone interest—in these roles. Most said they never thought of alternatives but considered themselves lucky to get a job in the first place. Very few tried to secure a position other than the one they were placed in.

When this did happen, it could only be phrased as a *request* to their superiors, seeking a transfer to other institutions under their control (which regularly included at least one larger cash installment to effect a transfer). Even if they did not like their position, their commanders could bar them from looking for alternatives, leaving the respondents effectively stuck:

> I still do not like being a policeman because my original vocation and training was in the military. But after the integration, military factions were not fully integrated yet. FUNCINPEC members remained in their faction, and we KPNLF members remained in our faction. And Sak Sutsakhan at that time had already become an advisor to King Sihanouk. When I met Sak Sutsakhan, I asked him if I could return to the military. But he told me to just stay in the police. (BAC-KPNLF -1)

Most said that they never really considered doing something else because their former commander decided their fate anyway. Only very few made a request to be transferred: "We could not control who got which position, it depended on the placement by our boss. I actually made a request to become a provincial governor, but it was rejected—probably because the money I offered did not meet the requirements" (BAC-KPNLF -4).

The boss decided, but money also had a say. Bribes for transfers within the network were costly, meaning that it was not an option for everyone. Veng Sereyvudh, a former member of FUNCINPEC, stated that at the time, "the price list quoted by FUNCINPEC officials for jobs in the administration ranges from 200 USD to 3,000 USD, depending on how good the position will be for extracting bribes" (cited in Roberts 2002, 105–6). Preexisting economic resources and the commander's position within the insurgent network determined which institutional pathways they would take during the transition to peace, effectively reproducing the internal hierarchies of these networks. Network position and the need to pay *and* receive bribes reinforced each other. Since all respondents remained in the roles they had initially been placed in by their commanders, leaving the network did not seem to be an option either. When asked whether they, at any point, thought of doing something completely different (not just in terms of an internal transfer, but outside of their network), all said they did not.

However, at the same time, their fate hinged on their commanders. While many make a comparatively good living nowadays, some were degraded in their positions within the apparatus and became impoverished. These were usually followers of commanders who died during an early stage of the peace process or were dismissed from the apparatus (after the July 1997 fighting, in particular). These respondents found themselves completely isolated within the newly established administration. Even being placed in a position as high as deputy governor of a province did not prevent these respondents from becoming impoverished due to "a lack of connections" (CC-FUNCINPEC -3). As another one put it: "In Cambodia, no matter how many millions of dollars you earn from your business, you will eventually lose everything if you do not associate with a political party" (BAC-KPNLF -1).

At first, many of these "loose molecules" seemed to fare well and to enter society and its institutions at a high level with good salaries and decorations. However, a currently retiring deputy director of the capital's anti-terror police unit, who now regrets that he did not take an offer to be resettled in the United States during the 1980s, explains how he became exhausted after a while:

> Looking back, I honestly must say that the resistance was useless. Why do I say so? Because after the integration we gained nothing. We lived a hard life. I became a deputy director of the city's anti-terror unit [in Phnom Penh]. I started off with a three-stripe rank but was not trusted at work. People still looked down on me as someone coming from the "forest people." So I started to lose my energy, because most people from the old resistance ran away [leaving him cut off and isolated in within the police unit after the factional clashes in 1997], and others became impoverished, living far away, selling their names [to hide their identity]. (CC-KPNLF -1)

For these former mid-ranking commanders, having been a member of the insurgency seemed pointless after losing the backing of their former superiors and colleagues. However, since others are even worse off, they saw no reason to complain:

> Of course, there is a huge difference between my life and that of the rich. However, there are also people whose lives are even worse than mine. Cambodia is like that. We think that we have a bad life, but there are actually a lot

of people whose life is much worse compared to ours. That's how we keep on living like that. (CC-KPNLF -1)

Although these respondents lived in poor neighborhoods (one even in a slum along the capital's railway track) or were homeless (sleeping in provincial storage houses or an old car) and clearly lacked economic resources, they still believed that as civil servants, they were slightly better off in social status than others. Still, some respondents within this group said a relapse into conflict, a time when they had enjoyed much higher status, would be a positive development, even today: "I would like to return to the time of war because—as a soldier—we want to do something to help the country, even if we are now getting older" (BAC-KPNLF -1). By and large, the members of patrimonial networks as a group experienced horizontal mobility after the war, securing positions similar to those they held within the insurgency. However, the political climate meant that they remained excluded from more profitable positions. Those whose network patron left the apparatus for some reason even faced a clear downturn in social status and income, becoming isolated within the state administration.

The post-war status of this group was closely linked to the fate of the head of their patrimonial network and their relation to their former commander within the CGDK, which is also their main symbolic resource. In a typical pattern for patrimonial networks (Scott 1972, 97), the stability of a patron-client cluster based upon particularistic vertical links relies heavily on the patron's performance and position. Hence, in post-conflict Cambodia, a patron-client network flourished or disintegrated depending on the network head's political fate. Some died, some had to flee the country, and some were sidelined, but others performed well and found a relaticely secure space for their network. Such networks also depended on the patron's interest in maintaining his vertical bonds. Intellectuals in particular often quickly lost interest in the fate of their former supporters, particularly the "uneducated" soldiers, maintaining only a distant and superficial bond. Followers of strongmen—as leaders who counted their patrimonial network as a central resource—either managed to be part of a network that was transferred to positions in the state apparatus or became impoverished alongside their sidelined or—in some cases and in later years—arrested strongmen patrons.

The importance of the patrimonial structure of these wartime networks shows how important it is to study network structures, densities, and dynamics during reintegration (Cardenas, Gleditsch, and Guevara 2018). However, these networks were comparatively less crucial for other groups in the mid-range, who were not so intimately connected to a wartime patron. While social resources are always relevant, the position of other groups within the armed group—and, correspondingly, in post-conflict Cambodia—did not rest solely upon their role within a patrimonial cluster, but also on other resources. The role, structure, and importance of patrimonial networks are different for different social groups within the field.

MILITARY CAREERISTS

Except for the strongmen who rose to leadership positions, very few respondents forged even a modest career within the insurgency. However, as former rank-and-file soldiers with a minimal but decisive military background, the respondents from this habitus group managed to rise to mid-ranking positions through military schooling institutions and wartime allegiance to an elite military commander. In their early lives, they were low-ranking military cadets in a training facility under Lon Nol. Some already had a father serving in the military. As very young soldiers, they fought against the Khmer Rouge during the 1970–1975 civil war. When the Khmer Rouge took over, they had to hide their backgrounds since they were high on the list for execution.

After getting into trouble with local cadres or having their backgrounds exposed, all respondents within this group eventually fled Democratic Kampuchea. Along the border, they met others trying to survive barehanded or with little more than a few weapons stolen from Khmer Rouge cadres. These groups, under the command of strongmen or old military elite commanders, were the predecessors of the non-Communist wings of the CGDK. But during the Khmer Rouge period, they—like many of their colleagues at that time— fought for their own survival. Only after the Vietnamese occupation, when aid and refugees began to flow into the border areas, did these groups manage to consolidate control over resources and refugee encampments. However, membership in the embryonic insurgent force, consisting of little more than a few dozen people, often meant that former low-ranking soldiers managed to become part of the entourage of former military elite commanders and their early resistance forces. These early allegiances became decisive as a resource for forging a career in the insurgent military.

All respondents who made even a modest career within the insurgency had a certain level of prior military experience and had been part of an early resistance formation. Like education, military experience was scarce and badly needed within the insurgent organization, especially given the killings of Lon Nol soldiers and commanders under the Khmer Rouge regime: "When I came to the border they really needed me as I had been trained in the state military before" (BAC-KPNLF -7). However, in contrast to the patrimonial loyalists, the careerists did not know the former elite military commanders before meeting them along the border and had not belonged to the mid-range of the military apparatus before. They only got to know them upon arriving in these groups, consisting of only a handful of men:

> At that time along the border, I met Youk Morn and some other former generals from the Khmer Republic, including Toun Chay, Ta Lout, and Ta Meng, among others. Later that year, they also gave us some guns. (BAC-KPNLF -6)

In later years and in combination with their primary socialization as soldiers, access to old military commanders during this early period also meant access to training abroad in Thailand, Singapore, and Malaysia, and of course in the coalition's military school in the Ampil encampment. All respondents were part of the very first cohort of graduates of Ampil. They steadily rose in rank from platoon leaders up to battalion commanders after they finished training at Ampil and abroad: "Tom 1" for low-ranking soldiers learning how to salute, crawl, use weapons, and basic military discipline, followed by "Tom 2" for mid-ranking commanders, who learned the strategies and tactics of guerrilla warfare, planning, and geographical and military preparation.

As with the military elite commanders and the patrimonial loyalists, military discipline and ethics stood at the center of the careerists' habitus. But unlike the loyalists, they did not put much weight on loyalty to the upper echelon, instead emphasizing that their units "had been rather independent" and that they "oftentimes dared to disagree" with their superiors (BAC-FUNCINPEC -2). In addition to the military ethics and knowledge they had gained through training, they stressed that they were always striving for success, claiming that they succeeded in their career due to their personal efforts: "All I did was to reach out for success" (BAC-KPNLF -6). Being promoted was a response to their "military merits and successes" and their "strong capabilities in [battle-related] decision-making" (BAC-KPNLF -5). For them, their life trajectory—starting as a rank-and-file soldier under Lon Nol, then being frequently promoted within the insurgency—was a result of their own efforts and capabilities as well as the merit they had earned within the military sphere. On a deeper level, it was a natural result of their good deeds and actions:

> I believe in the ethics that in doing good one eventually receives good returns, and in doing something bad one will receive something bad as well. Accordingly, I have never done anything bad, although I sometimes got quite angry with people. No matter what has happened, I would never curse or physically assault anyone. (BAC-KPNLF -6)

In their own view, their successful careers were not just the result of loyalty to their commanders or any other patrons within the insurgency but stemmed from the totality of the good deeds they had done, which in an animist and Buddhist cosmology had been answered with good returns.

Changes in Status and Resource Valuation during Transition

During UNTAC and after reintegration, all careerists became part of the RCAF military under their former commanders, and most former KPNLF commanders became members of FUNCINPEC. Like the old military elite commanders, they did not participate in the 1997 factional fighting. But when the simmering conflict finally broke out into outright violence, the careerists were also forced to choose sides. Some opted to stay in the military by making a deal with Hun Sen. Others claimed that military ethics prevented them from collaborating with a political party.

Those who made a deal with the government by promising to join the pro-CPP faction within FUNCINPEC and not to take part in the fighting attributed their decision to a combination of being abandoned and feeling concerned over possible civilian casualties:

> When the coup took place, I was a deputy commander within military region [omitted]. At that time, soldiers from both factions started to point fingers at each other. We [within FUNCINPEC] did not know who our leader was, because Prince Ranariddh ran away into exile, and Nhek Bunchhay disappeared [to the border]. Many of the high-ranking commanders also disappeared, and I was the only one left within my military region. Soldiers from three units stayed with me in [omitted]. We started to discuss how we should not engage in any of the ongoing battles because we did not want to cause any civilian casualties. I was also discussing this with another colleague of mine who was also a deputy commander at that time. There was no top commander left in the countryside, as those who did not disappear preferred to stay in Phnom Penh. While we were discussing all of this, Hun Sen suddenly asked for a meeting with me at his house in Phnom Penh. There he asked me about the cause of the coup, and I told him what I knew. Then he told me not to go anywhere and that I should join hands with the government, and I agreed. Later on, I went back to [place omitted] and I got promoted to be a top commander for a military region from 1997 until 1999. After that, I was assigned to be among the deputy army commanders in Phnom Penh. I was a three-star general at that time. However, in 2003, I asked to resign due to my poor health and they approved my request. I became a deputy governor of [province omitted] instead and also got a house there. When FUNCINPEC lost all its seats in 2013, I finally quit my job at the province. But they sent me back to the Ministry of Defense. But now I am fully retired. (BAC-KPNLF -6)

This group saw all their promotions, during both the years they spent in the CGDK and the years with the government, as the result of their relentless drive for success: "All of my efforts at work solely aimed at reaching success. Back then, I did not know what the result of my actions would be. And I was working hard while knowing that I might die any time. But when I returned to the interior, people knew me and kept promoting me" (BAC-KPNLF -6). Even though they stayed loyal to the Hun Sen government, today the dealmakers among the careerists are fed up with the mass of seemingly non-merit-based promotions within the ranks of the RCAF:

> Rank-and-file soldiers are only very rarely promoted to higher ranks, and in comparison, there are few lower ranking soldiers. In our country, there are a lot of commanders with high ranks. It seems as if everyone nowadays has a high rank, and I really wonder about that. Some youngsters hold four or five stripes. How is that possible? I am not saying anything bad about the government here, but I just think that the number of high-ranking commanders and the number of soldiers does not match up. In Singapore, only a handful of commanders hold a five-stripe position. But in our country, thousands hold a three-star position. (RC-FUNCINPEC -3)

They complain that other countries promote only those who earn it, and "care about their commanders' well-being," while in Cambodia commanders "have no cars" and soldiers "have no choice but to take a side-job as moto-taxi drivers or to borrow money from lenders" in order "to send their kids to school": "That's why there are not so many soldiers on duty within the barracks. But don't get me wrong, I am not criticizing the government here" (BAC-KPNLF -6). Like the old military elite, they feel that they are in a double bind: having to collaborate with the "victorious" Hun Sen government and facing what they perceive as a "lack of respect."

However, not every careerist stayed in the military. Some respondents quit during the factional clashes in July 1997. One respondent laid out his motive for leaving military service:

> [During the time of the clashes,] I told them that we could peacefully talk without them having to point their guns at us. I asked whether they didn't want to stop. We can just talk. Then they asked whether I would join the CPP. Then I said that, according to the country's law, we [as members of the military] would always have to follow the country's leaders. That is point number one. Number two, soldiers should not be biased. They need to be independent. If soldiers serve a party, this would mean that there is no democracy. But they did not share our view. They simply wanted to eliminate FUNCINPEC members. Then I thought that if I kept on insisting [on my principles], the situation could get worse because our top leaders had all been arrested or vanished. Therefore, I thought I should focus on my own survival first, so that I could continue to serve in my capacity as a commander. Then I asked for three hours

to think about their proposal, and my request was granted. They gave me two additional things to think about. First, if we joined the CPP, they were not sure what we could do there. Second, if we did not join, they would want us to quit from military service. That made me think that I had better quit that day. Then I processed the necessary paperwork and got approved. At that time, I left the military. (BAC-FUNCINPEC -2)

However, as mentioned in the section on network politics, this respondent did not just quit, but kept a foot in the door by telling his "brother"—a friend serving as a fellow commander in the CGDK—to join the CPP:

> However, I also had a brother who was also working with me as a commander in that military region. I told him that he should continue his service, but I would quit. I said that in the future if anything happens, we would be on both sides. You are here, and I am there [part of the opposition network]. That was my suggestion to him. So I left the military on July 5 or 6. (BAC-FUNCINPEC -2)

This meant that in case of a change of government in Cambodia, he would be prepared: "I do not know if, one day in the future, I might return to the military again. The country might change its leaders, and I might be asked to return" (BAC-FUNCINPEC -2).

Even though the careerists managed to rise in rank during the civil war and most were able to secure a position in the military afterwards, all had a difficult time dealing with their symbolic deprivation of status, and oftentimes also had to draw on additional sources of income to make a living (in most cases farming or a family trading business). Many obtained mid-range commander positions within the state military that were equivalent to their former ranks, but in terms of social status and income, reintegration meant a significant setback for all of them. In the end, therefore, they often returned to their pre-war social status, like most of the previous groups, and frequently articulated the wish to return to a higher status that would afford them more "respect," or to go back to a position within the state military. Being a (successful) commander is their main symbolic resource, and this is what they try to guard.

WARRIOR MONKS

Warrior monks are Buddhist senior monks and/or animist sorcerers, so-called *kru khmai*, who became mid-range commanders in the CGDK due to their socially and symbolically ascribed spiritual and magical potency and moral authority. While many Cambodian males serve as monks at least for a brief period in their life—mostly in order to receive education as children coming from poor households—these respondents were monks starting in early childhood, went to Pali schools in Phnom Penh, and became well-known senior monks within monasteries before the Khmer Rouge takeover, or practitioners of magic who were deeply respected by leading commanders and taken into their military and patrimonial entourages within the non-Communist factions of the CGDK.

Often, *kru khmai* are also former monks or learned their magical practices while in the monkhood; others claim to have gained their spiritual knowledge from Buddhist ascetics (cf. Harris 2005, 59–61). While not every *kru khmai* has an affinity for Buddhism, in the case of the warrior monks interviewed for this project, the line between being a *kru khmai* and a monk was almost impossible to draw. All respondents were highly regarded not only for their Buddhist knowledge and moral integrity as (former) senior monks, but also for their magical potency as sorcerers. Most of them had a long family tradition in the monkhood, and many also came from families with a tradition of being magical practitioners. One senior monk even came from a family with a particular tradition of creating protective items for Lon Nol soldiers, earning him an early part-time job as a novice monk and trainee *kru khmai*:

> I strongly believe in the potency of spiritual forces since serving as a soldier in the Khmer Republic. Both my father and my grandfather were *kru khmai*. And when I became a monk, they often asked me to help them to inscribe spellings and magical words on paper or cloth [for protection]. They gave me a hundred or two hundred riel for that, which was a lot given the value of the currency back then. The more I inscribed, the more I could earn, and most of our customers were soldiers. And when I was in the military myself, I realized that these items were the only thing I could use to protect myself. Besides these items, I also dreamt of incidents before they happened. (BAC-KPNLF -8)

Protective items, such as pieces of cloth called *yorn*, magical tattoos, and various amulets were often cited as possessing spiritual powers responsible for the respondents' survival of countless dangers under the Khmer Rouge and during the civil war.[1] However, on a deeper level, these items depended on two additional factors to unfold their power: a knowledge of portents and spiritually correct conduct. Portents tell the respondents what will happen in the near future; during the Khmer Rouge years, this often took the form of signs indicating which pathways to take while fleeing. Portents occur not only in dreams but also in waking life—for example, through a winking eye warning of dangers to come. Besides the capacity to read portents correctly, obedience to a spiritual code of conduct is essential. This code may take the form of explicitly Buddhist rules as taught by senior monks:

The most important thing is related to the five Buddhist prohibitions: killing, humiliation, robbery, having bad intentions towards other people, and having love affairs with other people's wives. During battle, we were prohibited from raping a girl, and we had to keep away from other people's wives. (BI-CGDK)

None of the respondents drew a clear distinction between animist and Buddhist belief systems (as some Buddhist leaders in Cambodia certainly would), and all were highly respected not just because of their position in the Cambodian *sangha*, but also as magical practitioners who could create potent items for warriors and higher-ranking commanders. Religion is always a process of syncretism of different belief systems and religious traditions, and Cambodia also has a long heritage in which Buddhism has adapted to local cults, and these cults to Buddhism (Ang 1988). Therefore, even former senior monks heading influential pagodas may adhere to a code of conduct with a number of elements relating to the spheres of ghosts and various animist forces, including rituals for powerful spirits such as *neak tā* or the "calling" and control of "souls," *brah liṅg* (compare Ang 2004, Thompson 2004 on the notion and control of *brah liṅg*).[2] Besides observing the five Buddhist precepts, as mentioned by the respondent above, many also stressed that it is important to keep the magical items and the wearer pure through ritual practice as well as dietary and hygienic regulations. For example, it is forbidden to wear an amulet while squatting on a toilet, to put a *yorn* in the back of one's trousers, or to eat pork (cf. Bultmann 2015, 148–49).

Most warrior monks considered magical items useless if their bearer was not also in strict compliance with the rules of *dharma*, or cosmic law and order. Transgressions destroy the potency of the items by making them unable to feed upon spiritual and cosmic forces. Within this Buddhist and animist cosmology, a person's fate is not only the result of deeds committed in previous lives, but also his lifetime obedience to spiritual discipline guided by a cosmic order. Or as one commander argued: "Without a proper belief in and respect for the potencies connected to items such as tattoos or the *yorn*, its powers are useless" (BAC-KPNLF -8). While almost all respondents within the project sample believed in a cosmic and spiritual world order, including magic and ghosts, the warrior monks positioned themselves as its true vanguards and the best instructors of proper spiritual conduct. They believed in their ability to instill military potency in others and saw themselves as possessing exclusive knowledge about "true" Buddhism and its teachings: "Ninety percent of the Khmer are Buddhists, but only very few of them actually understand Buddhist teachings" (CC-KPNLF -2).

All warrior monks were forced to disrobe under the Khmer Rouge, sometimes even to marry, and to work in the rice fields, all of which contravene

Buddhist principles. As former senior monks, some were put in charge of groups of former Buddhist novices and did well for a while under the Communist regime, even though they were officially regarded as "parasites" by Khmer Rouge cadres. This, however, seems to have changed when purges intensified at the end of 1977. After the removal of comparatively "humane" cadres, most chose to flee their cooperatives. Like the strongmen, they saw their journeys to the border as being enabled by spiritual forces. Both metaphysical signs and spiritually inclined people guided them along their way: "I met a man whom I could follow through the woods. He owned a horse and he was in possession of a spiritual soul [*brah liṅg*] that protected him from being shot. On our way [to the border], we suddenly saw Khmer Rouge with an oxcart carrying sacks of rice. The man told me to climb a tree while he stayed on the ground. I was afraid of dying, but [for some strange reason] they were not able to see us" (CC-KPNLF -3).

These former senior monks and *kru khmai* not only helped soldiers to protect themselves, but, due to their ascribed moral authority and potency as sorcerers, they also became teachers instructing top-ranking commanders on "good morality" (BI-KPNLF), or even mid-range commanders themselves. This might seem to contradict Buddhist teachings that strictly forbid practitioners from killing. However, one former instructor, now head of a pagoda in Siem Reap province, provided an allegory to explain how this could be seen as acceptable:

Respondent: Monks cannot even enter military barracks, nor can they look at military training. They cannot talk with soldiers who are carrying a gun in their hand. The morality of Buddhism is based on non-violence. We do not encourage someone to exploit or harm others. Now, let me give you an example. A monk sees a thief running right in front of him. Later, somebody comes and asks if he has seen the thief. If he says he has seen him, it seems like he is encouraging the police to arrest the thief. Yet, if he tells the police that he hasn't, he would be telling a lie. Both answers are wrong. So, what can the monk do to get himself out of this? When the monk saw the thief, he was standing here. If he just moves back a bit, and changes his previous position, he could tell the police: "While I was standing here, I did not see the thief." ((Laughs)) When the monk saw the thief, he was standing here. But when he moved here, he did not see him. So this is a win-win situation. The monk neither told a lie, nor has he told the police to arrest the thief. We did not intervene in the two of their affairs. You get it? When the monk saw the thief, he was standing here. If he just moves one step away, he could tell that he did not see him while standing here ((laughs)).

Interviewer: I am a bit doubtful and I would like to go back a bit to clarify something. The monk INTENTIONALLY moved a step in order to change his standing position?

Respondent: He did in order to survive. We do not want our words to have any bad effects on others. Just think about this example. And you don't have to wonder whether monks taught soldiers or not. [. . .] Buddhism prohibits killing (4), but this case [Vietnamese occupation] is exceptional. This had nothing to do with monks though. It's about sovereign defense. Let's say this is the border-line. This is Cambodia, and this is another country, be it Vietnam or Thailand. (1) Suddenly Thailand, let's say Thailand, invades our territorial sovereignty. In this case, shooting Thai soldiers dead is not considered sinful. Do you get it? It's not sinful because we were defending our sovereignty. Khmer did not mean to kill Siamese. When Siam invaded us, we had to shoot them or they would take our land. So we did not intentionally want to shoot them. We were just protecting our territory. But if Khmer soldiers invade Siam's territory and shoot Thai soldiers dead, that is considered sinful. This is Buddhism's rule. If we kill others to seize their land, we are sinful. If others invade us, we have the duty of self-defense. We did not INTEND to do it, though. This is not a sin. I want to clarify in case you are curious how we could defend our territory. If foreigners come, we cannot give them our land because it's our heritage. (cited in Bultmann 2015, 46)

Somebody who participates in an act of killing without intending to kill has not committed a sin. Many former senior monks, like this respondent, pretended that they were not training soldiers but were simply helping civilians protect themselves. As long as their disciples wore civilian clothes, they could "instruct" them without the "intention" of supporting them in their jobs as commanders or soldiers who would have to kill others. Traditionally, this principle is meant to relieve a Buddhist believer from unintentional sin—when, for example, he unintentionally crushes an ant. Yet, for the respondents, the same principle is at work here, making it possible, for instance, to train soldiers for combat using methods derived from the "Triple Veda": martial arts, predictive horoscoping, and protective charms (Kong 2009).

Others, however, also referred to the Buddhist principle of intentionality to explain why they planned and directly engaged in combat as mid-range commanders. These respondents were not officially serving as monks during the civil war, but their habitus was still defined through their symbolic capital as former monks. They referred to combat as an act of self-defense—and therefore an act of unintentional violence—whose aim was not to destroy the enemy. If it had been, everyone would be dead by now:

Interviewer: How did you manage to strike a balance between killing people in battle and at the same time following Buddhist teaching?

Respondent: Ok, I understand. As a soldier, we normally cannot be like that [follow the principle of non-violence]. We need to be able to weigh our options.

If we accidentally engaged in fighting and shot somebody, it was unintentional. And if someone was trying to shoot us, we had no choice but to self-defend. Even when we shot them, we never intended to kill them. If we had really intended to shoot them, all Khmer people would have been killed [no one would have survived]. Our enemies were parents of their children, and so were we. So we tried to avoid firing as much as we could. (CC-KPNLF -2)

Within this logic, Buddhist ethics prevented worse things from happening; Buddhism is not antithetical to combat but helps limit its negative consequences by prohibiting *intentional killing*. However, warfare remained a constant challenge to the respondents' ethical and spiritual universe, especially the fact that soldiers who died in combat were not disposed of properly through cremation or burial, and that their deaths were violent and sudden, causing the spirits of the deceased to wander around as ghosts (*khmaodj dtai haong*), caught in a confused state between life and afterlife (Bertrand 2004, Davis 2016). One respondent, for example, could still list exactly how many men he lost in battle and started to cry when talking about the fact that their bodies had to be abandoned in the middle of nowhere: "Their bodies might just have been eaten by animals" (CC-KPNLF -2).

Changes in Status and Resource Valuation during Transition

Sooner or later, all warrior monks returned to a position within the Cambodian *sangha*, the Buddhist monastic community. A few served in the civilian administration of UNTAC or as policemen before entering or even leading monasteries as senior monks. Re-entering the *sangha* was not always easy, particularly because the larger *Maha Nikaya* monastic order now has close links to the CPP government (Harris 2001). Despite royal patronage, the second largest monastic order, the *Dhammayuttika Nikaya*, remains a minority, and through its affiliation with the royal court it is connected to certain wings within FUNCINPEC. However, even though the *Maha Nikaya* is generally closer to the government and the *Dhammayuttika Nikaya* to the royalist opposition, neither order is entirely unified, which is why there are monasteries within both that serve as refuges for the warrior monks nowadays.

While some of these religious authorities remained in monastic orders within the camps, others held official commanding positions. When asked why they did not continue in their military roles, a common theme was that they drew a clear distinction between their honest and selves and the greed of others, not that they necessarily eschewed participation in organized violence. One, for example, explained why he left the military to serve the police, and why in the end he quit to return to a life as a monk:

If I had really done what I was planning to do, I would have been in a much higher position now. But I did not want people to think I was showing off. Why? It was due to my honesty. [. . .] Our leaders tried to stop me from quitting because they did not want the lower ranks to disunite. But while they asked us to work hard, they themselves did not. That is why I decided to become a policeman instead. (CC-KPNLF -2)

The problem, he went on, was a lack of morality:

There was no such thing as a good leader. Until today, those of them who managed to obtain high positions were the ones who only cared about themselves, and this applies to all factions, even to the KPNLF. All just tried to find a way to survive individually. No discipline, no morality, was guiding [them] whatsoever. (CC-KPNLF -2)

Greedy and immoral people might be successful in the short run, but they are "in constant danger" (BI-KPNLF). And in view of an inevitable death, being morally good and honest is what divides humans from animals:

I think everyone is the same. We all eat, sleep, and we are all afraid of death. Death is just inevitable. There is just one thing that distinguishes a person from others and that is their adherence to and belief in religious teachings. A person without it is equivalent to an animal. I strongly believe in this. (CC-KPNLF -2)

But it was not just honesty and morality that guided them to leave the military and return to their initial "vocation" as monks; it was also their reading of signs that appeared to them in dreams:

I simply quit, but before I did that I already contributed a lot to the country. I was a member of Battalion [omitted]. And when I was sleeping at [name of a pagoda], I was hoping for a dream to tell me whether I should continue [with my service in the military]. I discussed the [meaning of my] dream with some disciples who then held lights high in their hands until it became dark. That night, I did not dream, so I thought it was clear that my career should end now. Although I had a nine-day training, I just attended until it finished at 9 pm, and afterwards I simply stopped going to the military base. (BAC-KPNLF -8)

While the key fact for the respondent was that he did *not* dream about himself as a future member of the military, he also felt that his commander was too greedy because the commander feared the respondent might "grab" his position one day. This made it impossible for the respondent to work for him any longer.

All respondents are still afraid of revenge acts by the government, leading them to set up shrines and carry magical items for protection: "When I keep the holy cloth, I am not afraid of anything. But I am also required not to do anything [morally] bad; otherwise it becomes ineffective" (CC-FUNCINPEC -2). Many warrior monks talked at length about their fear that Cambodia was under the control of Vietnamese. They believed the Vietnamese were even behind the Khmer Rouge and were secretly responsible for the deaths that took place during the regime. One respondent said he believed this because he saw Vietnamese in Cambodia after the Khmer Rouge took over:

> We all volunteered to fight with *Yuon* because Pol Pot's leader was a *Yuon*. Let me trace back a bit. The Khmer Rouge were first created in Battambang, at Phnom Vaichab. King Sihanouk asked his subordinates to attack the Khmer Rouge, which included people like Khieu Samphan, Hu Nim, Hou Youn, [and] Pol Pot. But after the collapse of Lon Nol and the advent of Pol Pot, I saw a lot of *Yuon* in rural areas. I even gave them things to eat. A lot of Khmer Rouge soldiers were also walking with them. That really hurt me. (CC-KPNLF -2)

In his opinion, the Vietnamese never truly withdrew from Cambodia, which is why it was a huge mistake to engage in peace talks: "I was not happy about the negotiations. I told Grandfather Son Sann not to negotiate as there were still too many *Yuon* in the country." In the end, "*Yuon* remained in Cambodia" (CC-KPNLF -2). The only option left to him was to return to the pagoda: "I came here to calm my feelings down." Returning to monkhood helped him "to heal mentally. Monks need to be calm and practice meditation" (CC-KPNLF -2). In this way, many warrior monks also ended up returning to their pre-war social status.

BLANK-PAGE LEADERS

Using a Maoist metaphor, the Khmer Rouge preferred a very special type of recruit: "blank pages" on which the leadership could write anything they want (Hinton 2000, 33). In order to guarantee a perfect revolutionary transformation, the best recruits for the party's core apparatus were considered ideologically unspoiled children that could be molded like formless clay into standardized revolutionary socialist cadres. Children were perfect for this since, as the slogans went, "clay is molded while soft" and "only a newborn is free from stain" (Locard 2004, 143). According to Pol Pot himself, children are not just malleable, but also fundamentally honest: "If you wish to know how things happen, ask adults; if you wish to see them in a clear light, ask children" (cited in Locard 2004, 142). However, Pol Pot also emphasized the importance of working hard to form the revolutionary self, as humans age quickly:

Those among our comrades who are young must make a great effort to reeducate themselves. They must never allow themselves to lose sight of this goal. You have to be, and remain, faithful to the revolution. People age quickly. Being young, you are at the most receptive age, and capable of assimilating what the revolution stands for better than anyone else. (Cited in Locard 2004, 144)

Through constant indoctrination and self-improvement, these underage recruits were made to incorporate a socialist-normed practice prescribed by the intellectuals within the party leadership. Cadres for the security apparatus and the military, who usually joined from the ages of 14 to 16 (some were recruited even younger), had to come from poor rural households. Without exception, the movement's rank and file and security apparatus consisted of juveniles from impoverished rural households, heavily affected by the exigencies of civil war and the US bombardments (taking place until 1973), with many respondents experiencing the early loss of at least one parent. Sometimes it was pure poverty that orphaned them:

How did they [his parents] raise me? Well, my mom died of cholera. Both of my parents died when I was young. While I was walking along the road, a monk came with his ox-cart and took me to live in a pagoda. From then onwards, I called him "father." (BC-NADK 2)

Besides rural poverty, many said they joined the Khmer Rouge guerrilla forces as revenge for violence inflicted by the Sihanoukian and Lon Nol state militaries and authorities, as well as by the US bombings (cf. Ea and Sim 2001).

After Prince Sihanouk was ousted from power in 1970, the royal—with some additional pressure from the Chinese—joined the Khmer Rouge as part of a coalition in an effort to restore himself to power. His call to join the liberation forces in the forests, which he referred to by the French term *maquis*, led to a massive surge in recruits for the Communists: "My children, my grandchildren, come and join your father, your father who awaits you in the forest-*maquis*" (cited from Locard 2004). This proclamation by the freshly deposed Prince and head of state was often mentioned by respondents as their trigger for joining the Communist resistance. Respondents influenced by Sihanouk usually used the term *maquis* while speaking Khmer: "King Sihanouk told us to go into the *maquis* in order to survive because Lon Nol was staging a coup" (RC-NADK -1). Many of these recruits aimed to restore the old order but ended up inadvertently enlisted in an effort to forge a socialist utopia: "I was cheated by the Khmer Rouge propaganda, which on and off claimed that it would create a Socialist utopia in which everyone would be given equal rights. Back then, I was actually in favor of and expecting a leadership under Norodom Sihanouk" (BAC-NADK -4).

However, not everyone joined voluntarily. Some were simply picked by local authorities within the cooperatives when they were young: "I was chosen to be in the military during a session within my cooperative" (DC-NADK -1). As reported by a former cadre, Khmer Rouge leaders were looking for especially daring and dedicated people, so-called "absolutes," but not every recruit fully understood this term:

> They were looking for the "absolutes"; I did not understand what it was. When they looked for "absolutes," I raised my hand and I was picked. I was made a soldier. I was to be an "absolute" soldier. [. . .] I raised my hand because I saw others do so. (Suoy 2011)

Many became soldiers for the Khmer Rouge at a very young age, and the respondents within the group of blank-page leaders all spent their entire lives serving *Angkar*: "They chose me to become a member of the military, even though I knew nothing. I have been in the forest for the whole time" (CC-NADK -1). They were almost completely unable to remember their childhoods and families of origin. As one phrased it: "I was too young to be able to recollect anything about my parents" (RC-NADK -1). Some, however, remembered that they were recruited at a time when they were young and "hot-blooded," not initially thinking about anything else than their joy at being a soldier:

> They reason why I joined the military was because I wanted to carry a gun and fight. I did not have the idea of loving the nation or hating anyone else yet. I was a hot-blooded teen. I always prayed that I could go to fight because I really liked it. (BC-NADK 2, also cited in Bultmann 2015, 121)

Living in a society at war made being a soldier especially appealing for children; it may have promised a better and more "exciting" life. In some cases, it may simply have been a safer life, especially for partly or completely orphaned children. These recruits did not particularly care about the "master cleavage" of liberation or ending imperialism or capitalism. Interestingly, none of the respondents referred to any of these ideological concepts as a motive for joining the Khmer Rouge, or even mentioned them at all.

For these juveniles, there was no life prior to war and displacement. Important parts of their first socialization and basic habitus formation took place within the context of the Communist armed group itself. For all military cadres, recruitment started with a separation from their home communities and families. After separation, they underwent longer periods of training, constant indoctrination, and "rectification" through self-criticism sessions, in which they had to criticize themselves and others within their unit (cf. Procknow 2011). In order to rise in rank, Khmer Rouge soldiers had to prove their ideological commitment through being "absolute," meaning unconditional obedience to the upper command and constant dedication to practical work. Those who did not constantly work to forge their revolutionary selves and make an effort to fight counterrevolutionary spies supposedly hiding within the "masses" were quickly dubbed "enemies of the people." During the years the Khmer Rouge held power, many cadres died after being cast out as enemies due to even minor infractions of revolutionary conduct.

Being an "active" revolutionary therefore meant two things: a way of rising in rank as a perfect socialist, and a way of preventing oneself from being regarded as an enemy. Those who were "lazy" could be easily accused of being spies, even after 1979: "There were spies hidden in our forces. They did not work, so we fired them" (BAC-NADK -2). Rising in rank, at the same time, could put people at risk of being purged during the final stages of party infighting in late 1978 and early 1979. All blank-page respondents rose up the ranks from ordinary soldier to commander, with one even becoming a division commander. Within other armed groups, these people would be regarded as top commanders, but the organizational mode of the Khmer Rouge was different. Because they were not in a position to set out rules but only implemented orders handed down by the Central Committee and the military directorate, they were treated as mere operators implementing and at times adjusting commands.

In addition, many received their high ranks during the final stages of conflict, as a symbolic reward for their loyalty during UNTAC and the late 1990s. Some received these ranks at the very last moment before negotiating their merger with the state military within the "win-win" framework. Their careers hinged upon being "active and proving our willingness for two to three years" (DC-NADK -2) and through "learning directly in combat" (CC-NADK -1). However, some respondents within the higher ranks of the NADK also mentioned that they already knew someone within the apparatus. This might have enabled or accelerated their rise.[3] On top of that, most joined the Khmer Rouge during the movement's early years, when the military wing was still being created (it was officially founded on January 17, 1968). As veterans joining from lower ranks, they belonged to the core of the military apparatus, maintained a strong allegiance to the Khmer Rouge leadership, and had no other resources besides their formal rank and social resources within the Communist organization.

Having joined as juveniles, gone through decades of indoctrination, and lived in seclusion from the rest of society led to a strong incorporation of Khmer Rouge schemes into their habitus. Therefore, even when trying to adapt to contemporary society, respondents regularly referred to central concepts of Khmer Rouge ideology. Their discourse was shaped by what they regarded as their main symbolic resources: practical combat experience and obedience to the "collective," by which they meant the top command within the framework of "democratic centralism." While the top command of the Khmer Rouge envisioned a "normed practice" that included very formulaic prescriptions of what "correct" socialist practice would look like in all areas of daily life and military conduct, the blank pages within the military interpreted the discourse of the intellectual leadership—rather unintellectually—as "merely" practice-guided. As a result, they skipped the formulaic prescriptions that were passed down by the upper echelon of the party and translated the principle of "experience by normed practice" into "learning by doing," which meant that child recruits had to be sent into combat right away without any preparation. This, according to one commander who now serves in the local government, made them strong and brave fighters, making them valuable assets even today, when these now grown-up child soldiers fought against the Thais during the conflict over Preah Vihear in 2011:

> Sure, even soldiers at this height [pointing to a rather low level] carried a gun to fight. During the battle with Thai soldiers at Phnom Trop, those [during their initial recruitment] short soldiers never ran away from battle. Their height did not meet international standards when they joined. Some were just about 15 or 16 years old. But [having these battle-hardened former child soldiers, is the reason why] the Thais could not easily defeat us over here. (Cited from Bultmann 2015, 124)

Direct battle involvement was "good experience" in being able to "learn quickly" (RC-NADK -1). The upper intellectuals' discourse often translated into "learning by doing" via direct involvement in combat operations. Often, the respondents therefore began their careers as carriers, messengers, or cooks for more experienced fighters.

The second scheme can be described by the principle of "democratic centralism." Many respondents frequently claimed that what was lacking in contemporary Cambodian society was "democracy." However, their conception of democracy was, in fact, the anti-individualist stance of the Khmer Rouge. In their own narrative, democracy meant that soldiers, for example, should "not act too individually," but should "adhere to rules and regulations" and have regular self-criticism sessions in order "to have discussions with others," which is why, as one put it, "When we have democracy, we do not have individualism" (BAC-NADK -2). They complained that in modern Cambodia, individual self-interest was running rampant without "discussion" and approval by the collective (RC-NADK -2). The ideal of democratic centralism referred to the primacy of collective decision-making over that of individuals. The individual must accept the wisdom of what "the collective" demands. Therefore, respondents saw no contradiction in praising the advent of "capitalism," which means that "you can move freely, spend your money freely and may do your business freely," while complaining that current politics "lacks democracy": "When they [the current government] want to decide something, they do not ask for a meeting with everyone" (BAC-NADK -3). Likewise, being a good soldier or commander means that you are a loyal follower of commands—someone whose actions comply with the will of the collective (cf. Bultmann 2015, 123–24).

Narratives and Status Change during Transition

During interviews, the researcher and his Khmer assistant were accused of being "Vietnamese spies" at least three times. Throughout the interviews, respondents had largely drawn on two narratives to distance themselves from the killings and starvation under Democratic Kampuchea. One was to blame a Vietnamese conspiracy: "The reason why the conflict [over bad rice yields] arose was that the *Yuon* secretly came at night to transplant our seedlings," and, of course, "there were spies hidden in our forces" (BC-NADK -2). The other, which regularly came up among loyalists of Ta Mok, was to blame Pol Pot and his entourage: "People under Ta Mok's command along the border did not kill anybody; it was all done by Pol Pot's people in the interior" (BC-NADK -1).

The former Khmer Rouge blank-page commanders cited three reasons why they eventually defected to the government: the elections under UNTAC, infighting within the party, and, by far most commonly, the "win-win policy." As explained by a former member of the NADK in an interview with Dany Long from the Documentation Center of Cambodia, many hoped for reintegration via the elections but were left disappointed—"spiritually and intellectually" weakened—when the upper echelon of the Khmer Rouge decided to withdraw from the Paris Peace Agreement:

> *Chiem*: At that time [when UNTAC arrived], we were able to defend ourselves and struggle to maintain our power, but during the last few years, the situation was uncontrollable; for example, we did not participate in the Barey Agreement,[4] and thus were unable to participate in the election movement. What is more, Ta Mok set primary and secondary conditions that required us not to join the election campaign and to continue to attack the enemy. At that time, we held a meeting organized by Ta Mok near Chhatt [Umbrella] Mountain.
>
> *Dany*: What did he suggest during the meeting in Chhatt Mountain?
>
> *Chiem*: Ta Mok told Pol Pot that if Pol Pot decided to carry on with the fighting, he would follow the decision. It seemed that Ta Mok was no longer independent. The situation during the national resistance differed from the three-year resistance. When the Vietnamese forces attacked us, we were weak both spiritually and intellectually. (Tun 2010)

Especially among the lower ranks, disappointment with the non-participation in the elections was regularly cited as a source for "war fatigue," although this for several reasons did not necessarily translate into action such as defection. Still, the election made some wings within the Khmer Rouge military start to realize that they were not fighting the Vietnamese anymore, but fellow Cambodians. The discourse of being anti-Vietnamese freedom fighters lost its grip, even among the most secluded NADK units, who were receiving an unprecedented inflow of external information via UNTAC radio. Mass defections set in, especially within the lower ranks, reducing the fighting force of the NADK by one third during UNTAC. Yet, the secluded blank-page leaders remained profoundly mistrustful of the Hun Sen and Ranariddh government's intentions and usually did not defect until they were targeted as enemies by their own people in concert with defecting top commanders and leading figures, and/or they were promised protection and positions within the "win-win" framework.

The first major group of defectors (after the smaller group under Keo Pong in Oral district) was the group surrounding Ieng Sary and the two division commanders in his area, Y Chhean and Sok Pheap, who were prompted to act after a threat of arrest by Son Sen:

> [M]y forces did not want to be under the control of Son Sen. Son Sen planned to arrest many leaders, namely Sok Pheap and [Y] Chhean. This caused controversy among the leaders. One day, it was broadcast on air that Ieng Sary, Sok Pheap, and [Y] Chhean were traitors. After learning this, we, soldiers from the two units, rose up against the accusation. Now that we were accused of being enemies, we decided to defect to the Hun Sen government. (Tun 2010)

After lengthy negotiations, top commanders and lower-ranking soldiers in the Pailin area were transferred into the state military and received top positions within the local government. Others defected later, during the final months and weeks of conflicts in Anlong Veng and after the clashes between Ranariddh and Hun Sen in July 1997, when they realized that only Hun Sen was left to make a deal with.[5] They not only had to fear losing all the resources they had accrued during wartime and their higher status as military commanders, but also any assurance of safety, as the Khmer Rouge were widely feared and disliked. Both premiers promised positions and resources as well as legal and military protection, but the clash in July meant that those who opted for a deal with Ranariddh would be in acute danger: "After the coup, I had to flee and I went into hiding with others. There were rumors that we would be beheaded if we stayed home" (DC-NADK -3).

The "win-win policy" not only worked very well for the government (the Hun Sen faction in particular), but also for the insurgents, as it enabled a smooth reintegration and prevented them from falling back to a lower social status (which is literally why it was called the win-win policy). It also protected them from reprisals. Accordingly, all respondents spoke highly of the agreement:

> At first, I was a bit afraid of reintegration because before we used to be their enemies. But now they have given us both positions and money. [. . .] I do not face any challenges in my life anymore. I have got a full salary from the government. And meanwhile, I can even do some farming. I don't seem to have any major challenges in my livelihood. (BAC-NADK -3)

Most respondents either still worked in the local government, the military, or the Ministry of Defense as an "advisor," or had recently retired from such a job. The "win-win policy" worked quite well for these members of the higher echelons of the Khmer Rouge military. Since most of their leaders were dead and many of them had received their positions at the very end of the conflict, they felt they had gotten a good deal when they received positions in the government or military. As veterans who made their careers within the Khmer Rouge apparatus, they had not initially belonged to the core leadership before but were treated as leaders during the transition. When asked why they had received high-status positions, they often pointed to their strength and resources as soldiers, such as their fighting skills: "The government said that I was good at fighting, so they wanted me to stay in the military" (BAC-NADK -1). Some also confessed that they did not know why they got the jobs they did, saying simply, "It was arranged this way. They said we could keep our military structure, even though our position might be a bit lower than before" (BAC-NADK -3). Even though many had to accept a slightly lower formal rank than before (a rank they usually received right before "reintegration" anyway), their wartime status was transferred into the new military as well as the village and commune structure:

> It was good for us to defect to the government. Our ranking framework remains the same; thus, we are able to be independent. The win-win policy of the prime minister is very effective, and the government is implementing its promise. We are able to be the owners of the land, houses, and our personal property after we integrated with the government. Most noticeably, each village and commune implements decentralized management, which makes it possible for each village to play an independent role. The structure is divided into independent villages consist[ing] of [a] village chief [and a] deputy chief with an assistant. (Tun 2010)

During the defection process, former members of the Khmer Rouge generally tried to secure social positions equal to the ones they had achieved through decades of combat. The "win-win policy" smoothened this transformation by keeping political and military structures intact, but it also worked on a symbolic level: During official integration ceremonies, mid- and low-ranking combatants even showed up in their NADK uniforms to receive and immediately put on their new RCAF uniforms, visually enacting their symbolic conversion. Without the "win-win policy," the blank-page leaders would have had a hard time transferring their resources, which were almost entirely field-bound and restricted to the inner hierarchy of the Khmer Rouge apparatus, into a society at peace. At the same time, the policy made it possible for them to maintain their social structure in post-conflict Cambodia. The whole Khmer Rouge apparatus, with all its allegiances and loyalties, continues to exist in the border regions of Cambodia and within the current state military.

Control over natural resources in Khmer Rouge-controlled areas and a cut of economic revenues from various other sources were usually part of the deal. Although the former communists were often accused of greed, in fact both the government and the Khmer Rouge had primarily political rather than financial motives for seeking control over these resources, which were transformed into political commodities during the peace negotiations (O'Brien-Kelly 2006). At least at the beginning of the defection process, income from natural resources such as timber was spent on an as-needed basis only for items such as construction materials, medicine, food, and fuel, rather than systematically for profit (cf. Le Billon 2002).

The blank-page leaders feared reprisals from the populace and the government and hence were also in need of security. As reported by a brigade commander, the upper command of the communist guerrillas played upon fears within its entourage and kept them in a constant state of insecurity and seclusion:

> In my case, I was with the Khmer Rouge for so long, so I only got political teaching from the Khmer Rouge. They told us that if we went back to the country or allied ourselves with the government, we would be killed. Which is why we [soldiers] came up with the thought that if we went back, we had no choice but to be killed. However, if we stayed on, we at least had the choice in which either we die [in combat] or we survive. Actually, if we were asked whether or not we wanted to fight or go into war, we of course would have said "no." Yet I was politically influenced by the Khmer Rouge. The way they influenced me was through talking about death all the time. (BC-NADK -1)

Yet even after joining the ranks of the government and its military, many remain skeptical and some even complain of an overabundance of *Yuon* in the country. Feelings about the government are highly ambivalent, oscillating between praise, mistrust, and resignation:

We [members of the military in general] are the government's instruments. Working for the Hun Sen government now means that we are the government's instruments. Same goes for the commanders. Of course, they still have their soldiers. But they are just the government's instruments as well. And so is a one-star general. If the government betrays us all, we will die for sure. (RC-NADK -1)

Some fear remains about the central government's true intention. But almost all respondents within the sample of this study profited from the "win-win policy," with the notable exception of two. The first was cast out of the military after being injured. After becoming disabled, he seemed to be of no further use as a soldier: "I was only disappointed that my commander cast me out after my injury. But past is past. We just cannot do anything about it" (DC-NADK -1). He claims that he was loyal to the army until his injury but was not taken care of afterwards. Since he had "no skills whatsoever," all he could do then was to rely on his "physical strength," which was all he "could make use of to make a living": "I would have done anything for the nation, even die. But the nation has never returned anything for my service. There is just nothing we can do about it" (DC-NADK -1). For most part, he survived by asking neighbors for food and getting jobs doing light manual labor. However, many others within the sample are also disabled, but did make deals and live comfortably. Therefore, it is at least questionable whether his disability was actually the main reason why he was "cast out."

The second exception was a commander who made a deal with Ranariddh and had to flee Anlong Veng after the clashes between the two premiers. He was also disabled, but this does not seem to be the main reason he was unable to strike a deal. He himself stated that a "lack of connections" was the real reason for why he became poor, leaving him isolated and disappointed:

I did feel disappointed because I received no compensation for all the years of struggle. All my fellow soldiers died, some having their heads injured, others their bodies torn apart. Although I am disappointed, there is simply nothing I can do to change it because everything is over already. Now that the war has ended, all we can do is focus on our present life. (DC-NADK -3)

NOTES

1. One type of amulet believed to be particularly effective is the *goan krak*, an amulet made from a desiccated human fetus. Ian Harris mentions its increased usage during times of national upheaval: "[The] Issaraks, for instance, are known to have used them during the independence struggle. A husband is supposed to cut a fetus from his wife's uterus after several months of pregnancy. In theory, she has previously agreed

to offer herself up to him and dies in the process. The *goan krak* is then dried out over a fire and generally worn in a small wooden ball of two halves (*danlap*) around the neck" (Harris 2005: 61, compare also Ang 1986, 157–158). While amulets like these were mentioned by respondents, no one claimed to have possessed one themselves.

2. Most Cambodians belief in the existence of two separate types of souls, *viññāṇa*, described as the Buddhist moral consciousness eventualy taking rebirth in a new body, and the *braḥ liṅg*, a collection of nineteen animating spirits. While many Buddhist leaders deny the existence of the *braḥ liṅg*, often treating it as mere superstition, many—as Erik W. Davis noted—still warn against "the real and immoral magic one could practice by working with them" (Davis 2016, 43–44; see also Ang 2004, Thompson 2004). Among the most powerful spirits relevant to the guerrillas were spirits of the forest (*neak tā prey*) and the spirit of *Khleang Moeung*, who is believed to have been a general in Ang Chan's army (1806–1836) and who defeated the invading Thai (Harris 2005, 53). *Khleang Moeung* was also the name of a resistance group that pledged loyalty to the king after the formation of FUNCINPEC in February 1981 and was formally incorporated into the ranks of the ANS. The group has frequently resurfaced in politics since then.

3. In theory, each recruit had to be admitted through two veteran cadres. This rule was not always implemented in practice, especially after 1979 and in the lowest ranks. But it is likely that this background check via networks was more important in the higher ranks of the apparatus. Thus, it might be the case that the blank-page leaders all had previous connections vouching for them. Some mentioned previous connections (up to Pol Pot or even Tou Samouth), but it is of course impossible to ascertain whether these were decisive in their careers. However, it is clear that the contacts mentioned by the mid-range cadres came from higher positions (at minimum from the mid-range command, and often the upper echelon of the leadership), while those mentioned within the rank and file had been "veteran cadres" within the lowest strata of the movement.

4. "Barey Agreement" refers to the Paris Agreement of 1991.

5. Because of this, respondents turned not only against Pol Pot during the last months of Khmer Rouge infighting, but also against Ta Mok. They even joined the CPP in combat operations against the last remaining pockets of loyalists in Anlong Veng and Preah Vihear in late 1998, thereby—at the very last moment—securing high positions within the provincial and military administration in this area.

Chapter Five

Rank-and-File Soldiers

In terms of occupational status, the rank and file of the non-communist groups KPNLF and FUNCINPEC almost without exception experienced horizontal mobility, becoming farmers, unskilled manual workers, or small-scale traders after demobilization. In most cases, they simply returned to the occupation they or their parents practiced before the war. However, those who had faced war and displacement during an early age and who lived as soldiers for major parts of their adult life often tried to stay in the military (largely unsuccessfully). Otherwise, they had to take highly insecure manual labor jobs; many still cross the border to Thailand illegally as migrant laborers. War and displacement as children meant they had received barely any education.

For many of these soldiers, all they possessed was their physical strength and the symbolic resource of bravery as a combatant. None of these respondents managed to improve their social status after the war. On the contrary, they were stigmatized as former combatants *and* as former members of the besieged CGDK. Due to the social distance between them and the upper levels of the commanding hierarchy, very few rank-and-file soldiers were incorporated into the state military. These "lucky few" were usually part of the entourage of a strongman or of one of the few elite military commanders who brokered a deal with Hun Sen after 1997, thereby keeping their forces together—a valuable means of enhancing their own security and status during the transition process. But the remaining fighters had to find ways to support themselves.

Much of this holds true for the Khmer Rouge fighters as well. However, their mode of reintegration was slightly different for several reasons. Firstly, Khmer Rouge soldiers tended to have lived secluded lives since early childhood, which effectively separated them from life beyond their own military units and in most cases also from social relations within the interior. The unit was the only social reality they knew, which is why many waited until their commanders made a deal for integration into the state military and/or received land within the areas under Khmer Rouge control. Beyond seclusion and the restriction of their cultural, social, and symbolic resources to the social spheres of their units, all faced high levels of stigmatization as members of the Khmer Rouge, even those who were only short-term recruits. The symbolic blood on their hands meant that they had to make strenuous efforts—at least from their own perspective—to reconstruct their symbolic status within the community and society at large. They often found it easier to remain within the sphere of the Khmer Rouge after officially demobilizing.

PATHWAYS AND SYMBOLIC VIOLENCE

The rank and file of the non-communist insurgency was largely recruited from a displaced peasantry as well as workers in the refugee camps. While forcible conscription was very rare, most soldiers nevertheless did not have a heartfelt ideological commitment to the resistance but joined due to the exigencies created by civil war itself. This is a typical pattern for political conflicts, in which the lowest stratum of fighters generally do not join an insurgency to create war, but are driven to join due to the effects of war (cf. Arjona and Kalyvas 2012). Or as Stathis Kalyvas put it, many soldiers enter armed groups "driven by incentives and constraints that are byproducts of the war" (Kalyvas 2008, 1063). This holds true for the recruits of all three Cambodian insurgent groups, some of whom had already been part of the state military or a resistance force during the civil war from 1970 to 1975. Others had been part of the rank and file of the state military under Sihanouk.

Instead of talking about recruitment, therefore, the process of incorporation into an insurgent group is better described using the concept of "pathways." Under this framework, what is decisive is not just the individual's motive for joining, but also his or her *social mode of access*. Recruitment into armed groups does not simply stem from a centrally coordinated policy from above that is met by a rational decision made by socially loose individuals from below. Instead, most CGDK fighters joined through networks of friends, former colleagues, or even family members. As was the case for the upper ranks, the lowest rank of the insurgency was largely the result of the militarization of social networks (cf. Hoffman 2007). These networks can differ strongly from one another in terms of institutionalization and possible peer group pressures at their disposal, which may include occupational groups, political circles, religious groups, or networks of friends and family. In civil wars across the world, many rank-and-file members of armed groups say that their main reason for joining was friends, contacts within association or clubs, or a history of military service within their own families (cf. Argo 2009, Schlichte 2014). Close bonds of solidarity within the recruit's social milieu regulate access to armed groups. The networks lay out trajectories of access and also some basic patterns of disciplinary techniques securing loyalty to "the cause."

A large share of rank-and-file soldiers during the civil war that followed the Khmer Rouge regime's breakdown simply joined whatever group controlled the area or the refugee camp where they lived. Some stated that they had escaped a "miserable life" due to fighting in their villages (RF-KPNLF -3); many simply "got stuck in the camp" and saw no alternatives to a life as a soldier (PC-FUNCINPEC -1). Others thought that an armed group was the safest place to be, as "it was unsafe everywhere [else]" (GC-KPNLF -3). As Nordstrom remarked, "[t]he least dangerous place to be in contemporary wars is in the military" (Nordstrom 1992, 271). For many fighters, the experience of violence within their local communities as well as their own families, and the wish to retaliate, was a crucial factor in their decision to join (Fuji 2009, Balcells 2010). This also holds true for the Khmer Rouge soldiers, who cited US carpet bombings (until 1973) and violence exacted on them by the Lon Nol state military or even South Vietnamese troops as an important motive for joining the Communist guerrilla group in the first place.[1]

Other respondents said they had joined the military due to poverty and the fact that they had no relatives left and "no one to rely on" after the Khmer Rouge regime; they hoped becoming fighters would guarantee a certain amount of food and assistance (BAC-FUNCINPEC -2). A widely shared theme was that, during the chaos after the Vietnamese incursion in 1979, many respondents ended up in a refugee camp "by accident" and, as long as they were safe and had enough to eat, did not care exactly who led them: "I was fine with any faction, [. . .] and my friends told me I would die if I stayed in the interior" (GC-KPNLF -1). However, camp regulations also played a role here, because the UN tried to avoid feeding warriors by distributing food to women and small children only. Since food rations were not distributed to adult males, many felt forced to join an armed group, effectively turning the UN policy on its head and making it a machine for recruitment:

UNBRO supported us [the resistance as a whole], but they only gave [food] to women. So I kept my hair long pretending to be a girl only to get a ticket [for food rations]. When the Thais [the camp police force] found out that I was a boy, they hurt me. It was not easy. They checked and found my penis, so they beat me up. Therefore, I registered to join Son Sann, because that was where I was staying. (GC-KPNLF -1)

When boys had grown "too old" for food rations, many saw no alternatives to a life as a soldier within the camps. Young men also had almost no skills after childhoods spent under the Khmer Rouge: "I was too old to study in the camp, so I joined the resistance" (GC-KPNLF -2). Others tried to make a living in cross-border smuggling, but it was still "easier" to do that as a member of an armed group, as combatants had weapons to protect themselves and easier access to goods to trade with (RF-KPNLF -2). Very few of the soldiers interviewed throughout the years said they had joined the resistance due to a deeply felt hatred for the Vietnamese or the central government. Although anti-Vietnamese sentiment did play a role, it was interestingly almost never mentioned when respondents explained their primary motivation for joining a particular armed group along the border. Since anti-Vietnamese slurs came up quite regularly throughout the interviews, the omission of the sentiment within the narrative of joining the insurgency does not seem to be the result of an intent to adapt to an imagined discourse of a foreign interviewer.

One major factor causing individuals to join an armed group was symbolic violence. For many, if not most, combat soldiers, it seemed normal to become a soldier and take on the role of a fighter during wartime due to their positions in society (cf. Bultmann 2018b). Or as one put it, "we [as 'ordinary' people] simply followed what we were meant to be" (RF-KPNLF -2). People within armed networks do not take up their positions simply because they crave money or want to kill people they hate. They tend to come from lower social milieus from which it is normal to be recruited as combat soldiers within the lowest spheres of an armed group. Symbolic violence, in this context, refers to misrecognized obedience by the agents in which an arbitrarily imposed symbolic power and the resulting social order are accepted as legitimate, or simply beyond one's own agency. Many rank-and-file soldiers saw themselves as merely the "pedals of power" (cited in Bultmann 2015, 145). Combat was difficult, but in the end, it was "a business-as-usual situation for us. This was our life and there was nothing we could do about it" (SC-KPNLF -4).

Perhaps, as Tarak Barkawi argues, citing Field Marshall Lord Wavell, it is time to decolonize our conceptions of war and perpetration, since "many battles and campaigns have been won by men who had little idea of why they were fighting, and, perhaps cared less" (Barkawi 2015). In Cambodia, certainly, the insurgency reproduced the peacetime social order, as top commanders saw it as "normal" for the "ordinary people" to become soldiers in wartime, when nothing is "normal" and human psychology becomes twisted:

Respondent: The file and rank was recruited really from the ORDINARY refugee [hm]. It was—it was not very difficult AT ALL.

Interviewer: To recruit?

Respondent: To recruit. BECAUSE, you know, those years—more than ten years—it was STRANGE, special years. Because I think that PEOPLE seem to lose a LOGIC of a NORMAL of human being. The psychology was really in war time. You—you see people do things that they NORMALLY don't do [hm]: rape, stealing, you know, KILLING (RC-KPNLF -2, see also Bultmann 2015, 135)

Recruits, from his perspective, were "ordinary" people with basically two options during these "special years": to be a "refugee" living a harsh life (without food rations) or a soldier with a "much better" status. To opt for a life as a fighter was "normal" or a "logical choice," as he said elsewere for "ordinary refugees" in extraordinary times, because it entailed a rise in status.

Yet the rank and file of the insurgency remained in some sense *terra incognita* to the top command, who were former members of the Cambodian elite. These soldiers barely knew who these superiors were, and even during times of war, they did not expect anything from them: "I never expected [to receive] anything from them. We did not even know what these commanders did, as they had been so distant from us. We never talked to each other. [. . .] We had merely been low-ranking soldiers, so there was a huge [communication] gap between us" (GC-KPNLF -1). This social distance could also be seen in the discourse of the top commanders, who had no idea why rank-and-file soldiers followed their orders (except for suggesting that it must be in their nature) or what their former fighters did after the war (except for speaking abstractly about their miseries and setting up foundations as a means of support).

There was just one exception: The strongmen maintained small entourages of fighters who guarded them on their heavily fortified and secure compounds during "peacetime." However, members of the old elite from both the political and the military upper class did not care what their soldiers did. Their soldiers also stated that they did not expect anything from their commanders (as they had not expected any substantial care before either). However, as will be discussed below, some did complain that the commanders "should have taken care of their former armies" (GC-KPNLF -2). But for large parts of the former fighting force, vertical support and cohesion did not materialize during the transition to peace. During and after the war, most rank-and-file soldiers were not part of patrimonial networks of commanders from higher ranks. Instead they relied on subsistence ethics and—if possible—on horizontal support networks of family, friends, and home communities to enable and foster transition. Only the small rank-and-file entourages of strongmen entered patrimonial relations, and even fewer could actually benefit from that relationship after the war. Many eventually ended up with an imprisoned strongman as patron.

DISPLACED PEASANTRY

For former peasants who had joined a militia from a village along the border, or who were able to return to a community they had some previous connection to, reintegration was a comparatively smooth process, and they generally returned to their previous social status. According to a survey by the International Labor Organization (ILO), about half of the rank-and-file fighters from the non-communist factions strove to become peasants during UNTAC (Bernander 1993). Roughly a third planned to open a small business, while the remaining former belligerents planned to make a living through manual labor. Within the sample of this study, the decisive factor in reintegration seems to have been at which age the combatants were socialized into the armed forces, and how long they served as fighters. Peasants who were displaced as adults struggled to varying degrees to find suitable available land (promises by the UN were not met because secure land was scarcer than had been believed), but because they had a former life they could return to, they were able to re-establish their former social status with comparative ease. Most resettled in border areas in the provinces Oddar Meanchey, Banteay Meanchey, and Battambang. However, those who had been displaced and socialized into war and military service as children found it much harder to pick up former lives, social resources, and skills as peasants. They had been members of the insurgency for a much greater part of their youth and adult life, while others had been part of ebbs and flows of recruits in cycles of militarization.

Cycles of Militarization

Within the rank and file of an insurgency, it is difficult to draw a clear line between being a full-time member, a part-time supporter, a combatant, a mercenary, or a person who has joined for a brief period (Guichaoua 2012). Especially before the arrival of UNTAC, all factions hastily recruited combatants to fill their ranks for the demobilization process, which was supposed to disarm 70 percent of their forces. Besides inflating their numbers, they called various former fighters back into service or recruited poor villagers for short-term service with the lucrative prospect of being subsequently demobilized. As interviews with self-demobilized soldiers indicate, the eventual suspension of the demobilization program meant that they did not receive these expected benefits, which was likely one reason why so many short-term combatants defected during this period (Steve Heder was part of the team interviewing NADK self-demobilizers, see Heder 1996; many of the interviews are currently stored at the Australian Defence Force Academy, UNSW Canberra, and will be discussed below).

Yet not only did the lowest rank consist in large parts of "hop-on and hop-off guerrillas" at its margins, but the insurgent groups also recruited most of their soldiers from neighboring villages along the Thai border to which the soldiers returned after their service, as reported by an ILO survey (Bernander 1993). The insurgent movement was part of an economic opportunity structure within the surrounding villages that provided for an ebb and flow of short-term combatants and mercenaries. A considerable share of combatants commuted between service and farming or other economic activities in their home villages nearby, which is why many villagers were part of the insurgency at different stages of the conflict—and for different factions. Short-term service to one or multiple groups was a means to ameliorate their poverty. As one former part-time FUNCINPEC, KPNLF, *and* Khmer Rouge combatant said, he constantly rejoined the most proximate military "as I was illiterate and there were no other jobs for me" (RF-MF -5).

Being a part-time guerrilla with at least some prospect of reintegration incentives was an important factor drawing some to join the insurgency during its late stages, even when this meant becoming part of the infamous and already crumbling Khmer Rouge: "We were extremely poor, so I joined" (RF-NADK -3). Since demobilization was halted after a while, many soldiers went to the civilian refugee camps in order to try to get the reintegration packages for civilians. Around the time UNTAC's demobilization program began, the KPNLF also started to screen for fighters who would devote themselves fully to the military, demobilizing those who were married and keeping single people as core combatants:

> *Interviewer*: Who told you about the demobilization? Were there some people still working?
>
> *Respondent*: My commander told me about it. Only those who were single were allowed to stay.
>
> *Interviewer*: Why only singles?
>
> *Respondent*: It was due to the fact that they can work more, while married people cannot. (RF-KPNLF -3)

For many combatants, reintegration was merely a matter of losing a side income within the local economy.

Stigma, Patronage Exclusion, and Group Reintegration

Of course, not everyone was a commuter who could return to (or stay in) nearby villages. Combatants without supporting community and family networks within the interior—usually also those who had served in an armed group for more than 10 years—faced particular difficulties in entering village communities after (re)integration. Like civilian refugees, they were excluded from village patronage systems (cf. Hensengerth 2008, 38–42). Returning soldiers lacked the support networks and connections to people of influence essential to make a living in the village community. Not only were they unable to build upon inherited networks within the community, but they also faced stigmatization by the long-established members of the villages:

I MYSELF have EXPERIENCED—I myself as a refugee—people—when I RETURNED—in the (incomprehensible) of repatriation supported by United Nations. They just give FIFTY dollars [yeah]. Like the money you can spend to build a HOUSE, yeah. Then they provide us a PLOT of LAND. But the land that they provide US is not as SECURELY, it is NOT a safe land. When we leave [to live there] at that time, you know, its UNSECURED. Anytime the local authority come to THREAT us, yeah, BECAUSE they-they-they feel like a REVENGE statement [hm]. They say that: "YOU live free, you live for FREE in the camp, you receive support, yeah? for FREE by United Nation. BUT US we don't have ANYTHING." (MS-FUNCINPEC -1)

Due to this stigmatization, these returnees remained excluded from the political and economic system in village communities and constantly feared reprisals and the loss of assets or land, which is why many of them established support systems among groups of former refugee warriors, or settled in areas that were closely connected to the insurgency along the border. Others, particularly former child soldiers without reliable support networks or professional skills, had no choice but to become illegal migrant workers:

It is HARD for [making a] living. And SO far, based on economic upside down, there are no WORK for the people. And WHO got negative effects from the economy in Cambodia? Most its to the former Khmer REFUGEE [hm]. So they decide to MOVE to close—to live close to the border [hm]. Easy to access to Thailand ILLEGALLY to find a work. (MS-FUNCINPEC -1)

Many—especially those without support networks in the interior and without farming skills—moved to live in the so-called "camp villages" (*phum djumrum*) that were set up by the UN on the outskirts of the cities of Battambang and Pursat, where the whole village community consisted of former civilian and non-civilian refugees. These people had nowhere else to go, as they had been refugees for too long. Today they mainly survive by migrant work or cheap manual labor and—particularly the disabled former combatants—through external support from international NGOs and UN programs. This support included the provision of plots of land to build houses (but despite initial promises to the contrary, without enough land for farming) and the distribution of building materials. It also extended to the regular provision of food, creating highly dependent communities that still remain largely dependent on external support (SC-KPNLF -3). These communities are also frequently stigmatized as UN-supported "camp villages," adding heavily to their isolation. The "children of war" discussed in the next chapter faced numerous problems during the transition to peace, especially those who were combatants and had no memory of life before war and displacement.

CHILDREN OF WAR

All respondents from this group said that they could not remember a life before war and even, sometimes, before being a soldier. They not only served as soldiers for longer periods of time but had experienced their primary habitus formation within armed groups or as displaced children in war zones. Some were as young as 14 or 15 when they were recruited to fight, while the rest grew up in war zones and refugee camps, and as children under the Khmer Rouge, which meant that they lacked key cultural knowledge and social resources and had experienced a deep rupture in their education:

> Due to the war, we became illiterates. Me, for instance, when I was studying in grade nine [the fourth year of schooling], the Khmer Rouge took over and they had no schools. And after that, during the [People Republic of Kampuchea], I was too old already, just about old enough to carry a weapon to go into battles. [. . .] For me, education is like the running water that never comes back. (GC-KPNLF -2)

Even though many like this respondent had not been child soldiers in a strict sense, with some joining a military in their early 20s, all were children of war and displacement, which strongly affected their ability to reintegrate after the war's end.

In terms of habitus formation, a focus solely on the age of recruitment into an armed group seems too narrow. Both the Khmer Rouge regime and the conditions within refugee camps had a major impact on the education and well-being of these children. Their primary socialization took place in conditions of constant danger, fear, and violence. War was normal to them, and most importantly, there was no community or social status they could possibly return to. They learned, as one respondent put it, "to be extreme" during a life in which "life and death go hand in hand" (SC-KPNLF -4). Childhood became a distant memory: "I cannot remember much from my childhood, except for being a soldier" (SC-KPNLF -2). In a typical pattern for child soldiering, the high number of poor, orphaned, and desperate juveniles within the refugee camps served as a perfect pool for recruitment (Achvarina and Reich 2010). In the Cambodian case, this was additionally supported by the UN policy not to distribute food to juveniles over a certain height (Thibault 2015).

Many saw no alternatives for themselves as illiterate teenagers besides joining an armed group in times of war; some even tried to flee conflict zones, only to end up in the military again:

> I was running away from the [state] military [at the age of 15] but after my flight I just ended up in another military at the border. I never wanted to become a soldier. I was forced to join the military. Before, I never thought about joining at all. I had no choice but to look for a safe place, which is why I went to the border, only to end up suffering yet again. (SC-KPNLF -3)

Interestingly, unlike their commanders, the low-ranking soldiers did not buy into the ideology of cleavage that was the theoretical basis for the conflict. They did not refer to a war against occupation and seldom mentioned that they were motivated to join the insurgency to fight the Vietnamese. If they did mention the Vietnamese, they still stressed that "it was a war of Khmer against Khmer, not Khmer against Vietnamese" (SC-KPNLF -3). As many previous studies have noted, the lowest ranks are usually the least ideologically firm members of an insurgency, with most only paying lip service to the official cause of their side (cf. Kilcullen 2009). For the rank and file, the conflict was in many ways beyond the scope of their agency and possible influence. Their motivation in fighting was often to survive, or ameliorate the exigencies created by war and displacement.

War has a deep impact on the habitus of recruits who are socialized into it, as it reduces their time-horizons, giving them "a very strong preference for current consumption even at the expense of future consumption" (Murshed 2010, 117). A former child soldier now working as an illegal manual laborer in Thailand reported how this short-term orientation affected his decision-making during reintegration:

> I am currently in a bad living condition as I am renting a house. I decided to take money, not land, following repatriation. UNHCR then was giving us land, but I was so short-term oriented that I decided to take the money in an attempt to start a business. However, soon the money was already used up. This is my story. Nowadays, I am renting this house [a poorly cobbled together wooden shack over a mud hole for which he pays 5 USD a month]. (Cited in Bultmann 2015, 180; GC-KPNLF -1)

His short-term orientation led him to opt for the immediate economic benefit.

Narratives and Status Change during Transition

As outlined by a respondent who was working on others' rice fields and as a manual laborer on the side, making a living after the war's end was a matter of "physical strength. [. . .] To work on farms is a bit tiring, but that is normal. I do some other odd jobs as well to earn some extras. At least we do not have to run away from bullets anymore" (RF-KPNLF -1). On a certain level, it seems as if not much has changed for former foot soldiers, as they are still reduced to their bodily strength—by society and, in a sense, also by themselves. The only difference lies in the fact that their life nowadays is less dangerous.

As noted before, the lowest ranks had been largely decoupled from the leadership and mid-range command. They did not interact with each other and had no social relations. The social distance between these layers of the insurgency meant that almost no commander actually cared about the fate of their former soldiers, although they sometimes had abstract feelings of responsibility (e.g., one commander set up a foundation to help people living along the border with Thailand). While pretending that they did not expect anything from their former superiors during transition, former fighters nonetheless expressed high degrees of frustration:

> *Respondent*: I didn't have any expectation because our leaders didn't care about us anyway.
>
> *Interviewer*: Why do you say that your leaders didn't care about you?
>
> *Respondent*: To put it briefly, as long as there was a war going on, they needed brave people, but as soon as peace set in, they only needed the knowledgeable. We [the rank-and-file soldiers] are illiterates, so they don't value us. At least I can count myself lucky that I am not handicapped. I would even dare to say that all rank-and-file soldiers of Son Sann were simply ignored [after signing the peace agreement]. (SC-KPNLF -1)

Not being handicapped was the best a soldier could hope for after war's end. For many, the main division in post-conflict Cambodia lies between those who are able to perform physical labor and those who are handicapped by war and cannot work. All former children of war of the non-Communist factions interviewed for this project became untrained manual workers, and, from their own perspective, lost something vital in the transition to peace: the symbolic resource of being a brave warrior. Suddenly, their main skill, fighting, was not needed anymore, and their previously important selves became deeply problematic, something that had no place in a society at peace.

However, the respondents still perceived their position within post-conflict society as the result of a natural order in which what they received depended on their power and status. When asked why they did not receive benefits like land, as others did, a typical response was: "I am [a] normal [person]. My position is low. When you are in a high position and you have some power, then you would have received a plot of land" (RF-KPNLF -2). Society gives to those who have power and connections:

> Of course, I want a good position and to have cars like others. Nowadays, those who are still working [in the military] have strong connections to run a business. And if you do not have any power, you cannot do anything, not even cut wood to build a house. (RF-KPNLF -3)

Many respondents hoped to return to a life as a soldier, particularly those who had dedicated large parts of their youth and adulthood to the military as members of the insurgency, and who did this at great personal cost. However, only a few managed to join the newly formed state military or the entourage of a strongman who treated them, as one respondent said in high praise, "like a father would" (GBC-KPNLF -1). Many of these respondents' attempts to join the state military were rejected, as there was no need for so many rank-and-file soldiers:

> *Interviewer*: Have you ever thought of returning to the military?
>
> *Respondent*: Yes, but they would not let me in.
>
> *Interviewer*: Why would you like to return?
>
> *Respondent*: Because I do not want to be looked down upon. It is not that I would like to kill anyone, I just want to escape from my current living condition. (RF-KPNLF -1)

Another respondent had expected to transfer to the state military, but when he attempted to do so he realized that "there was no one to sign my documents [for the transfer]" (RF-MF -3). Others waited to be called back into service: "I thought that all troops, at least those who were still alive, would be called into service, but then nobody was calling me. And now all [my former commanders] have passed away anyway, so there is nothing I could possibly do about it" (RF-MF -4). For these former fighters, it was quite clear that they could not receive a transfer because they had no vertical social resources: "To be frank, they do not value us. They simply forgot their former soldiers in arms" (RF-MF -5). As child soldiers who had spent their lives within these organizations, they were in a difficult situation. Like child soldiers in general (Vermeij 2011), they were highly identified with their group, which almost served as a surrogate family for them. But they could not stay with that group and received no support after the war.

Despite all the politics involved, almost all respondents viewed their current lives as a direct result of their destiny: "I think that I cannot change my life, as destiny has already determined it" (SC-KPNLF -4). While acknowledging that those who joined the CPP were better off, they saw even the ability to join the party as a matter of fate:

> *Interviewer*: Do you regret that you have not joined the CPP?
>
> *Respondent*: Yes, sometimes I feel sorry about that, but again, this is the result of my destiny. We cannot do anything [that contravenes destiny], just let it be. (GC-KPNLF -3)

Looking back, they felt risking their lives for the sake of the nation had been meaningless since in the end nobody cared about them. Even those who actually died in service were not honored afterward, and their families did not receive support:

> A lot of my friends died in the battles. I really appreciate that children today have a chance to receive education [and to become something other than a soldier]. For me, I joined the military since I was 16 or 17. I did not know what else I should do, so serving in the military was the only option for me. When we joined the military, we had to do what we were asked to; otherwise, we would not get any rice to eat. Very soon, I had enough of the military. At least, I was lucky because sometimes I was almost hit by a bullet, but I was fine. During this period of my life, I was so scared. Unfortunately, the lives of those who died were just meaningless because their family members are now having an even more difficult life. No one pays attention to them. This is the life of fighters. (RF-KPNLF -2)

His view reflects a common opinion among the former rank-and-file soldiers of the insurgency: Combatants of the CGDK died for nothing. But at the same time, the soldiers are unsure whom to blame for this state of affairs:

> Right at the moment, the primary source of income for me as well as for others is working in Thailand. There is nothing to do in Cambodia. We received no land [during reintegration], so what else could we possibly do? So most of us cross the border to work in Thailand. No one thinks about us, but we do not know who to blame here. If we were given what we were supposed to get [according to the initial announcement by the UN] and then still ended up poor, it would be us to blame. But in our case, we received nothing, so now we do not know what to do. We also borrowed some money from the bank to buy an old motorbike and to be a motodup driver to have an additional income for a living. But what we earn is just enough to repay the debt and to buy some food. This is not just the case for my family, but for everyone else. (GC-KPNLF -2)

There was, however, at least one consolation in being a soldier from the lowest ranks of the insurgency. During the military confrontation between Ranariddh and Hun Sen in mid-1997, many were afraid that they might be targeted as well. They saw that many of their former commanders were being killed or threatened. "But us simple troops? They would not care about us" (SC-KPNLF -2).

BLANK-PAGE SOLDIERS

In terms of class background and access to the guerrillas, almost everything that was written about the blank-page leaders (chapter 4) holds true for the blank-page soldiers as well. The only difference is that the blank-page soldiers did not manage to rise in rank within the Communist military. This was either because they did not prove as "active" in following orders as those who eventually became leaders, because they did not have the necessary connections to mid-level or upper echelon cadres (some did have previous contacts, but within the rank and file), because they joined comparatively late (during the Khmer Rouge's years in power, at the earliest), and/or because they were only short-term recruits at the margins, who were useful for combat purposes but would not be entrusted with activities at the core of the apparatus. The difference in years of service and time of recruitment is often decisive for the recruits' habitus, as well as their reintegration.

The rank-and-file of the Khmer Rouge was almost entirely recruited from poor rural households and consisted almost without exception of juveniles and—especially for those who were conscripted during the years in power—children. There were only a few exceptions, such as when recruits were hastily added in the early 1990s in order to bolster the fighting force right before the arrival of UNAMIC and UNTAC and its demobilization program. The Khmer Rouge at that time needed a bigger force to have stronger leverage during negotiations and gain more dispensable members for eventual demobilization. The Khmer Rouge therefore consisted of a core of long-serving soldiers who had been recruited as minors, and a margin of members who had usually been recruited between the ages of 18 to 22, or sometimes even later. Many of these hastily recruited soldiers had also been members of several other factions as well and served essentially as mercenaries who tried to make a living in zones of war, displacement, and conflict.

Much of the following focuses on core members, who strongly resemble the blank-page leaders in habitus and life course. They do not tend to remember anything of their childhoods or natal families, and schooling is also a hazy memory at best: "I do not remember for how long I went to school" (RF-NADK -2). Those who were recruited before 1975 cite either the loss of family members during the civil war or the US bombings, or Norodom Sihanouk's call to join him in the *maquis*, as their prime motivation for entering the guerrilla forces in the first place. Some, however, also mention that they as minors were easily "persuaded" by cadres. One respondent likened himself to a child being given a cookie: "They convinced me to join. They would say things like, 'Oh, you are so brave' and stuff like that, so I just followed them. It is not very different from how you convince children to eat a cookie" (SC-NADK -1). For others, propaganda against spoiled children in the elite worked well. One respondent, for example, said that songs sung by the Khmer Rouge in his village made him angry: "They sang, 'Big bellied youths spin the stick around as they are afraid of dogs. They never stay apart from their mum and keep begging her until she finds a woman for them.' That made me angry" (GC-NADK -1).

Like other rank-and-file soldiers, Khmer Rouge cadres sometimes used irony to talk about their recruitment. When asked how they felt after being "chosen" to become a soldier, one, for instance, said: "Of course, I felt as happy as an insect playing with the light" (RF-NADK -5). Others noted the social distance and symbolic violence underlying their recruitment, stating that they simply "felt normal" when recruited since they were "only rank-and-file soldiers, who had no relation to commanders and the upper leadership" (RF-NADK -4). Like the blank-page leaders, they were thrown into battle right away and had to prove their "activeness" from day one. The exact meaning of being "active," however, remained abstract for many, and they tended to interpret it as being hard-working and willing to engage in battles: "We had to be active. Active meant to work without getting sick of it. We had to show up at all three to four battles per week. Inactive would have been if you only show up during two of them" (RF-NADK -2). The mode of reintegration heavily depended on their years of service.

Narratives and Status Change during Transition

Besides using interviews by the author, this chapter relies on interview memos by members of the UNTAC program for Khmer Rouge "self-demobilizers." During UNTAC there were essentially two options for NADK defectors to reintegrate, one through UNTAC and one through the SOC government. The main difference between these programs is described by Steve Heder, who conducted many of the UNTAC interviews with Khmer Rouge defectors being used in this chapter:

UNTAC did not actively seek to persuade NADK combatants to self-demobilize, and the material incentives and security guarantees provided were generally meager. The UNTAC program existed alongside a SOC program to bring about NADK defections that had been in existence and vigorously pursued for many years. The SOC program aimed to "bring back into the national fold" individuals and groups from NADK ranks who "confessed" the error of their ways and admitted that they had been "misled persons." These misled persons were generally subjected to brief periods of "reeducation" before being allowed to return home. During the UNTAC period, it appears that NADK combatants wishing to break with the PDK more often did so via SOC's misled persons program than UNTAC's self-demobilization program. This was especially the case when the local situation was such that the best chance of obtaining viable security assurances was through personal arrangements between the former NADK combatant and SOC local authorities. (Heder 1996, 75)

Besides a short period of "re-education," in which they had to attend training sessions on various areas of national law and political discourse, defectors within the "misled persons program" received a one-time cash allowance of 30,000 riel and were able to make deals with local SOC authorities, who registered them, as one respondent who took part in it put it, "like normal people" (RF-NADK -4). The "misled persons program" was in a way a forerunner of the "win-win policy." As noted by Heder, who personally interviewed around one hundred Khmer Rouge self-demobilizers, many were former member of the Cambodian People's Armed Forces (CPAF) who had been abducted by the Khmer Rouge to fill their ranks. A large number of these defectors did not belong to the core of the Khmer Rouge.

Statistics gathered by the author from thirty-six of the UNTAC interview memos stored at the John Sanderson Manuscript Collection of the Australian Defence Force Academy at the UNSW Canberra show that many of those opting to self-demobilize via UNTAC had been short-term recruits (most had been members for three years maximum, some even just for a few months). Very few had served longer than three years. And of those defectors, who had dedicated much of their youth and adolescence to a life within the fold of the Khmer Rouge, most if not all were interested in continuing their military career within the Cambodian People's Armed Forces (CPAF). Together with the interviews conducted by the author, this tells us a lot about the mode of demobilization of the Khmer Rouge, as well as its main impediments. The following boxplot graph shows that almost all (except for one, who served for 18 years) of the defectors who served for three years or less wished to become farmers, return to a family business, or become manual workers. By contrast, those who had served for at least nine years all wished to be integrated into the state military. This was at a time when the "win-win policy" was not yet in place. Instead, ad hoc deals had to be made with local authorities and commanders of the CPAF.

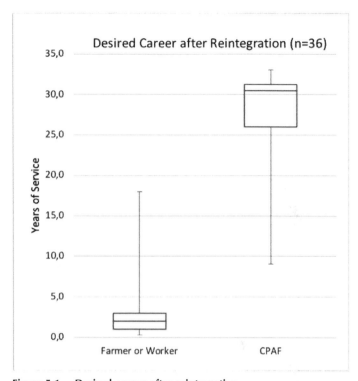

Figure 5.1. Desired career after reintegration
Own design using data from interviews stored at The John Sanderson Manuscript Collection, Australian Defence Force Academy, UNSW Canberra.

After spending decades within the Khmer Rouge disciplinary apparatus, the blank-page veterans from the core of the apparatus incorporated its discourse as normal; they had nothing else besides the resources they have gathered over the course of their membership. For them, everything hinged on the close-knit community they had established with their comrades. This made it difficult for them to leave this cosmos, as pointed out by a defector during UNTAC:

> Guys like him [his former comrade] won't ever surrender to UNTAC or anybody else. He's too politically dedicated. For the newcomers like me, we simply couldn't put up with it anymore, and that's why we surrendered. (Saroeun 1993)

The "newcomers" he is referring to usually could not adapt to the harshness of life within malaria-ridden units of the NADK. Most of these defectors cite sickness, poverty, and disappointment with the withdrawal from the peace process as their reasons for defecting. Participating in warfare came at a great cost for them. By contrast, in some areas commanders could do quite well by profiting from the war economy, and wood sales in particular. This led to rising inequality, which was also sometimes mentioned as a reason to leave the guerrilla life:

> Soldiers are dissatisfied because they have no money, do not even have a bicycle. They see their commanders, who offer sweets or cakes to their children when they cannot afford to do so. If you are an officer and have power you can get money, but if you are an ordinary soldier you cannot. Soldiers are very unhappy with this situation. (Roeurn 1992)

Besides having incorporated a life as a NADK soldier into their conception of what was normal, and having no economic and symbolic resources beyond this, the blank-page veterans also had no chance to establish resources outside of their units. Staying in the military would have meant carrying on with their previous life, which is why many said during the interviews that they wished to do so: "I have served there for so long already" (RF-NADK -1). As soldiers who had fought for the Khmer Rouge for almost their entire lives, they were isolated from Cambodian society. Therefore, most simply did not know where to go during UNTAC:

> People do not want to stay [within the NADK] but do not know where to go. (1) some do not have relatives left in [C]ambodia and therefore do not know where to go, (2) some do not know their birthplace because they were children when they were separated from their families by DK, (3) others know there is no land available at their home villages and expect to get land from DK because DK keep[s] promising land to soldiers who stay in the army. (Roeurn 1992)

Echoing a central pillar of the impending "win-win policy," the defector Roeurn in the UNTAC program for self-demobilizers went on:

> Most soldiers would like to return home, but cannot return because they are afraid of the Vietnamese and of the Heng Samrin authorities there if they return. But if they had guarantees for their safety upon return, all of them would go, would return. For the moment they wait. (Roeurn 1992)

Having spent their entire lives with their comrades often created a close-knit community with a strong sense of solidarity, and increased the soldiers' emotional detachment from people within the interior, as reported to a team from the Documentation Center of Cambodia by residents of Malai:

Some of these residents told our team that they have lived very far from their homelands for so long that they do not have much emotional connection to their relatives, old friends, and neighbors in their home villages. Instead, they have lived with their Malai comrades for more than 30 years and over this period, have developed a strong sense of solidarity with each other, resulting in a close-knit community. (Long 2010, 30)

Living in such seclusion also meant that before defecting, many did not know much about the current conditions within the interior. During their interviews with UNTAC officials, many asked a lot of rather basic questions about safety, how to navigate the interior, and the current political situation, prompting notes by the interviewers such as: "Obviously, he had no idea about the current conditions in Cambodia" (Anon. 1993c). Lack of information was a real problem for the members of the NADK—not only because of the nature of warfare, but also because of Khmer Rouge policies. Since inception, the Khmer Rouge kept their subjects strictly separated from each other and from the world outside of their work cooperatives. They stuck to that policy until the very end. Some defectors, therefore, mention that simply managing to get ahold of a radio and listening to Radio UNTAC was a meaningful window into the world outside their military units.

Still, very few defected on their own. Those who did faced a harsh life, as they had to conceal their backgrounds upon return and "somehow had to make a living while those who stayed in their units received land from their leaders" (RF-NADK -5). Since they hoped to receive benefits during "reintegration" and since they were afraid of the interior and of the reaction of the populace upon their return, many defected in groups or waited until their commanders made deals in order to return as a community. Some smaller units even chose one defector to enter the interior on his own first as a "probe"; he then had to report whether it was safe for the others to return (e.g., Im 1993). While waiting to determine whether it was safe, many heard rumors about abuse of defecting comrades and of the ongoing presence of Vietnamese soldiers:

As for Vietnamese military units, I have not seen any myself, but several of our people who have been captured and taken to Pursat have been interrogated by Vietnamese interrogators. This was in late 1992. (Im 1993)

While those who defected on their own faced harsh conditions, those who waited for a deal between their commanders and the state authorities usually received land to farm or other job opportunities within the Khmer Rouge strongholds in Anlong Veng, Pailin, Samlaut, Veal Veng, and others. As a rule of thumb, those who had served the Khmer Rouge since their early childhood and joined before 1975 were also the ones who benefitted from the "win-win policy" by receiving land and positions from their superiors and staying within their sphere of influence, while those who belonged to the margins of the Khmer Rouge apparatus usually received nothing and had to make a living on their own. They were dispersed without support networks over various communities throughout the country and often had to migrate to Thailand as manual laborers. However, this also meant that the cadres from the core had to remain under the influence of their former commanders; in some cases they still directly serve them today (SC-NADK -1). Their social, symbolic, and economic resources remained closely associated with their former units and hinged on the goodwill of their superiors. Their seclusion as soldiers and cadres of the secretive *Angkar* was reproduced during the transition to peace, and long after.

Reintegration as a close-knit community also had its benefits, of course. The Khmer Rouge were very familiar with resettlement and with creating ad hoc organizational structures in unfamiliar and hostile environments. This benefitted them in cases when they had to be resettled from the border to the interior:

> The Khmer Rouge have, over the years, specialized in the controlled movement of their own cadre—soldiers and their families—under arduous circumstances. Such experiences have, in a perverse way, made them uniquely adaptable to the difficult repatriation circumstances they faced in Repat[riation phase] 2. For example, returnees in both Saml[au]t and A[nlong] V[eng] reported that the circumstances of repatriation were not much different from their previous experiences migrating from place to place in mountainous and jungle environments. As a result, they knew how to work together to quickly establish temporary shelters and forage in the jungle to compliment subsistence food rations. (Bellard 2002, 50)

While many units stayed together after the war, the Khmer Rouge units had the strongest bonds:

> The primary socio-political linkages within the former Khmer Rouge communities have been structured both vertically and horizontally. Within vertical linkages, individuals and families have been linked to various leaders according to the internal ethics and logic of patron-client relationships based on political and/or military order, affiliation, and loyalty. In horizontal linkages, individuals and families have been linked to one another through a strong sense of communal identity based on group solidarity and mutual protection honed by years of adversity. (Bellard 2002, 58)

Staying within their community was essential in maintaining their identity. Those who contemplated returning to their home villages, where relatives often helped make deals with the village chiefs, feared being stigmatized as former Khmer Rouge. The symbolic blood on their hands made the prospect of return difficult: "I would like to return home, but I do not dare because I am afraid that I will be in trouble. If it was not for the security concern, I would return home" (Saroeun 1993).

For the rank-and-file soldiers of the NADK, the most difficult—if not impossible—transition concerned their symbolic status within Cambodian society at large. Their past will always be associated with the horrors of the Khmer Rouge's years in power from 1975 to 1979: "I am not proud [of my service as a soldier] as I am afraid that people will always hate me" (SC-NADK -1). For most respondents, their status as former low-ranking combat soldiers made reintegration particularly difficult, as Cambodians tended to differentiate between "the ones who just talked" and "the ones who actually did something" and who "usually made the mistakes": "We [the combat soldiers and not those, who just talked within the upper levels of the Khmer Rouge] were the ones, who were hated" (GC-NADK -1). This "perpetrator discourse" particularly concerns the lower ranks of the Khmer Rouge who face stigma as "murderers," those who did the actual killings, even if they joined after 1979 or did not belong to the core (cf. Hennings 2017, 7).

Like the strongmen, but to a higher degree, the Khmer Rouge soldiers had to find symbolic pathways to construct a narrative of change and personal transformation into a new and "better" human being. And like the strongmen, they often turned to Christianity to cleanse the symbolic blood from their hands and to distance themselves from their former deluded selves. Symbolically reconstructing their status in society meant that many converted to Christianity or, in some cases, became Buddhist monks. At the same time, they constructed narratives of an ongoing struggle for national salvation and democracy, and a heroic opposition to Vietnamese plots.

NOTE

1. Another major reason cited by Khmer Rouge cadres was Norodom Sihanouk's call to join the resistance in the *maquis* after he was toppled by Prince Sirik Matak and General Lon Nol in mid-1970.

Chapter Six

Blank Pages' Symbolic Reconstruction

While a disproportionately high number of former Khmer Rouge seem to have converted to Christianity, this is not the only type of religious conversion they underwent. During their years in power, the Khmer Rouge put an end to *all* religion. Hence, becoming a monk—or reconstructing the Buddhist self—can also be considered an act of religious conversion. The following chapter deals with three ways in which ex-Khmer Rouge tried to symbolically reconstruct their social status in their local communities as well as in wider Cambodian society. Similar to the strongmen, the Khmer Rouge struggle with a stigma in which their virtual social identity, as it should be, does not fit their actual social identity (Goffman 1963). This leads to a mismatch which they try to bridge, or a "spoiled identity" which they try to get rid of by creating a new (positive) virtual social identity which their current actual social status can fit into and which will lift them up in status again. The first section deals with conversion to Christianity. The second section lays out respondents' narrative of a return, or (re)-conversion, to Buddhism. The third section, in contrast, deals with a narrative that does not claim change, but frames respondents' actions as Khmer Rouge members as motivated by an existential battle against the Vietnamese, thereby constructing themselves as heroic members of a threatened Khmer nation.

CHRISTIAN CONVERSION

Probably the most famous Khmer Rouge convert to Christianity is Kaing Guek Eav, alias Duch, the head of the Khmer Rouge's central prison, Tuol Sleng (code-named S-21). Before being imprisoned and put on trial at the Extraordinary Chambers in the Courts of Cambodia, he converted to Christianity in 1995, built a church in his home village, and converted dozens to his new-found faith (Carmichael 2015). While standing trial, he pleaded guilty and said he was eager to "confess" all his sins. But on the very last day of the proceedings, to the surprise of many observers, he asked to be acquitted and released from prison. It seems that, for him, complete confession meant that he would be relieved of future punishments. This understanding of Christian redemption also came up during interviews with other converts. Recently, another Khmer Rouge functionary, Im Chaem, who was charged by the hybrid court with crimes against humanity, also converted to Christianity (Khemara 2018).

Before discussing the findings, a short note on the different quality and flow of the interviews. While it was usually difficult to get non-Christian converts within the Khmer Rouge community to speak openly about what they did as commanders, soldiers, or cadres (with many even skipping this period in their narrative), the Christian converts—especially those who seemed to be "strong" believers—were almost eager to confess their "sins," making interviews comparatively easy. It seemed as if they were habituated to confess by Khmer Rouge practices such as self-criticism sessions, but even more so through the act of reaching redemption through relentless confession to God and Christian priests. At the same time, this means that they had ready-made and fine-tuned storylines they often pulled out when meeting foreigners, researchers, or journalists. Still, for the purposes of this chapter, a polished narrative of conversion is exactly what is most interesting as it represents the picture of themselves that these converts would like to submit to the wider populace.

The exact number of Khmer Rouge who have turned to Christianity is impossible to ascertain. However, in the former stronghold of Pailin, which has only 70,000 inhabitants, there are currently twenty-two Christian churches of various denominations, including Marist, Baptist, Evangelical, Presbyterian, and Seventh-day Adventist churches. According to one source, there are more than 600 Christians in Pailin, while reports of Khmer Rouge converting to Christianity across the country reach into the thousands, (with one missionary alone claiming to have converted 4,000 Khmer Rouge, Chen 2017). These cited numbers of "Christians" within the Khmer Rouge community have to be taken with a pitch of salt, as many were likely motivated by poverty rather than a deep-felt need to convert. The high number of churches distributing resources and providing pathways to education in these poor Khmer Rouge communities during the mid- and late 1990s might be the main reason why there are so many people in these areas who identify as Christian. As Pol Leang, vice-governor of Pailin and himself a former Khmer Rouge cadre, put it, missionaries were "buying souls" through their support for livelihoods, education, and health care (Anon. 2004).

In interviews about their religious beliefs, respondents in Pailin cited four primary reasons for joining a Christian church, from the worldly to the "metaphysical": 1) the reception of material benefits (including hopes for a better education for their children), 2) the experience of the magical force of prayers, 3) a fear of the afterlife, and, closely related to that, 4) the hope for forgiveness (both by Cambodian society and by God). However, much of what the respondents said about Christianity remained within the framework of animist and Buddhist cosmologies.

Respondents were surprisingly frank about their initial motivation in becoming Christian. When asked about which Christian teachings sparked their interest at the beginning, most did not mention any specific doctrine, but referred to receiving medicine, food, or schooling for their children: "[The Christian belief] is good because the church assists my children financially. Otherwise, I could not manage to send them to school" (FC-NADK -4). They pointed to the practice of gift-giving as a central benefit of Christianity over Buddhism, which instead collects money and food from adherents to give to monks and use for the construction of pagodas. For them it boils down to the difference between giving and taking: "Buddhism just takes, takes, takes— and Christianity gives" (FC-NADK -3).

For one missionary at a Marist church, the material benefits that attract former Khmer Rouge to Christianity carry a larger spiritual meaning. To him, sharing is an act of showing love and respect to everyone, even to former cadres of the Communist movement:

These Khmer Rouge they HOPE for many GIFT—gift from GOD, from Christianity. Just share LOVE, FOOD and things. Christianity, it-it is DEEP love, yeah; clothes, medicine and so on. It is just LOVE. I have some FOOD and give to YOU. It shows RESPECT. (Missionary 2017)

Respondents usually did not know much about Christian doctrine, let alone the contents of the Bible. Most stated that they just attended church and listened to the songs, but did not understand what the priest was preaching: "I just go to the church regularly, sing a song about Jesus, and meet my fellow believers. But with regard to the teachings and of what they say during the preaching, I don't understand much" (FC-NADK -2). Or as another respondent put it: "There are elders who know about the teachings. I myself do not know [much]" (FC-NADK -4). Other respondents simply did not understand questions about Christian doctrine and the contents of the Bible at all, and remained silent when asked about it.

When talking about the benefits of their newfound Christian belief, all respondents primarily emphasized its supposed spiritual potency. In so doing, they were implicitly integrating it into an animist cosmology in which Christianity is a competing force with other spirit beliefs, such as for instance different kinds of *neak tā* spirits. Ian Harris divides the *neak tā* into three categories:

> The first contains spirits associated with natural phenomena, such as mountains (*neak tā phnom*), rivers (*neak tā tuk*), trees (*neak tā dam*), paddies (*neak tā sre*), swamps (*neak tā beng*), and forests (*neak tā prey*). Ancestral spirits both male and female, come next, while *neak tā*, derived from Brahmanical gods and various mythical heroes, make up the final category. (Harris 2005, 53, cf. Souyris-Roland 1951, 162)

Christianity becomes a competing protective force to all the tutelary spirits in the Buddhist-animist cosmos. All Khmer Rouge respondents explained that they initially started to believe in the potency of God and Jesus when they got into trouble, lost family members, or suffered from poverty. At this point, they realized that the old spirits did not have the power to protect them, as claimed by their local *kru khmai*:

> Before I did not believe in this religion; instead I believed in traditional beliefs like *neak tā*, various kinds of spirits, sacred soil and hungry ghosts that surround us.[1] I was regularly offering foods and burning offerings to provide for the hungry ghosts, especially to those of my ancestors. I thought that if I failed to practice this, they would put a curse on me and possibly even take the life of one of my relatives or family members. And I had already lost three relatives. When I discussed that with the *kru khmai* in my village, he said it is due to *ah reak* [a ghost which represents the destruction of human happiness]. Then I prayed for blessings and burned some offerings and food to seek the ghost's forgiveness for my unintentional wrongdoings. Yet this did not work. But now, since my whole family has started to believe in Jesus, we rarely have any problems, especially health issues, and enjoy a peaceful life in happiness. As for my husband's family and relatives, all have converted to Christianity by now and abandoned their traditional beliefs, be they animist or Buddhist. (FC-NADK -2)

At the very beginning at least, it was not the doctrine, the morality, or the metaphysics of Christian doctrine that convinced the respondents, who stated that they did not understand these things anyway. It was the worldly potency of God. His benevolent power ensures that those who believe in him do not suffer from starvation and yield profits from their businesses, or at least sufficient income to live:

[Since starting to believe in Christ,] my business has been going well. In the past, we earned very little, so we had to live from hand to mouth. Upon changing my belief to Jesus, he won't let us die from starvation anymore. We have enough food, at least enough to make our ends meet. (FC-NADK -2)

Another respondent, a Jesuit, explained that God shows his kindness and charity through the acts of others, and thereby proves much more useful than the old spirits. He remembers how he converted a friend by showing him the workings of God through the reception of cash from various sources:

For example, there was a lady who fell into a debt of nearly 20,000 USD with the bank. We tried to persuade her to believe in Jesuits. I went to her house in Sihanoukville to talk to her and saw some spirit objects inside her house. I said, 'Believe me, it is useless. Look! You are still in debt.' And she said to me, 'What else should I do then?' And at that time, there was a group of Jesuits from Hong Kong visiting places nearby her house to pray for God. Then they gave her 700 USD without hesitation. I believed this was due to God's help. Even though his help is not given directly, he sends it through other people's actions. It is not just a mere coincidence that they had been nearby. Afterwards her relatives in Phnom Penh also sent her 200 USD right away. This amount of money was very helpful for her to pay the bank's interest. So, it is more useful ["practical"] and her husband as well decided to believe in Jesus. (MC-NADK -1)

God has the power to change everything; he is an almighty *neak tā*. Even children change after finding God: "After starting to believe in God, my children got smarter" (FC-NADK -2). Most importantly, however, the respondents' stories depict God as a protective force securing their survival and basic subsistence. God is like a patron in a cosmos guided by the moral economy of subsistence ethics (Scott 1976). Prayers have the power to provide food security:

As soon as I know that tomorrow I will not have enough food to eat, I pray to God and tell him about it. Then, the day after, I have food coming up from somewhere. One day, for instance, Jesus heard my call for support and [the day after] the elders in the church all of the sudden brought food for me. You know, they [the elders] do not know whether I have food or not and actually we do not live together, so how could they know it? You see? It must have been that Jesus heard my prayers and ordered them to bring food for me. (FC-NADK -4)

For the respondents, the omnipotence of a benevolent God becomes visible through miracles, especially the healing of the sick without the use of medicine:

If there is a patient, someone who fell sick, all of us just pray to God. Some-times, they get better. We do not even need medicines and treatment. It is a miracle. Without witnessing miracles like that ourselves, we would not have believed it. But miracles do exist because of God. For example, when we suffer from a serious illness and there is a group of people praying for us, we might recover from the disease right away. (MC-NADK -1)

All respondents at some point referred to a miraculous act of healing that changed their lives:

All of my family members, including me, are in a healthy condition now. My life has turned to a completely new page. When my husband, for instance, used to suffer from a stroke, everyone recommended us to seek help from a sorcerer. But I responded with confidence that I would not go because we are children of Jesus now [who protects us]. (FC-NADK -2)

Yet the stories usually went on to claim that believing in God not only provided them with new sources of income and health care, but also that it changed them so deeply that they were effectively reborn after becoming Christians:

At the beginning, I suffered from chronic diseases, such as pneumonia, high blood pressure, and fainting. Back then, I was brought to the hospital. And the people around me, including my children, suggested that I pray to God to ask for a better health condition. Then I prayed to Jesus and asked for his help: "Please help me to continue my life in this world; please help me to recover from the diseases. If you do so I will dedicate myself to Christianity." From day to day, I felt better and better despite not yet completely believing in Christianity. [. . .] I believe that I was reborn on that day. (FC-NADK -4)

This brings us to the concept of symbolic reconstruction. Besides seeing God as an almighty patron and potent force in the spiritual order, respondents constantly claimed that turning to God changed them so drastically that they became totally different people. In her classic study of a Cambodian village in 1959–1960, May Ebihara refers to the possibility in Khmer culture that even individuals with "a checkered past" can achieve limited respect and authority within segments of society by making a "clean break with their past" (Ebi-hara 1968, 202). For her, this possibility of shifting status through claiming a complete change in personality marks a "general feature" in Khmer society:

The ability and freedom to shift status, within certain limits, at will and to make a clean break with the past, is highly prized. [The] shift in status must be clear and abrupt . . . and must be publicly announced. . . . Once a person has made such a shift, he does not wish to be held to the obligations and responsibilities of his former roles or to be considered liable for the policies and actions which he then advocated. (Ebihara 1968, 202; referring to Hanks 1962, 273)

At least for the former Khmer Rouge cadres, it was clear that they experienced a clear change for the better in their personality: "If compared to my life before, I have changed to a totally different and good person" (MC-NADK -1). Finding God made them realize how bad they were before: "Believing in Christ has changed my personality, I feel so sorry for my wrong actions in the past now" (FC-NADK -2). Their claim of being reborn as better people receives recognition and support from their environment and certain segments in their community, at least from members of local churches: "if they believe in GOD, they-they become better people" (Missionary 2017). Many respondents were surprisingly frank about their actions as combatants and commanders, particularly when compared to non-Christian Khmer Rouge fighters, who usually shied away from talking about negative acts perpetrated in past times:

> Before [turning to God], I did many bad things, for example killing, stealing, looking down on somebody, taking advantage from others, having love affairs with other wives, drinking alcohol, and so on. In the Bible, drinking alcohol is not prohibited. But Jesus warns, "You can drink, but do not get drunk." So now I have noticed that I have changed completely. I now have a good attitude toward all the people around me, such as all my family members and my neighbors. I am trying to do a lot of good things in the name of Jesus. (MC-NADK -1)

Signaling a changed personality, the Khmer Rouge tried to support their political and economic goals with a symbolic conversion, demonstrating that nobody has to be afraid of them anymore and reconstructing their standing in certain segments of society.

However, this calls for an explanation for why exactly Christianity reconstructed them as socially good people, while Buddhism did not. A common explanation was that Buddhism is also good in terms of its ethics and morality, that there is nothing "wrong" with Buddhism, but that it is too hard to practice because it leaves its adherents alone, without a moral authority watching over them. In Christianity, by contrast, God has the power to make you morally good: "Buddhism is good, but Buddha is just a human being, not a powerful God like Jesus. His teaching is good, but nobody can practice it. It is too idealist" (MC-NADK -1).

All respondents emphasized that they continued to see Buddhism as good, and in their daily lives even visited pagodas and participated in Buddhist ceremonies in their community. But while doing that, they stayed committed to Christian beliefs: "Sometimes, I bow in front of the Buddha statue, but inside my heart, I speak to Jesus" (FC-NADK -4).

Another benefit of Christianity over Buddhism for these respondents is that Christianity tells you that you are already full of sin as a newborn:

> In Buddhism, a newborn baby is seen as a pure person, but in Christianity, to the contrary, it is already aligned to sin simply because it is a human being like Eva and Adam have been. If we say that we do not have sin, we lie to ourselves. Trust is not inside your heart. But Jesus is pure and ready to forgive us everything wrong that we have done so far. We just have to accept our mistakes and sinfulness. That's enough. (MC-NADK -1)

This qualification is interesting in light of Khmer Rouge ideology, which viewed newborns as pure and unsullied by the taint of capitalist and individualist ideology. To a certain degree, the respondent seems to be merging his interpretation of Buddhist and Khmer Rouge thought. Hence, he believes that what went wrong for him was that he had an improper state of mind during the Khmer Rouge period, and unquestioningly accepted the Khmer Rouge tenet that children are pure and morally good, like him when he was recruited as a juvenile. He has now come to understand that this ideology was totally incorrect, and that children are actually born weak and full of sin. They need to be taught how to live a morally good life in which they do not kill, rape, drink, or steal. As long as people do not accept the doctrine that humans are sinners at birth and need to turn to the one true God, they will continue committing sins in a state of weakness and "false consciousness."

Only if you believe in God do you receive his strength to actually act good and overcome your natural sinfulness. Respondents did not see Buddhism as bad; many even claimed that it "teaches the same morals" (FC-NADK -3). The only problem with it is that humans are too weak to become good on their own. They need a superior power and authority to make them good. In the respondents' reading of religions, all Buddhism does is instill fear by threatening people with suffering in hell. Here, the selective reading of the Bible and a popular understanding of Buddhist afterlife become most prominent: "In Buddhism it is just about HELL, HELL, HELL—and in Christianity, we are VERY clear that-that we have ETERNAL life with HIM" (Missionary 2017). The respondents all claimed that they would go to heaven, only because they started to *believe and confessed their sins.* Or as one said:

> *Interviewer*: In case I myself want to be in heaven, what should I do in my life?
>
> *Respondent*: It is easy. Just believe in God and confess. (MC-NADK -1)

According to the respondents, you can atone for your sins comparatively easily. This seems to be another major advantage of Christianity over Buddhism, which is guided by a notion of cause and effect in which no one can escape the karmic consequences of his prior actions, as highlighted by Robert Carmichael:

> I would say that Christianity has some advantages over Buddhism in terms of the idea of atoning for one's sins. [In Buddhism], life is a cycle of birth, death, and rebirth, and one's behavior in this life dictates how one will come back in the next life. There is no escaping one's crimes in Buddhism, and I suspect that for many of the converts, this is a powerful motivator. (Cited in Chen 2017)

According to the selective reading of Christian doctrine by the former Khmer Rouge, entering heaven can be very easy. All you need to do is to believe and Jesus Christ will then nullify all your sins: "He died and rose again. He took on all our sins for us" (MC-NADK -1). Therefore, "as long as I believe in God, I will go to heaven" (FC-NADK -2). One respondent even quoted his favorite passage from the Bible, which, according to his interpretation, shows that Jesus has already promised him a place in heaven:

> This is the message we have heard from Him and announce to you, that God is Light, and in Him there is no darkness at all. If we say that we have fellowship with Him and *yet* walk in the darkness, we lie and do not practice truth; but if we walk in the Light as He Himself is in the Light, we have fellowship with one another, and the blood of Jesus His Son cleanses us from all sin. If we confess our sins, He is faithful and righteous to forgive us our sins and to cleanse of from all unrighteousness. If we say that we have not sinned, we make Him a liar and His word is not in us. —Cited from The First Letter of John (1, 5) as read out by (MC-NADK -1)

After reading out the passage from the First Letter of John, he delivered his own interpretation of what God promises everyone on earth:

> The most important thing is the fact that he said that if we believe in him, he would bring us to heaven. And if we committed one or two wrongdoings before turning to him, he can forgive us. Yet, of course, this does not mean that we can repeat the same mistakes all over again. If we do so, he would not help us anymore. Therefore, those who have already decided to believe in him are also feeling very much afraid to do something wrong. (MC-NADK -1)

This means that God gives you the strength to do good, but at the same time, there is a catch: you need to adhere to his moral laws or risk falling into disgrace. God cleanses you from your sins, but only your *past* sins. In this, the former Khmer Rouge deliver yet another explanation for why one should trust the new Christian believer *in the future*. God—and, one might add, society—forgives you all your sins, but Christianity requires you to continue engaging in moral behavior now and ever afterwards:

Before, I had sin; now, I need to do something good. God never complains about my past and the wrongdoing that I have committed. He has never condemned it. (FC-NADK -4)

God promises forgiveness and salvation. But interestingly, no respondents saw a major difference in the moral codes of Khmer Rouge–style communism, Buddhism, and Christianity. They only differed in the view of whether the believer needs to be supported in acting good or not, whether they are capable of doing good on their own or whether they are in need of a superior authority to *make* them do good.

This interpretation of Christianity has more affinities with Khmer Rouge ideology than most of the respondents liked to admit. Under the Khmer Rouge, it was the collective, *Angkar*, which rectified adherents' "sins" of capitalist delusion and individualist thinking, and which demanded complete obedience to its leadership and moral codes. Even the act of confessing your sins in front of others mirrors Khmer Rouge practices of self-criticism, writing one's "autobiography," and extracting confessions under torture in the "reeducation" and "security centers" (Chandler 1999, Em 2002). In the end, the respondents' interpretation of Christianity is highly framed by the Khmer Rouge thought they imbibed during their primary socialization and habitus formation. Pol Pot's former bodyguard, Uk Sarith, who also converted to Christianity, summed it up by saying that he saw Christ as merely a new authority demanding respect and obedience:

Today is a good feeling. I believe it [my conversion] will help me for all the things I have done in my life. In the end, the Khmer Rouge is just like Christ. The Khmer Rouge taught us to avoid bad things like robbery and cheating. [It] had a lot of rules. Christ is the same; believing in him is like having a leader you respect and obey. (Anon. 2004)

These people's symbolic reconstruction, and their interpretation of religion as such, remain in the framework of the schemes of thought incorporated into their habitus during their socialization within the Communist movement, and carry many culturally indigenous understandings. Ex-Khmer Rouge Christian belief becomes an assemblage of Christian, Buddhist, animist, and communist thought systems aimed at a symbolic reconstruction of social status in society. Their interpretation of Christianity hews close to Khmer Rouge ideology, making it easier for the former Khmer Rouge cadres to adopt.

In a way, the respondents created a Khmer (Rouge) adaptation of Christian doctrines in order to claim symbolic conversion and seek salvation and forgiveness from both Cambodian society (in this life) and God (in the next). On a side note, while all Khmer Rouge were used to the practice of confessing their misdemeanors and some were even familiar with being interviewed by international scholars or journalists, the Christian converts' interviews were distinctly different from those of non-Christian former Khmer Rouge. These interviews heavily resembled acts of confession in style and structure, in which wrongdoings in the past were willingly admitted at the beginning, followed by a declaration of reformation, showing clearly that they had been accustomed to confessing their "sins" and in narrating a process of purification and change. Of course, not every Khmer Rouge turned to Christianity. Some—particularly high-ranking commanders—instead became Buddhist monks.

BUDDHIST (NON-)CONVERSION

Although it is true that the respondents usually had been Buddhists before joining the Khmer Rouge (some even serving as monks for a certain period), they may—on a symbolic level—count as converts if they later took up positions within the Buddhist *sangha*, a community they aimed to destroy during their years in power. However, they tend to depict this movement not as a return to their roots, but rather as a continued effort to adhere to the Buddhist morality that guided them through all stages of life—even when they were serving as cadres for the state of Democratic Kampuchea, during which Buddhism, like all other religions, was abolished and monks persecuted as "parasites" against the people.

In their own view, they acted in perfect accordance with the principles of Buddhism throughout their lives. And, of course, there is a tiny kernel of truth to this, as there are many elements within Khmer Rouge ideology that were influenced by indigenous cultural understandings, including Buddhist notions. Broadly, both ideologies urged adherents to renounce worldly goods, the family, and the self by following a specific moral discipline (*viney*). They also shared a number of ritual practices, such as an initiation in which neophytes have to change their names and put on new clothes, as well as "the way in which they intone their respective litanies, all the way down to the incorporation of similar thrills at the end of each stanza" (Harris 2005, 187; see also Bizot 2004). Yet, despite these affinities, the Khmer Rouge treated Buddhism as competing bourgeois ideology that they sought to destroy.

The respondents who became monks after reintegration often tried to claim that the Khmer Rouge were not anti-Buddhist. On one hand, their motives for becoming monks resemble those of the Christian Khmer Rouge; they wanted to regain respect within the context of Cambodian society: "I wanted to be a good and respected citizen with high morals again and Buddhism is a path to realize my dream" (BAC-NADK -4). They also claimed that they changed after joining the monkhood: "Buddhism made me more tolerant, peaceful and calm" (CC-NADK -2). But at the same time, they tried to depict themselves as being Buddhist at heart throughout their lives. They did this by claiming that they never actually killed any living beings. However, they always made interesting exceptions, mostly related to enemy combatants, whom they did not conceptualize as human:

> I have never intentionally killed any living being, not only human, but even small animals. I have not had bad intentions toward anybody, even though the Khmer Rouge used to teach me how to kill people. There is only one exception: I used to open fire towards other soldiers; of course, these were not civilians. (BAC-NADK -4)

This enemy was not just an ordinary enemy, but the biggest existential threat to the Khmer people: the Vietnamese and their "allies." These respondents felt that the Vietnamese were so nefarious that they tested the limits of tolerance, even for the most heartfelt Buddhists. One respondent tried to depict himself as tolerant while calling for intolerance against all Vietnamese, a longer passage worth quoting in full:

> *Respondent*: Even if people treated me badly [under the Khmer Rouge], I stayed calm and practiced tolerance. Eventually, I would overcome the hatred [of others].
>
> *Interviewer*: Did tolerance have limits?
>
> *Respondent*: No, but if you were tolerant, others did not regard you as a successful person.
>
> *Interviewer*: Did tolerance have limits with regard to the Vietnamese?
>
> *Respondent*: This situation is totally different. We needed to resist them.
>
> *Interviewer*: How is it different?
>
> *Respondent*: It relates to their intention. Yuon do not have a good intention and they follow a strategic plan to destroy us. They are dishonest, and they steal everything from our country.
>
> *Interviewer*: Before you mentioned that you need to be tolerant even with those who treat you bad. Why is Vietnam different?
>
> *Respondent*: If we act like this, we will lose our country. I feel very worried about this.
>
> *Interviewer*: So Vietnamese intentions are more evil than others?
>
> *Respondent*: Yes, these people speak sweet, but their intentions are fundamentally bad.

Interviewer: How to protect Cambodia then?

Respondent: All Cambodians have to join hands and to create an alliance against them. According to what I personally saw since 1979, the Yuon stole gold, property, even dogs and cats, and a lot more from Cambodia. Its spies are everywhere across the country. That is why I refused to work for them [during the early 1980s]. Yuon are born as thieves. Some Cambodians work for them, so they become thieves too. It is true, believe me. [And] they created the story about Khmer killing Khmer. I saw myself how a Yuon ordered a Khmer Rouge to kill another Khmer Rouge. In reality, Yuon killed Khmer. (BAC-NADK -4)

In this view, Buddhist ethics simply do not apply to the Vietnamese due to their evil intent. If you practice tolerance toward the Vietnamese, they will capitalize on your kindness and destroy you. This was a common theme among the Khmer Rouge. In their view, they did not kill any Khmer people, but were simply rooting out Vietnamese spies who aimed to secretly wipe out the Khmer, and who toppled the country's leadership in order to create a false narrative of Khmer killing Khmer, with the ultimate goal of occupying the country. Even now, the respondents believe they were fighting for a good cause, and frequently declared that they would have continued their resistance against the Vietnamese occupiers and their "puppet regime" if they had not grown too old:

If I were not too old already, I would fight against the Yuon, especially against those who take our lands at the moment. When I was still with the Khmer Rouge, I was not afraid to die in battles with Yuon soldiers. My friends also were brave, but now most are dead already. I have been wounded several times and all I want in this life is to destroy the Yuon. I told the younger generation that they should go on with the resistance now. (CC-NADK -2)

According to the respondents, fighting the Yuon was necessary to preserve the country for the Khmer people. But for them, "Vietnameseness" is determined not just by ethnicity or citizenship, but by factional loyalty. Mirroring Khmer Rouge discourse, those who oppose them are labeled "Yuon" and should (and morally can) be killed. At the same time, this—in Maoist terms— "life and death contradiction" also means that there will inevitably be losses for the Khmer people:

Do you hate the Khmer Rouge leaders such as Pol Pot, Ieng Sary, or Khieu Samphan? Think about it: Those people only followed orders. They were just struggling for the nation. The loss of lives could be not avoided. (RF-NADK -4)

These former veteran Khmer Rouge serving the organization for decades since early childhood depict their struggle as a constant battle to save the

Khmer people, a struggle that demands certain sacrifices but is necessary to thwart the evil plan of the Vietnamese and emerge victorious. They pursue a double strategy to reconstruct their social status: On one hand, they claim that they have changed for the better and become calm and good monks striving for peace. On the other side, they claim they are part of a larger struggle to protect the Khmer people. This claim, ironically, mimics the manner in which the Khmer Rouge drew the line between "their people" and "the enemy boring from within" and "rotting the party and society." The respondents reproduced a narrative of "toxification," which provided a "lens of legitimacy" for the killings against those who actually or allegedly opposed their rule (Williams and Neilsen 2016). The Khmer Rouge discourse that legitimated and drove violence within and by their party apparatus was so thoroughly incorporated by the respondents that it still constitutes the lens through which they look at current politics.

This lens seems particularly strong among the second-wave defectors, the followers of Ta Mok, and those who faced a stark downturn in status: "During the war they need the brave, but during peace they need the educated. Therefore, I could not do anything after the war's end but ordain myself as a monk seeking refuge in a pagoda. Here, I try to act good and to improve my rebirth" (CC-NADK -2). Under the "win-win policy," it was not just their level of education that decided their status in post-war Cambodia, but also the time of their defection. The anti-intellectual intellectuals who reintegrated—or rather, surrendered—after the elections in 1998 kept a low profile as well, with some of them also finding refuge in pagodas. Chan Youran, for instance, a former lawyer and public administrator with a doctorate who held positions within the government even before 1975, now lives as a lay devotee in a pagoda in Phnom Penh. Here he is waiting for the end of his painful life, in which he struggled as a "child of Cambodia":

> Now I am an observant lay devotee of Buddhism at Tuol Tumpoung Pagoda in Phnom Penh. Since 1998 I have lived in peace in the shade of Buddhism and in independence. Let me also inform you that I am tired and bored of my life, which has been a life of pain; as the Lord Buddha said, life is pain. It is my understanding that I have fulfilled my missions as a child of Cambodia to our nation, religion, and King in accordance with my personal propensities and virtues. Now I wish to tell you frankly that I have prepared myself to leave this world in supreme peace and quiet. (Chan 2009, 2)

NOTE

1. Hungry ghosts—or *pretas*—are former human beings "reborn in a hell as a consequence of usually quite venial sins, such as pride, momentary stinginess, or inadvertently killing an insect" (Davis 2016, 159).

Chapter Seven

Note on Female Combatants of the Khmer Rouge

Although it is still unknown how many women served as cadres or in the military apparatus of the Khmer Rouge as commanders and soldiers, the movement clearly had many female combatants. While females at the upper level of the military seem to be rare, they could be found comparatively often within the mid- and lower ranks of the movement's military and executive apparatus.[1] Throughout the world, female combatants are often found in socialist movements, which claim gender equality as a leading principle. Within these conflicts, female combatants to a certain degree "broke traditional social norms in these societies. Some provided household, logistic, or medical services, but some served as combatants: the mix varied across groups" (Wood 2008, 552). In the case of the Khmer Rouge, most served in logistical support units, but it seems that there was also at least one large and exclusively female combat unit. Especially in the movement's earlier years, their role within the military was restricted to traditional female jobs, fulfilling medical, logistical, and communal responsibilities. But this changed over the course of the conflict, with female cadres taking on increasingly higher responsibilities and traditionally male functions (according to Youk Chhang, Farina So and Suzannah Linton, who are currently preparing a larger study on this issue, personal communication; see also Crane 2015).

Despite great efforts, the author was not able to collect sufficient data on female combatants and their reintegration. There are three possible reasons for this. First, female combatants might not have felt comfortable speaking to a male researcher. Although the author was able to find many potential female respondents, many declined to be interviewed either at initial contact or shortly before scheduled meetings. Another possibility, connected to the first, relates to the fact that these female combatants have now returned to more traditional gender roles and feel uncomfortable talking about their roles as combatants, since these run contrary to currently hegemonic societal gen-der norms in which women are meant to be subservient (Jacobsen 2008). The point is that after a period of war, many gender roles that might have been weakened over the course of conflict, largely because of an increased demand for personnel to carry out traditionally male functions such as soldiering, are often quickly reversed (cf. Wood 2008). A third, also related point is that all contacts and interview brokers with whom the researcher spoke in order to find former female combatants were themselves males who obviously thought that the women's role had been insignificant. Because of this, they might not have put much effort in finding and convincing respondents to speak, despite being urged to do so.

In the end, only five female combatants were interviewed. Interestingly, four of these were found during a search for Christian converts in Khmer Rouge communities, rather than a search for female combatants specifically. However, the lives of all five involved a relapse into traditional gender roles after the war's end. At the beginning, they all fulfilled rather classic female functions within the military, but this—in their own view—was mostly just due to age. As one respondent put it:

> When I first joined, they did not let me do much as I was still young, [which is why I] just connected telephone cables in the forest and prepared food for the soldiers. I was too little [14 years], so they did not let me fight, only deliver food to soldiers. (FC-NADK -1)[2]

All five female respondents had been recruited at a typical age for Khmer Rouge combatants, between 12 and 14 years old. Looking back on their mo-tives for joining, all stressed that they had been too young to think critically about what was happening, which is why they were easily convinced to join the revolution. On top of that, as one respondent stressed, they constantly feared dying, which made them focus on the short term:

> When fighting along the border, we had enough to eat due to external support. We had canned fish and rice and much more. I just did what they told me to do. When they said to deliver these bullets, I just did it. Since I was young, I did not think these things through thoroughly, which is why I was easily dragged into doing what I was told to do. I encountered several difficulties. There would be bullets flying around and we would run into bunkers crying and missing family at home. Life under bullets was unpredictable. We never knew when we would die. We never expected to survive that long until today. That is what war is like. (FC-NADK -2)

For her, as for many other former cadres, the Khmer Rouge were nevertheless morally good people. Although the rules had been strict and the child soldiers remember that they cried a lot at the beginning, in their view the rules of the

Communist movement complied with the moral dictates of Khmer culture, in which males and females had to be kept separate. In this way, the Khmer Rouge were the true defenders of the nation's moral order; the only problem was that combatants were not only separated by gender, but also from their families, which made them homesick, as stressed by another female combatant:

> [Men and women] were not allowed to stay with each other. And if someone had an issue with this regulation, these people were warned not to commit any misconduct going against our Khmer culture. The Khmer Rouge were so nice to us. They took good care of us. The only thing was that we were separated from our families, which made us homesick quite often. But we never received any punishments and never starved. We had enough to eat, just like when we had been at home. (FC-NADK -3)

In her opinion, the Khmer Rouge were good people and took excellent care of their combatants, just like a family would have done. And indeed, in Khmer Rouge ideology, the Communist collective was considered the new family. Initial separation from the family of origin did cause some pain, but this was seen as a necessary move done for the sake of the larger and truer collective: *Angkar*. However, since this respondent—like the other four—married a high-ranking cadre at the end of the conflict (he was not present during the interview), statements like hers have to be taken with a grain of salt. After marriage, even before the end of the war, she and her female comrades returned to comparatively traditional gender roles: "I quit military service and took care of the children, while my husband fought on until 1997" (FC-NADK -1). As another one said: "After war, it was just normal. I married and had children, while my man makes a living as a manual worker" (FC-NADK -4). The life course of these female combatants fits a pattern of weakening gender roles during conflict and a comparatively neat return to classic patterns after the war's end. The social order and inequalities between the sexes were ultimately reproduced and returned to "normal."

NOTES

1. Within the upper political leadership, namely the Central Committee, Ieng Thirith is among the best known exceptions. But in view of the research focus of this project, there seem to have been even fewer female *military* commanders. Although there were only a few, some are still comparatively well known and are part of the current government.

2. One *male* respondent referred to a test designed to assess whether recruits were ready for combat purposes: As long as the AK-47 was touching ground while being carried over the shoulder, recruits were considered unsuitable for actual combat yet (C-CPK -1). Cadres quite literally grew into being soldiers.

Chapter Eight

The Diaspora

Throughout the years of resistance, first against the Khmer Rouge, then with the Khmer Rouge against Vietnamese occupation, and finally during and after the transition to peace, the diaspora played an important role. At the beginning, most Cambodians within the diaspora in the United States or France were students or members of the political elite who stayed abroad after the Khmer Rouge took power. Those who did not already possess a second passport suddenly became stateless: "The radical Khmer Rouge took over the country, and my status changed from 'diplomat' to 'stateless.' I became a refugee" (GS-KPNLF -1). Many of these students and members of the political elite who were abroad in mid-1975 began to engage in political lobbying work and formed groups to protest against the Communist takeover and to inform the public and the political establishment within the United States and France about human rights violations perpetrated by the Khmer Rouge. These constituted the earliest connections between the diaspora and the resistance—at that time embryonic.

Throughout the Khmer Rouge regime, many smaller political associations were formed in the diaspora. In the United States, for instance, there was the Association of Khmer Refugees, Angkor on the East Coast, Seiha on the West Coast, and two newspapers, Sereikar and Conscience. The Cambodian diaspora in the United States was very small at that time, but already growing due to the US support for the Cambodian political and military elite during the civil war between 1970 and 1975 and an influx of students studying in the United States. In France, which had a longer history of a Cambodian diaspora due to the country's colonial history as a French protectorate, the General Association of Khmer Abroad, or Association General des Khmer á l'Etranger (AGKE), was established. Later, a forerunner of the KPNLF, the Comite Provisoire d'Animation pour l'Union Nationale Khmere (COPAUNAK), was created when the Vietnamese toppled the Khmer Rouge (cf. Corfield 1991). Except for the strongmen, most of the later leaders of the KPNLF (and also quite a few leaders of FUNCINPEC) joined these associations before leaving for the frontline, including members of the old military and political elite of the Sihanouk and Lon Nol years.

These early political associations—of in many cases suddenly stateless people—within the United States and France gained additional strength and leverage when the first members of the Lon Nol military resettled to the diaspora in 1975 and 1976. Despite their disappointment over "being left alone to fight the Khmer Rouge" when the United States pulled out in 1973 (LN-C -2), most of them fled to the their former ally, the United States, because they did not know where else to go, as well as for the simple reason that the United States was accepting Lon Nol soldiers who managed to flee the country. Some members of the Lon Nol military and political elite had been evacuated by US army helicopters right before Khmer Rouge took power; others were not so fortunate (or high-ranking) and had to fight their way to a military base in Thailand. Many felt that they only lost the war because of the vacuum created by the United States pulling its military out of the region in 1973, and many still harbored grievances against the United States or those within its political system whom they saw as "responsible" for the decision to leave them "defenseless" (most put the blame on the Democratic Party). In their view, they would have won the war if the US army only had stayed; without US support, they felt like easy prey for the Communists, who had international backing of their own. Yet during their flight from Cambodia, they saw no alternatives to resettlement in the United States.

At the beginning, they had to apply for political asylum, which, according to the respondents, was very different from having official refugee status. As asylum seekers, they did not receive much support from the government upon arrival in the United States:

Interviewer: Did you receive any SUPPORT at the beginning?

Respondent: NOTHING. We received nothing like that; just short scholarship and after some MONTHS—you are on your OWN. (LN-LG -2)

By contrast, refugees who came via the UN resettlement schemes few years later, during the 1980s, were able to apply for welfare support (but, as highlighted by one respondent, only if they had a family). The Lon Nol soldiers felt stuck in the United States and tried to make a living with day-to-day manual work in fields and factories, as burger cooks, and even in car washes. They felt trapped, unable to return to Cambodia but also unable to fully adapt to American society. Some still feel stuck today: "I came here in July 1975 and then I got stuck HERE until now. (laughs) [. . .] That was kind of HARD as we looked like a MONKEY, stay here from the jungle in AFRICA, something like that. We don't know ANYTHING" (LN-LG -1) After years as workers in day-to-day odd jobs, they applied for a green card and US citizenship.

Perhaps the most frustrating aspect of this experience for them was that their former social status did not matter at all:

> It just doesn't count that you were a military COMMANDER. I put in the RE-SUME like second lieutenant general, high school and all that. RIGHT? And THEY like "Oh, SORRY. This only job we HAVE." [pointing to his colleague sitting nearby] Even for HIM, being an English INSTRUCTOR back in Cambodia; it does NOT COUNT. You start from the SCRATCH, from the BOTTOM, working day by day in FACTORY. (LN-LG -3)

Being a "servant" to others was a whole new experience for most of the exiled military commanders. Some who had already lived abroad and who did not have to digest a comparable status loss felt it was a matter of—maybe inflated—pride:

> My experience and of other people's experience: In Cambodia they are RICH, its EASY. They want to go to [the US] or France [. . .] but it's the THINKING of these people that they don't want to SERVE. They are PROUD of themselves, they don't WANT to be SERVANT. (E-US -2)

While working in jobs that did not fit the status the commanders felt entitled to, they were frequently active in political associations or even created their own, perhaps as a way of recreating a feeling of political significance. Some tried to return to Cambodia to join the early anti-Communist resistance but struggled to do so as they did not know what was happening in the country and could not enter without endangering their lives. At the very beginning, very little information came in and the commanders did not know whether the reports they heard of mass executions were actually true. Some believed atrocities were occurring, but others did not. Many expected to return home eventually, but after a while most gave up, or started new lives and families in the diaspora that could not be easily abandoned.

Political lobbying grew increasingly important to the exiled members of the military and the political elite. They collected information via a network of soldiers and commanders who were still active along the border. Contacts in the border region sent videotapes of refugees reaching Thai soil. The political associations in the United States used these as a means to mobilize the diaspora, screening the self-made videos in theaters in Long Beach, California. Their lobbying yielded financial results, which in turn also increased the information flow from these ad hoc resistance groups:

We collect MONEY from ALL—ten dollar from EACH—to send to the border. And the group we call [name omitted], after sending money, we got INFOR-MATION the country is THIS and THAT and the MOVEMENT grow. It was a growing ANTI-communist movement (LN-LG -4)

Political associations within the diaspora over the years collected consider-able sums to support the armed resistance, first against the Khmer Rouge and later against the Vietnamese and the government in Phnom Penh. However, the support was not merely financial. The insurgency was a transnational field throughout its existence, and many commanders came from the diaspora to serve on the frontlines. Some former Lon Nol commanders even organized something they called a "headquarters" on US soil for the resistance until 1981: "We organized the HEADQUARTER here until 1981 and sent GEN-ERAL from here to the border. It was BIG staff here" (LN-LG -1). This aspect of their organization was highly secretive: "If you talk to the WRONG people, they don't KNOW about it" (LN-LG -3).

Also, after 1981 and after the creation of the two anti-Communist insurgent groups, many members of the resistance commuted between the diaspora and the Thai-Cambodian border to serve as commanders or members of the Gen-eral Staff. These people, however, were all members of the elite, not ordinary soldiers or members of the mid-range. To do this, they also needed to have a US or French passport, another marker of elite status, as these documents were only available to those who had already lived abroad in the past. In the end, those who returned needed a passport and had to live away from their families for long periods, which is why many former commanders preferred to stay in the diaspora:

We start a FAMILY already that's why we STAYED here. And also the Thai—they don't LET us step on their LAND as we are NO US citizens. NO, only US citizen. So we had FRIENDS who COULD join. They were FRENCH or US citizen. We support them from the BEHIND (another respondent interven-ing:) NO, we NOT just support: We build HEADQUARTER, we the COM-MANDER from here [oh ok]. We COMMAND from HERE. And we SENT the people from here—to JOIN [oh ok INTERESTING]. But mostly the HIGH ranking, the TOP. (LN-LG -1)

Supporting the resistance and sending commanders to lead the newly formed organizations, however, depended heavily on the goodwill of Thai authori-ties, mostly those directly along the border:

We could not make the THAI ALLOW US at all. We started to make—CON-NECTED with a MAYOR in Thailand at the Thai-Cambodian BORDER. He joined as well because HE wanted the RESISTANT troop to fight from THAI-LAND (laughs). So finally we CONNECTED and HE got the MONEY to put

in the BANK [hmhm]. To ASSURE, ONE of us to go. A FRIEND said now we
CONNECTED, we can have DIEN DEL go. (LN-LG -2)

The diaspora did not only send people and money. It also served as a refuge
for those who fought along the border. While the only refugee camp under
the control of UNHCR that engaged in resettlement, Khao-I-Dang, was only
open for a brief period after the end of the Khmer Rouge regime (being officially closed to new "arrivals" after January 1980), some commanders found
ways to get resettled even though they served in camps that were under the
control of an armed group and did not have resettlement schemes. Some
were able to receive support from friends and colleagues within the diaspora
to organize resettlement for them as political refugees. Others had to be a
bit more creative. One commander, for example, married a woman and had
a child with her, then sent her to Khao-I-Dang to apply for resettlement in
France. When he got into trouble with Thai authorities in 1987, he used her
and his child to apply for resettlement as a family member (GS-FUNCINPEC
-1). The diaspora did not only serve as a refuge during the years of civil war.
Many members of the political apparatus and the military—especially during
the period of two-headed government that lasted until 1997—have migrated
to the United States because they, in their own words, became "a non-trustable person" while working in the Cambodian government after 1997: "That
is why I came here [to the United States] with my family" (BC-KPNLF -5).

Since resettlement was not open to members of the military within the
camps under the control of the CGDK, ordinary soldiers were usually not able
to take refuge in the United States or France; only members of the leadership
had the resources and contacts to do this. But indirectly, the diaspora played an
important role for some former mid- and low-ranking soldiers as well. Since
some had family members who managed to resettle to the diaspora as civilians,
they continue to have an extra source of income to this day, receiving periodic
cash injections from abroad. This additional source of income did not escape
the attention of former colleagues fueling grievances: "some people are better
off than us, as they have relatives who are living abroad" (GC-KPNLF -1).

Despite a formal peace agreement and an end to armed resistance, for many
activists and members of political associations within the diaspora, the civil
war is still not truly over, and the ultimate purpose of resistance—to expel the
Vietnamese—has not yet been fulfilled. Although many did not even return
to Cambodia for fear of political violence, instead doing political advocacy
work and providing organizational support from afar, the members of the
diaspora who were interviewed for this project were considerably more anti-
Vietnamese than respondents in Cambodia. The whole peace process, for
them, was only the result of external pressures: "all [warring factions] did not
agree with each other AT ALL. BUT we HAD to agree PRESS-PRESSED by
BIG power, you HAVE to agree, yeah?" (BC-KPNLF -5)

It seemed obvious to all respondents within the diaspora sample that the Vietnamese had never actually left the country. Instead, they staged a kind of political theater for international observers, pretending that they withdrew their forces while secretly returning afterwards:

> [in Khmer:] The Yuon officially at least left the country in 1989, but then you see them returning in cars, disguised as civilians at nighttime. [switching to English:] United Nations they do not KNOW, WHO are YOU? (laughs) Khmer or Vietnamese (laughs). Difficult to SEE, yeah. We wanted to dismantle the government but HE (meaning Hun Sen) did not accept. (BC-KPNLF -5)

For these respondents, Hun Sen is seen as a Vietnamese puppet who sometimes pretends to be closer to China (as for example in the South China Sea issue), but "this is just a trick" (MPA-France -1). The disarmament process was also rigged, and Hun Sen simply hid his weapons: "After the PEACE agreement, they want ALL to drop ARMS. But the Hun Sen government STILL HIDE arms" (LN-LG -1). For the respondents, the Vietnamese are behind virtually every event that has unfolded in Cambodia over the past half century. Even the Khmer Rouge are seen as tools of the Vietnamese who killed Khmer people indiscriminately, paving the way for the Vietnamese invasion. For the purpose of concealing their secret control, the capital, Phnom Penh, was divided into two parts during the Khmer Rouge regime:

> The Khmer Rouge were under the VIETNAMESE ORDERS. The Vietnamese are HIDING in a hiding place; we cannot SEE them. One part is for Vietnamese, the other for Khmer Rouge. [. . .] The Vietnamese KILL ALL the Cambodian people, but the TRICK is: nobody knows, it is very SECRET like in the GENOCIDE time. They kill at NIGHT time or they kill by STARVATION. (MPA-US -1)

Even now, many activists and members of associations in the diaspora seem traumatized by what happened to them in Cambodia and are afraid to return their country of birth. They fear they would put themselves at risk of being executed by the Cambodian government if they returned. Some have carried that fear with them since the early 1980s, when they were refugees along the border.

> If I had to return [from a refugee along the border or during later years] I would have DIED because Cambodia is under the VIETNAMESE. I am SURE I would have been KILLED, my WHOLE FAMILY, it would have been KILLED too. (MPA-US -1)

The perceived ongoing but secretive occupation of Cambodia calls for an ongoing struggle against the ruling party, "for a proactive response," as one respondent put it, describing the reasons why he joins protests in the United States. These protests are not just aimed at the Hun Sen government's human rights violations and authoritarian actions, but at the Vietnamese lurking behind and killing protesters and members of the opposition:

> That's why I KEEP protesting. I don't want to fight the against the Cambodian People's Party but I think that BECAUSE of INVASIONS Vietnamese troop—every time like during COUP D'ETAT—Vietnamese troop [hm] was there [interviewer: you think they were present?]. YEAH, they were DISGUISED as the [hm] Hun Sen troop to fight back Nhek Bunchhay troop [hm], including ME. You see a lot of kill; LUCKY me [for having survived] (laughing). (ABC-FUNCINPEC -1)

For the respondents, Cambodia continues to remain under the control of the Vietnamese. The populace is either powerless or misinformed about the political reality of who is governing them. Due to poverty and low education among Cambodians, and the deceit of the Vietnamese, most respondents said that they saw no possibility of political change coming from the inside. The only chance is change from the outside, either via lobbying international powers or through a revitalized armed struggle:

> We still have a CHANCE for resistance [interviewer: from WHERE?]. From OUTSIDE. People [within the diaspora] that are YOUNGER than me, they know [what really happens inside Cambodia]. No CHANCE with election because they CHEAT, they cheat the WHOLE population, AGAIN. (MPA-US -1)

Some even claimed that there were secret armies hiding in Cambodia that could be mobilized by external leadership: "My former commander, he is still HIDING because he is part of ROYAL FAMILY. He STILL feel not good because of Hun Sen" (LN-C -1). Since most respondents are already elderly, they engaged in essentially unrealistic visions of armed struggle, or imagined what they would do if they were still younger: "if I was YOUNGER, I would—create a GROUP of FREEDOM fighter—of—I want to FIGHT that stupid prime minister" (MPA-US -1). However, they all held onto a hope for change believed there would be a force toppling the "puppet regime" one day. Some believed a strongman would arrive to lead this force very soon. This would be their last resort and hope: "I expect, I-I HOPE that Cambodia will have a STRONG man—who SAFE Cambodian lives" (MPA-US -1). This respondent claimed to know of a particular strongman who would rise very soon, but refrained from naming him, saying it was a highly secret affair.

It is hard for most members of the opposition within the diaspora to understand why so many former colleagues and brothers-in-arms who stayed in Cambodia eventually "flipped" and joined the CPP. They are convinced

that those who made a deal with the CPP did so entirely out of material con-
siderations. The government's strategy of buying off adversaries played out
quite well and was sometimes attributed by respondents to a morally negative
Cambodian "mentality" that harmed the former insurgent movement and its
political successors:

> You know, that is the problem, they [those who "flipped"] are up for material
> comfort. If they are offered money and a good job, they TAKE it and MOST of
> them DO. EASY. They do not think of the FUTURE, the LONG-run. And it is
> not just KPNLF, its CAMBODIANS in general. (E-US -2)

For the diaspora activists, the fight against an ongoing Vietnamese occupation was seen as a good and noble cause. But Vietnamese trickery and flaws
in the nature of Cambodians made this struggle for national salvation ultimately unsuccessful.

The political role of former members of the Khmer Rouge military within
the current diaspora seems marginal. There are Khmer Rouge who resettled
to France or the United States via refugee camps in the early 1980s, right
after the end of the Democratic Kampuchean regime, or who had strong connections within the political elite, which enabled them to seek refuge in the
diaspora, but the author could not find any members with clear connections to
the military apparatus who resettled during the unfolding of the peace process
throughout the nineties. Those who took refuge in the diaspora largely fall
into two categories: lower ranking cadres who fled from Vietnamese invasion
and resettled as refugees via Khao-I-Dang, who therefore do not fall into the
scope of this study (e.g. RF-NADK -6), or members of the upper strata of the
Khmer Rouge intellectual leadership, who had no clear connection to the military (therefore also not falling into the scope of this study) and who were not
willing to be part of any study about their engagement in the Democratic Kampuchea regime or their role as political actors within the diaspora after 1979.

Since many Khmer Rouge military cadres were child soldiers, some were
resettled in a third country by the Red Cross. Germany, for example, admitted
more than one hundred orphaned children, some of whom had been Khmer
Rouge cadres. After years of service to the communists and a long and painful flight to the border after the Vietnamese invasion, these child recruits
primarily cared about being fed: "When they asked me whether I would like
to resettle in Germany, I simply said it would be fine as long as I receive regular food" (C-CPK -1). In Germany, despite the fact that they received some
schooling, they suffer from high rates of disease, low education, trauma, and
unemployment. All claim to be completely uninterested in politics, and say
they only want to engage with the cultural aspects of their Cambodian heritage and avoid being caught up in struggles between the ruling party and the
opposition, in Cambodia or the diaspora.

Conclusion

Insurgent groups comprise multiple social groups sharing similar resources, a similar origin and life course, and a similar habitus. They are not only divided by rank and vertical symbolic valuation, but also by horizontal distinction, almost like castes. Hence, armed groups in transition should not be treated as homogeneous entities (cf. Bhatia and Muggah 2009). Each group has a different pathway into the military organization of the insurgent movement, and each group faces a revaluation of resources during warfare, as social resources and the cultural resources of military expertise and soldierly strength are upgraded, while others may lose relevance. However, most decisive is symbolic status within society, holding sway over positions and influence in the inner hierarchy of these groups and within the peace process itself. Status gains during times of war, such as for strongmen or military careerists, run a serious risk of devaluation during transition. This book has traced how each group within the insurgency is, in view of their resources and dispositions, differently prepared to handle this transition, thereby offering opportunities to some groups and posing threats to a successful "reintegration" for others. Most of the groups examined here strove to reconstitute their pre-war status (especially the military and political elite, as guerrilla warfare meant a status loss for them); only those who benefitted from warfare pushed for deals securing their wartime gains.

The Cambodian peace process, which involved several steps and phases for each habitus group, shows how hierarchies, resource valuations, and network structures are reproduced throughout the transition to peace, but it also provides insights into the mechanisms that might support or hamper post-conflict transformation. The Cambodian peace process saw the formal integration of three militaries into one state army. But despite this, the Khmer Rouge fought on, and informal conflicts within the military along previous network loyalties likewise lingered until negotiations with the Khmer Rouge for the upcoming second elections triggered factional clashes in mid-1997. But not every habitus group took part in the clashes. Resistance against CPP forces, for example, was led by FUNCINPEC's and KPNLF's strongmen, those who stood to lose the most from an end to armed conflict. Members of the military elite were more skeptical; most did not take part but complained about the losses they faced due to being associated with the "coup" because of their former membership in the resistance. By and large, they kept quiet and remained within the ranks of the RCAF, in positions that were technically high-level although effectively powerless. Some still control large units along the border but seem uninterested in returning to warfare.

The beginning of the peace process enabled members of the political elite (in this case, the intellectual commanders) to return to politics, or at least the state apparatus. However, after the factional clashes, many found refuge in the newly emerging civil society. The alternative space that civil society opened up for the deposed political elite helped ease political tensions after 1993 and especially after 1997, because many of these people were able to reconstitute their networks within this sphere. However, this seems to be one reason why Hun Sen still views large parts of the civil society as an enemy to his rule (Coventry 2017). Many intellectuals are not very keen to talk about their time as commanders, almost skipping this period completely when they tell their life stories. What also becomes clear is that network loyalties, especially within the upper ranks, were not restricted to formal groups such as FUNCINPEC or KPNLF but ran across these groups. Some respondents even described how their network tried to get a foothold in all groups in order to stay afloat if one broke down. These networks (*khsai* in Khmer) are opaque and become only very rarely legible to an observer. At the same time, cross-network trust is extremely low, even between seemingly close party members (likely a result of decades of war and conflict).

To a large extent, symbolic violence—like the acceptance of an arbitrary but naturalized social order—explains not only the cohesion of the insurgent groups during war (Bultmann 2018b), but also the smoothness of their eventual reintegration. Hierarchies are maintained by incorporated social orders guiding the perception of one's own and other's value within the field. For many, it was normal to become soldiers to secure their subsistence as dislocated peasants, and it was likewise normal for them to return to subsistence farming afterwards. It was, as one said, simply a matter of becoming "what we were meant to be" (RF-KPNLF -2). Symbolic violence seems to be the strongest force securing the reproduction of social inequalities, even within armed groups during their transition to peace.

However, in accordance with Ted Gurr's theory of relative deprivation, a desire to return to fighting was expressed most often by those respondents who had faced a stark downturn in social status during the transition to peace, and who felt that they did not receive the benefits they deserved (cf. Gurr 1970). This was the case for strongmen, who lost their warrior ethos and could not make any deals; for intellectuals, who did not belong to the core of the leadership, but rose to higher positions due to the scarcity of education as a resource, then found that they did not have enough connections (social resources to the political elite) to make a proper living after the war's end and after the factional clashes; for patrimonial loyalists, who lost their patrons; for careerists, whose military expertise from military schools along the border could not be transferred and whose leaders did not include them in their integration networks; for the children of war, who acquired all their skills and resources during wartime, who lost their symbolic resource of bravery and battle experience and who now oftentimes work as illegal migrants in Thailand (only very few managed to be part of the state military and to keep their symbolic resource alive); for the military commanders and soldiers within the diaspora, who faced a steep downturn in status as refugees within the United States or France; and of course, for the Khmer Rouge, for whom the blood associated with their years in power posed a heavy obstacle to their integration into politics and the symbolic universe of Cambodian society. Others also felt that they had not received what they were entitled to either, but "limited" their expressions of frustration to anti-Vietnamese slurs without voicing the wish to return to warfare. This was the case, for instance, with the military elite commanders, who were frustrated by their lack of power, but for whom guerrilla warfare had already meant a loss in status in the first place. This did not make a relapse into civil war seem very tempting for them.

The "win-win policy," which in itself came about in several steps and did not deliver benefits equally to all factions of the Khmer Rouge, enabled a seemingly smooth transfer into politics and into the military, but not a complete symbolic conversion. This symbolic conversion happened, instead, through a discourse of religious conversion (similar to the strongmen who could not make a deal and had no place in the military and political opposition elite) and through discourses claiming an ongoing struggle for democracy, nationalism, and Khmer-first ideology that opposed Vietnamese plots threatening the existence of the Khmer people. All of the groups that faced a stark downturn in status tended to favor a relapse into civil war and engaged in anti-Vietnamese slurs during the interviews, sometimes quite heavily. The key is not only the type and amount of resources they received during the transition, but also the incorporated self-perception within their social milieus, which guided their strategies during the post-conflict transition to peace and how they dealt with and tried to prevent losses in status.

Reinsertion packages provided by the UN seemed helpful to a wide range of belligerents, but in a limited way. They mainly served as a means for low-ranking soldiers to *reconstitute* their previous social status and resume lives as peasants, workers or small business holders. They were not useful and mismatched for low-ranking soldiers, who had been socialized during war and often even started their military service as child soldiers. These packages did not fit their social status and life course and they did not have the skills to make proper use of land or money gifts to start a life outside a military framework. These packages were the result of an early one-size-fits-all thinking within the UN and academia at that time, in which "money works" (Willibald 2006). In addition, DDR packages during the early nineties were mainly support instruments embracing short-term security goals within the clearly defined time frame of an intervention with a lower focus on long-term reintegration than today.

It is impossible to draw a neat line between war and peace. In Cambodia, for example, peace was not a sudden event, but came about gradually, in several phases, while lingering conflicts beneath the surface erupted periodically, most explosively in 1997. Following Tarak Barkawi, among others, the Cambodian peace process can be seen as a "liquid state" between outright battle and other forms of repression and conflict (Barkawi 2016), in which for some, warfare never truly ended or remains an ideal or fond memory. Some former belligerents went on to "struggle" against Hun Sen's actual as well as alleged repression, and his supposed control by the Vietnamese. In their own view at least, there is no clear break between the goals they pursued during and after the official end of war.

However, while many loyalties were rather loose and horizontal, vertical allegiances also changed constantly. Even during the war, the field of insurgency, like all non-state armed groups, was not a unitary bloc, but consisted of cores and peripheries with mercenaries, short-term recruits, and "hop on-hop off" guerrillas (Guichaoua 2012, Giustozzi 2008). For short-term recruits, the transition back to their old lives was rather easy and their loyalty to "the cause" rather low. On top of that, there was a clear drop-off in loyalty between the upper echelons and the foot soldiers. While loyalties between mid-range and top commanders often ran deep, cohesion between the lowest and upper ranks was not based upon personal loyalty and only rarely on ideological commitment. The upper ranks were largely connected by patrimonialism, while the lower ranks strove for subsistence and tried to evade the exigencies created by war (cf. Bultmann 2015, 135–42).

Rank-and-file soldiers did not expect any support in their transition from vertical networks, but relied when possible on family, friends, and—if existent—connections in their home communities. Only those who belonged to a strongman's entourage were able to enter and to maintain their patrimonial relationships after the war's end. Usually, however, these did not offer any substantial benefits. On top of that, following a typical pattern within patron-client clusters, these networks flourished and disintegrated depending on the wartime and post-war fate of the network's patron and the clients who served as mid-level patrons below them (Scott 1972, 97). The stability of patrimonial clusters during transition rests heavily upon the structural position of the patron in a post-conflict setting. These structures and different degrees of horizontal and vertical allegiances need to be taken into account in understanding the process of integrating insurgent groups. Network structures, and networks' density and cohesion, are important for successful integration. Current research increasingly points to the importance of analyzing network structures, their densities, and their entanglement with illicit activities such as drug production and trafficking, all calling for special attention (Cardenas, Gleditsch, and Guevara 2018).

Criticizing a widely held view in academia and among practitioners, Séverine Autesserre challenged the notion that international interventions should put an end to illicit activities for fear they might hinder a successful transition to stability and peace (Autesserre 2017). Instead, as was the case in Cambodia, illicit activities can create a basis for "negative peace" (an absence of direct violence), which in turn might make durable peace possible in the long term (for the concept of "negative peace," compare Galtung 1964, 1969). It is true that various deals between Hun Sen and members of the resistance made possible an initial transfer of the social order and its hierarchies from the insurgent movement into the state military and the political field (not just the "win-win policy" with the Khmer Rouge, but also multiple large- and small-scale deals with members of the military and political elite from the non-communist parties, most notably after the factional clashes in 1997).

However, in the end, Hun Sen turned on his former adversaries after the dust of war had settled, downgrading the rank of former CGDK members over the years or even jailing them over illicit activities that—in all likelihood—had previously been part of the deal they struck with him (e.g., former strongmen being imprisoned due to their role in the drug trade, which had been tolerated for years after their defection). The arrest of former military commanders of the CGDK usually happened shortly before elections (this was the case before the 2013 election and appears to be playing out in similar fashion at the time of writing, few months before the 2018 election). The strategy of a partial opening followed by a gradual closure of the military and political elite has worked well for the incumbent government, but it has also increased tensions within the political and military network on the ground, something the author felt clearly during his field research over the past seven years. The old political and military elite was effectively prevented from re-entering the country's upper ranks, additionally fueling current conflicts over socio-economic inequalities within a fast changing Cambodian society (Deth and Bultmann 2016). This back-and-forth opening and closing of the state and military apparatus to adversaries also explains the oscillating number of officers with the rank of general in the RCAF. While there was an initial surge to 2,000 officers with the rank of general in 1994 when the RCAF was created, their number was quickly reduced to 400 in 1995. However, not least due to the "win-win policy," the number surged yet again, reaching 613 in 2006 (Bartu and Wilford 2009, 13). In 2010, the defense minister, Tea Banh, announced another surge in numbers, to 2,200 generals, and as of early 2018 RCAF was adding yet another 300 generals.

While the reintegrated field of the CGDK military and its political networks was comparatively calm during the first rounds of interviews in 2011 and 2012, conflicts surrounding the elections in 2013, as well as a surge in arrests and violence before the elections in 2018, meant that interviewees clearly felt less comfortable talking about the politics of reintegration and their past and current relations with the incumbent government. Many respondents are involved in the ongoing conflicts with the Hun Sen government and either "flipped" to the government side (which by no means would mean that they are being trusted) or are still active within the opposition (within the CNRP or in the civil society). Today's political opposition, although it appears to comprise entirely new parties, is still heavily shaped by the ideologies and networks of these civil war factions. As written above on several occasions, for many respondents the war is not really over. Through a combination of carrots (government positions despite multiple election losses) and sticks (arrests), the Hun Sen government has taken great care to prevent a remilitarization of the old armed apparatus.

Of course, this study is by no means comprehensive. It has several limitations that affect the picture that was drawn here. Some are obvious: There was a lack of access to certain groups. The author was not able to talk to a sufficient number of female combatants; leading Khmer Rouge, who were either dead, imprisoned, or afraid of the Khmer Rouge tribunal; or deal-makers within the government and the state military, who were too worried about my intentions. There are certainly more habitus groups within the CGDK than are accounted for in this study. The groups discussed here are the ones the author was able to find and interview.

In the end, decisive for the creation of a habitus group—which is always a theoretical act by the researcher—is whether it is a social group whose social background, habitus, or resources make a difference during transition. Hence, there might be many more habitus groups, making a difference in terms of advancing theoretical insights on the social mechanisms of armed group transformation. But in the end, this study was able to detect differences in the transition of various habitus groups and to explain many patterns throughout the multi-phased transformation to peace. The study highlighted the importance of understanding the social structure of armed groups during their integration as well as the need to analyze the behavioral patterns guiding their strategies in securing the positions in post-conflict society they believe they are entitled to. It also highlighted the importance of the network structure and of symbolic violence as a cohesive element before and during the peace process. Understanding the strategies of individuals is impossible if they are not seen in the context of the entire social field they are part of, and to which their belief systems and actions relate. And last but not least, the book shows how status losses during transition translate into a wish among former combatants and commanders for a relapse into civil war.

Bibliography

Achvarina, Vera, and Simon Reich. 2010. "No Place to Hide: Refugees, Displaced Persons and Child Soldier Recruits." In *Child Soldiers in the Age of Fractured States*, edited by Scott Gates and Simon Reich, 55–76. Pittsburg, PA: University of Pittsburg Press.

Alden, Chris, Monika Thakur, and Matthew Arnold. 2011. *Militias and the Challenges of Post-Conflict Peace: Silencing the Guns*. London/New York: Zed Books.

Ang, Chouléan. 1986. *Les êtres surnaturels dans la religion populaire khmère*. Paris: CEDORECK.

Ang, Chouléan. 1988. "The Place of Animism within Popular Buddhism in Cambodia. The Example of the Monastery." *Asian Folklore Studies* 47:35–41.

Ang, Chouléan. 2004. *Braḥ liṅg*. Phnom Penh: Reyum Publishing.

Anon. 2004. "Khmer Rouge: Christian baptism after massacres." *Asianews.it*, January 12, 2004. http://www.asianews.it/news-en/Khmer-Rouge:-Christian-baptism-after-massacres-243.html.

APTN. 2002. Senior Khmer Rouge military leader dead at 68.

Argo, Nichole. 2009. "Why fight? Examining Self-Interested versus Communaly-Oriented Motivations in Palestinian Resistance and Rebellion." *Security Studies* 18 (4):651–680.

Arjona, Ana M., and Stathis Kalyvas. 2012. "Recruitment into Armed Groups: A Survey of Demobilized Fighters." In *Understanding Collective Political Violence*, edited by Yvan Guichaoua, 143–71. London: Palgrave MacMillan.

Ashley, David. 1998. "Between War and Peace: Cambodia 1991–1998." *Accord* 5:20–29.

Autesserre, Séverine. 2017. "International Peacebuilding and Local Success: Assumptions and Effectiveness." *International Studies Review* 0:1–19.

Ayres, David M. 2000. *Anatomy of a Crisis: Education, Development, and the State in Cambodia, 1953–1998*. Honolulu: University of Hawai'i Press.

Balcells, Laia. 2010. "Rivalry and Revenge: Violence against Civilians in Conventional Civil Wars." *International Studies Quarterly* 54 (2):291–313.

Barkawi, Tarak. 2015. "Subaltern Soldiers: Eurocentrism and the Nation-State in the Combat Motivation Debates." In *Frontline: Combat and Cohesion in the Twenty-First Century*, edited by Anthony King, 24–45. Oxford: Oxford University Press.

Barkawi, Tarak. 2016. "Decolonizing War." *European Journal of International Security* 1 (2):199–214.

Barma, Naazneen H. 2017. *The Peacebuildung Puzzle. Political Order in Post-Conflict States*. Cambridge: Cambridge University Press.

Bartu, Peter, and Neil Wilford. 2009. Transitional Justice and DDR. The Case of Cambodia. New York: ICTJ.

Becker, Elizabeth. 1998. *When the War was Over. Cambodia and the Khmer Rouge Revolution*. New York: Simon & Schuster.

Bellard, Brett. 2002. "Reintegration programmes for refugees in South-East Asia: Lessons learned from UNHCR's experience." Geneva: United Nations High Commissioner for Refugees, Evaluation and Policy Analysis Unit and Regional Bureau for Asia and the Pacific.

Berdal, Mats R., and Michael Leifer. 2007. "Cambodia." In *United Nations Interventionism, 1994–2004*, edited by Mats R. Berdal and Spyros Economides, 32–64. Cambridge: Cambridge University Press.

Berdal, Mats and David Ucko. 2010. "Introduction: The Political Reintegration of Armed Groups after War." In *Reintegrating Armed Groups After Conflict. Politics, violence and transition*, edited by Mats Berdal and David Ucko, 1–9. Abingdon: Routledge.

Bertrand, Didier. 2004. "A Medium Possession Practice and Its Relationship with Cambodian Buddhism. The Gru Pāramī." In *History, Buddhism, and New Religious Movements in Cambodia*, edited by Elizabeth Guthrie and John Marston, 150–247. Honolulu: University of Hawai'i Press.

Bhatia, Michael V., and Robert Muggah. 2009. "The Politics of Demobilization in Afghanistan." In *Security and Post-Conflict Reconstruction: Dealing with Fighters in the Aftermath of War*, edited by Robert Muggah. London: Routledge.

Bizot, François. 2004. *The Gate*. New York: Vintage Books.

Bohnsack, Ralf. 2013. "Documentary Method." In *The SAGE Handbook of Qualitative Data Analysis*, edited by Uwe Flick, 217–33. Los Angeles: Sage Publications.

Bourdieu, Pierre. 1985. "The Social Space and the Genesis of Groups." *Theory and Society* 14 (6):723–44.

Bourdieu, Pierre. 1986. "The Forms of Capital." In *Handbook of Theory and Research for the Sociology of Education*, edited by John Richardson, 241–58. New York: Greenwood.

Bourdieu, Pierre. 1990. *The Logic of Practice*. Stanford: Stanford University Press.

Bourdieu, Pierre. 1996. *Vilhelm Aubert lecture: Physical Space, Social Space and Habitus*. Oslo: University of Oslo & Institute for Social Research.

Bourdieu, Pierre. 2010. *Distinction. A Social Critique of the Judgement of Taste*. New York London: Routledge.

Bourdieu, Pierre, and Loïc J. D. Wacquant. 1992. *An invitation to reflexive sociology*. Chicago: University of Chicago Press.

Bremer, Helmut. 2005. *Von der Gruppendiskussion zur Gruppenwerkstatt. Ein Beitrag zur Methodenentwicklung in der typenbildenden Mentalitäts-, Habitus- und Milieuanalyse.* Münster/Hamburg/London: LIT.

Brown, MacAllister, and Joseph J. Zasloff. 1998. *Cambodia Confounds the Peacemakers 1979–1998.* Ithaca, NY: Cornell University Press.

Bultmann, Daniel. 2014. "Analyzing the Cambodian insurgency as a social field." *Small Wars & Insurgencies* 25 (2):457–78.

Bultmann, Daniel. 2015. *Inside Cambodian Insurgency. A Sociological Perspective on Civil Wars and Conflict.* Burlington, MA: Ashgate.

Bultmann, Daniel. 2017. *Kambodscha unter den Roten Khmer. Die Erschaffung des perfekten Sozialisten.* Paderborn: Schöningh.

Bultmann, Daniel. 2018a. "Introduction: The Social Structure of Armed Groups. Reproduction and Change during and after Conflict." *Small Wars & Insurgencies* 29 (4):1–21.

Bultmann, Daniel. 2018b. "The Normality of Going to War: Aspects of Symbolic Violence in Participation and Perpetration in Civil War." In *Perpetrators. Dynamics, motivations and concepts for participating in mass violence* edited by Susanne Buckley-Zistel and Timothy Williams, 99–116. Abingdon: Routledge.

Cardenas, Ernesto, Kristian S. Gleditsch, and Luis C. Guevara. 2018. "Network Structure of Insurgent Groups and the Success of DDR Processes in Colombia." *Small Wars & Insurgencies* 29 (4).

Carmichael, Robert. 2015. *When the Clouds Fell from the Sky: A Disappearance, A Daughter's Search and Cambodia's First War Criminal.* London: Mason-McDonald Press.

Chandler, David. 2017. *Peacebuilding: The Twenty Years' Crisis, 1997–2017.* Basingstoke: Palgrave Macmillan.

Chandler, David P. 1999. *Voices from S-21. Terror and History in Pol Pot's Secret Prison.* Berkeley: University of California Press.

Chandler, David P. 2008. *A History of Cambodia.* 4th Edition ed. Boulder, CO: Westview Press.

Chen, Dene-Hern. 2017. "The Former Khmer Rouge Cadres Who Turned to God for Salvation." *South China Morning Post Magazine,* February 16.

Collier, Paul. 2000. "Doing Well out of Civil War: An Economic Perspective." In *Greed and Grievance: Economic Agendas in Civil Wars,* edited by Mats Berdal and David M. Melone, 91–111. Boulder, CO: Lynne Rienner.

Collier, Paul, and Anke Hoeffler. 2004. "Greed and Grievance in Civil War." *Oxford Economic Paper – New Series* 61 (1):1–27.

Collier, Paul, and Nicholas Sambanis. 2005. *Understanding Civil War: Evidence and Analysis.* 2 vols. Washington, D.C.: World Bank.

Conboy, Kenneth. 2013. *The Cambodian Wars: Clashing Armies and CIA Covert Operations.* Lawrence: University Press of Kansas.

Corfield, Justin. 1991. "Title." Working Paper.

Coventry, Louise. 2017. "Civil Society in Cambodia: Challenges and Contestations." In *The Handbook of Contemporary Cambodia,* edited by Katherine Brickell and Simon Springer, 53–63. Abingdon: Routledge.

Crane, Brent. 2015. "Female Cadres of the Khmer Rouge." *The Phnom Penh Post*, August 1.

Davis, Erik W. 2016. *Deathpower. Buddhism's Ritual Imagination in Cambodia*. New York: Columbia University Press.

de Vries, Hugo, and Nikkie Wiegink. 2011. "Breaking Up and Going Home? Contesting Two Assumptions in the Demobilization and Reintegration of Former Combatants." *International Peacekeeping* 18 (1):38–51.

Deth, Sok Udom, and Daniel Bultmann. 2016. "The Afterglow of Hun Sen's Cambodia? Socioeconomic Development, Political Change, and the Persistence of Inequalities." In *Globalization and Democracy in Southeast Asia*, edited by Chantana Banpasirichote-Wungaeo, Boike Rehbein and Surichai Wungaeo, 87–110. London: Palgrave MacMillan.

Doyle, Michael W. 1995. *UN Peacekeeping in Cambodia: UNTAC's Civil Mandate*. Boulder, CO: Lynne Rienner.

Doyle, Michael W., and Nicholas Sambanis. 2000. "International Peacebuilding: A Theoretical and Quantitative Analysis." *American Political Science Review* 94 (4):779–801.

Dy, Khamboly. 2015. "Genocide Education in Cambodia: Local Initiatives, Global Connections." Doctor of Philosophy, Rutgers University, New York.

Dy, Khamboly, and Christopher Dearing. 2014. *A History of the Anlong Veng Community: The Final Stronghold of the Khmer Rouge Movement*. Phnom Penh: Documentation Center of Cambodia.

Ea, Meng-Try, and Sorya Sim. 2001. *Victims or Perpetrators? Testimony of Young Khmer Rouge Comrades*. Phnom Penh: Documentation Center of Cambodia.

Ebihara, May Mayko. 1968. "Svay, a Khmer Village in Cambodia." Doctor of Philosophy, Faculty of Philosophy, Columbia University.

Em, Sokhym. 2002. "Criticism and Self-Criticism." *Searching for the Truth* 31:18–19.

Etcheson, Craig. 1984. *The Rise and Demise of Democratic Kampuchea*. Boulder, CO: Westview Press.

Ferry, Tiphaine. 2014. "How Disarmament, Demobolization and Reintegration Programs Could Have Facilitated the Establishment of Long-Term Conflict Prevention in Post-conflict Cambodia." *Cambodia Law and Policy Journal* 3:128–153.

Findlay, Trevor. 1995. *Cambodia. The Legacy and Lessons of UNTAC*. Oxford: Oxford University Press.

Fortna, Virginia P. 2004. "Does Peacekeeping Keep Peace? International Intervention and the Duration of Peace After Civil War." *International Studies Quarterly* 48 (2):269–92.

Fortna, Virginia P. 2008. *Does Peacekeeping Work? Shaping Belligerents' Choices after Civil War*. Princeton, NJ: Princeton University Press.

Fuji, Lee A. 2009. *Killing Neighbors: Webs of Violence in Rwanda*. Ithaca, NY: Cornell University Press.

Galtung, Johan. 1964. "An Editorial." *Journal of Peace Research* 1 (1):1–4.

Galtung, Johan. 1969. "Violence, Peace and Peace Research." *Journal of Peace Research* 6 (3):167–91.

Gilligan, Michael, Eric N. Mvukiyehe, and Cyrus Samii. 2013. "Reintegrating Rebels into Civilian Life." *Journal of Conflict Resolution* 57 (4):598–626.

Giustozzi, Antonio. 2008. *Koran, Kalashnikov and Laptop: The Neo-Taliban Insurgency in Afghanistan*. New York: Columbia University Press.

Giustozzi, Antonio. 2012. *Post-conflict Disarmament, Demobilization and Reintegration: Bringing State-building Back In, Global Security in a Changing World*. Burlington, VT: Ashgate.

Giustozzi, Antonio. 2016. "Introduction." In *Post-conflict Disarmament, Demobilization and Reintegration. Bringing State-building Back In*, edited by Antonio Giustozzi, 1–27. Abingdon: Routledge.

Glassmayer, Katherine, and Nicholas Sambanis. 2008. "Rebel-Military Integration and Civil War Termination." *Journal of Peace Research* 45 (3):365–84.

Goetze, Catherine. 2017. *The Distinction of Peace: A Social Analysis of Peacebuilding*. Ann Arbor: University of Michigan Press.

Goffman, Erving. 1963. *Stigma. Notes on the Management of Spoiled Identity*. London: Penguin Books.

Gottesman, Evan. 2004. *Cambodia after the Khmer Rouge: Inside the Politics of Nation Building*. New Haven: Yale University Press.

Granovetter, Mark. 1973. "The strength of weak ties." *American Journal of Sociology* 78:1360–380.

Guichaoua, Yvan. 2012. "Circumstantial Alliances and Loose Loyalties in Rebellion Making: The Case of Tuareg Insurgency in Northern Niger (2007–2009)." In *Understanding Collective Political Violence*, edited by Yvan Guichaoua, 246–266. New York: Palgrave MacMillan.

Gurr, Ted. 1970. *Why Men Rebel*. Princeton: Princeton University Press.

Haas, Michael. 1991. *Cambodia, Pol Pot, and the United States: The Faustian Pact*. New York: Praeger.

Hanks, Lucien M. Jr. 1962. "Merit and Power in the Thai Social Order." *American Anthropologist* 64:1247–1261.

Harris, Ian. 2001. "Sangha Groupings in Cambodia." *Buddhist Studies Review* 18 (1):65–72.

Harris, Ian Charles. 2005. *Cambodian Buddhism: History and Practice*. Honolulu: University of Hawai'i Press.

Heder, Stephen. 1996. "The Resumption of Armed Struggle by the Party of Democratic Kampuchea." In *Propaganda, Politics, and Violence in Cambodia. Democratic Transition under United Nations Peace-keeping*, edited by Stephen Heder and Judy Ledgerwood, 114–33. New York: Routledge.

Heder, Steve. 1995. "Cambodia's Democratic Transition to Neoauthoritarianism." *Current History* 94:425–29.

Heindel, Anne, and John D. Ciorciari. 2014. "Experiments in International Criminal Justice: Lessons from the Khmer Rouge Tribunal." *Michigan Journal of International Law* 35 (2):369–442.

Heininger, Janet E. 1994. *Peacekeeping in Transition. The United Nations in Cambodia*. New York: Twentieth Century Fund Press.

Hennings, Anne. 2017. "With Soymilk to the Khmer Rouge: Challenges of Researching Ex-combatants in Post-war Contexts." *International Peacekeeping* 24 (4):1–23.

Hensell, Stephan, and Felix Gerdes. 2017. "Exit From War: The Transformation of Rebels into Post-war Power Elites." *Security Dialogue* 48 (2):168–184.

Hensengerth, Oliver. 2008. "Transitions in Cambodia. War and Peace, 1954 to the present." In *Working Paper*. Duisburg: Institute for Development and Peace (INEF), University of Duisburg-Essen.

Him, Chanrithy. 2001. *When Broken Glass Floates: Growing Up Under the Khmer Rouge*. London: W.W. Norton & Company.

Hinton, Alex Laban. 2000. "Revenge in the Pol Pot Period." *Searching for the Truth* 12:32–34.

Hoffman, Danny. 2007. "The meaning of militia: Understanding the Civil Defence Forces of Sierra Leone." *African Affairs* 106 (425):639–62.

Humphreys, Macartan, and Jeremy Weinstein. 2007. "Demobilization and Reintegration." *Journals of Conflict Resolution* 51 (4):531–67.

Jacobsen, Trudy. 2008. *Lost Goddesses. The Denial of Female Power in Cambodian History*. Copenhagen: NIAS Press.

Jodhka, Surinder S., Boike Rehbein, and Jessé Souza. 2017. *Inequality in Capitalist Societies*. Abingdon: Routledge.

Kalyvas, Stathis. 2008. "Ethnic Defection in Civil War." *Comparative Political Studies* 41 (8):1043–68.

Khemara, Sok. 2018. "Ex-Khmer Rouge Official Converts to Christianity Guided by Pastor She Once Enslaved." *Voice of America*, February 17.

Kiernan, Ben. 2002. *The Pol Pot Regime: Race, Power, and Genocide in Cambodia under the Khmer Rouge, 1975–1979*. Second Edition ed. New Haven: Yale University Press.

Kiernan, Ben. 2004. *How Pol Pot Came to Power: Colonialism, Nationalism, and Communism in Cambodia, 1930–1975*. Second Edition ed. New Haven: Yale University Press.

Kilcullen, David. 2009. *The Accidental Guerilla: Fighting Small Wars in the Midst of a Big One*. Oxford: Oxford University Press.

Kong, Thann. 2009. Phnom Penh.

Le Billon, Philippe. 2002. "Logging in Muddy Waters. The Politics of Forest Exploitation in Cambodia." *Critical Asian Studies* 34 (4):563–86.

Levy, Marc. 1999. "No Command for Lay Virak." *The Cambodia Daily*, February 19.

Locard, Henri. 2004. *Pol Pot's Little Red Book: The Sayings of Angkar*. Chiang Mai: Silkworm Books.

MacKinley, John. 2007. "Defining Warlords." *International Peacekeeping* 7 (1):48–62.

Marriage, Zoë. 2010. "Flip-flop Rebel, Dollar Soldier: Demobilisation in the Democratic Republic of Congo." In *Reintegrating Armed Groups After Conflict*, edited by Mats Berdal and David Ucko, 119–43. Abingdon: Routledge.

Metelits, Claire. 2018. "Bourdieu's Capital and Insurgent Group Resilience: A Field-Theoretic Approach to the Polisario Front." *Small Wars & Insurgencies* 29 (4).

Muggah, Robert. 2010. Innovations in DDR policy and research. Reflections on the last decade. In *Working Paper 774*: NUPI.

Münch, Philipp. 2018. "Forces of Heresy versus Forces of Conservation: Making Sense of Hezb-e Islami-ye Afghanistan's and the Taleban's positions in the Afghan insurgency " *Small Wars & Insurgencies* 29 (4).

Murashima, Eiji. 2009. "The Young Nuon Chea in Bangkok (1942–1950) and the Communist Party of Thailand: The Life in Bangkok of the Man Who Became "Brother No. 2" in the Khmer Rouge." *Journal of Asia-Pacific Studies* 12:1–42.

Murshed, Syed Masoob. 2010. *Explaining Civil War. A Rational Choice Approach.* Cheltenham, UK: Edwar Elgar.

Nem, Sowath. 2012. *Civil War Termination and the Source of Total Peace in Cambodia: Win-Win Policy of Samdech Techo Hun Sen in International Context.* Phnom Penh: Reahoo.

Nhek, Bunchhay. 1998. Phnom Penh.

Nhem, Boraden. 2013. *The Khmer Rouge: Ideology, Militarism, and the Revolution that Consumed a Generation.* Santa Barbara, CA: Prager.

Nordstrom, Carolyn. 1992. *The Paths to Domination, Resistance, and Terror.* Berkeley: University of California Press.

Norén-Nilsson, Astrid. 2013. "Performance as (Re)incarnation: The Sdech Kân Narrative." *Journal of Southeast Asian Studies* 44 (1):4–23.

O'Brien-Kelly, Martin. 2006. "The Role of Natural Resources in the Khmer Rouge–Royal Government of Cambodia Peace Negotiations and Reintegration Process." Master of Arts Program in International Development Studies (MAIDS), Chulalongkorn University.

Özerdem, Alpaslan. 2012. "A Re-conceptualisation of Ex-combatant Reintegration: 'Social Reintegration' Approach." *Conflict, Security & Development* 12 (1):51–73.

Özerdem, Alpaslan, and Mark Knight. 2004. "Guns, Camps and Cash: Disarmament, Demobilization and Reinsertion of Former Combatants in Transitions from War to Peace " *Journal of Peace Research* 41 (4):499–516.

Perrazone, Stephanie. 2017. "Reintegrating Former Fighters in the Congo: Ambitious Objectives, Limited Results." *International Peacekeeping* 24 (2):254–79.

Podder, Sukanya. 2012. "From Recruitment to Reintegration: Communities and Ex-combatants in Post-Conflict Liberia." *International Peacekeeping* 19 (2):186–202.

Porto, João Gomes, Chris Alden, and Imogen Parsons. 2007. *From Soldiers to Citizens: Demilitarization of Conflict and Society.* Aldershot: Ashgate.

Procknow, Greg. 2011. *Recruiting and Training Genocidal Soldiers.* Regina: Francis & Bernard.

Pugel, James. 2009. "Measuring Reintegration in Liberia: Assessing the Gap Between Outputs and Outcomes." In *Security and Post-Conflict Reconstruction*, edited by Robert Muggah, 70–102. London/New York: Routledge.

Rehbein, Boike. 2011. "Differentiation of Sociocultures, Classification, and the Good Life in Laos." *Journal of Social Issues in Southeast Asia* 26:277–303.

Roberts, David. 2002. "Political Transition and Elite Discourse in Cambodia, 1991–99." *Journal of Cummunist Studies and Transition Politics* 18 (4):101–18.

Robinson, Major T. P. 2001. "Twenty-First Century Warlords: Diagnosis and Treatment." *Defence Studies* 1 (1):121–45.

Rowley, Kelvin. 2005. "Second Life, Second Death. The Khmer Rouge after 1979." In *Genocide in Cambodia and Rwanda. New Perspectives*, edited by Susan E. Cook, 201–225. New Brunswick: Transaction Publishers.

Sanderson, John. 1998. "Yale-UN Oral History Project." Canberra, Australia, July 10, 1998.

Schlichte, Klaus. 2003. "Profiteure und Verlierer von Bürgerkriegen: Die soziale Ökonomie der Gewalt." In *Politische Ökonomie der Gewalt: Staatszerfall und die Privatisierung von Gewalt und Krieg*, edited by Werner Ruf, 124–143. Opladen: VS.

Schlichte, Klaus. 2009. *In the Shadow of Violence. The Politics of Armed Groups*. Frankfurt: Campus.

Schlichte, Klaus. 2014. "When 'the Facts' Become a Text: Reinterpreting War with Serbian War Veterans." *Revue de synthèse* 135 (4):1–24.

Schneckener, Ulrich. 2017. "Militias and the Politics of Legitimacy." *Small Wars & Insurgencies* 28 (4–5):799–816.

Scott, James C. 1972. "Patron-Client Politics and Political Change in Southeast Asia." *The American Political Science Review* 66 (1):91–113.

Scott, James C. 1976. *The Moral Economy of the Peasant: Rebellion and Subsistence in Southeast Asia*. New Haven: Yale University Press.

Scott, James C. 1987. *Weapons of the Weak: Everyday Forms of Peasant Resistance*. New Haven: Yale University Press.

Selbmann, Frank. 2016. "The 1979 Trial of the People's Revolutionary Tribunal and Implications for ECCC." In *The Extraordinary Chambers in the Courts of Cambodia: Assessing their Contribution to International Criminal Law*, edited by Simon M. Meisenberg and Ignaz Stegmiller, 77–102. Berlin/Heidelberg: Springer.

Shibuya, Eric Y. 2012. *Demobilizing Irregular Forces*. Cambridge, UK: Polity.

Short, Philip. 2006. *Pol Pot: Anatomy of a Nightmare*. New York: Henry Holt.

Slocomb, Margaret. 2001. "The K5 Gamble: National Defence and Nation Building under the People's Republic of Kampuchea." *Journal of Southeast Asian Studies* 32 (2):195–210.

Slocomb, Margaret. 2004. *The People's Republic of Kampuchea, 1979–1989: The Revolution after Pol Pot*. Chiang Mai: Silkworm Books.

Söderstrom, Johanna. 2011. "Reintegrating Ex-Combatants in Liberia: What role can DDR play for democracy?" ECAS, Uppsala.

Souyris-Roland, André. 1951. "Contribution à l'étude du culte des génies tutélaires ou 'Neak ta' ches les Cambodgiens du Sud." *BSEI* 26 (2):161–74.

Staniland, Paul. 2012. "Organizing Insurgency. Networks, Resources, and Rebellion in South Asia." *International Security* 37 (1):142–77.

Staniland, Paul. 2014. *Networks of Rebellion. Explaining Insurgent Cohesion and Collapse*. New York: Cornell University Press.

Stedman, Stephen J. 1997. "Spoiler Problems in Peace Processes." *International Security* 22 (2):5–53.

Strangio, Sebastian. 2014. *Hun Sen's Cambodia*. New Haven: Yale University Press.

Swartz, David. 2013. *Symbolic Power, Politics, and Intellectuals: The Political Sociology of Pierre Bourdieu*. Cambridge: Cambridge University Press.

Tabeau, Ewa, and They Kheam. 2009. "Demographic Expert Report: The Khmer Rouge Victims in Cambodia, April 1975–January 1979: A Critical Assessement of Major Estimates." Phnom Penh: Extraordinary Chambers in the Courts of Cambodia (ECCC).

Thibault, Christel. 2015. *L'archipel des camps. L'exemple cambodgien.* Paris: Presses Universitaires de France.

Thompson, Ashley. 2004. *Calling the Souls: A Cambodian Ritual Text.* Phnom Penh: Reyum Publishing.

Torjesen, Stina. 2013. "Towards a Theory of Ex-combatant Reintegration." *Stability: International Journal of Security and Development* 2 (3):1–13.

Torrens, Shannon M. 2016. "Allegations of Political Interference, Bias and Corruption at the ECCC." In *The Extraordinary Chambers in the Courts of Cambodia: Assessing their Contribution to International Criminal Law*, edited by Simon M. Meisenberg and Ignaz Stegmiller, 45–76. Berlin/Heidelberg: Springer.

Turner, Victor. 1969. *The Ritual Process.* London: Penguin.

Tyner, James. 2017. *From Rice Fields to Killing Fields: Nature, Life, and Labor under the Khmer Rouge* Syracuse, NY: Syracuse University Press.

UNDDR. 2017. "The Integrated DDR Standards (IDDRS)." United Nations, accessed September 14. http://www.unddr.org/iddrs.aspx.

Ung, Loung. 2005. *First They Killed My Father. A Daughter of Cambodia Remembers.* Edinburgh: Mainstream Publishing.

Uvin, Peter. 2007. Ex-combatants in Burundi. In *Working Paper*: World Bank.

Veit, Alex. 2010. *Intervention as Indirect Rule: Civil War and Statebuilding in the Democratic Republic of Congo.* Frankfurt: Campus.

Vermeij, Lotte. 2011. "Socialization and Reintegration Challenges: A Case Study of the Lord's Resistance Army." In *Child Soldiers: From Recruitment to Reintegration*, edited by Alpaslan Özerdem and Sukanya Podder, 173–190. Basingstoke: Palgrave Macmillan.

Vester-Lange, Andrea. 2007. *Habitus der Volksklassen.* Münster/Hamburg/London: LIT.

Vinci, Anthony. 2007. "'Like Worms in the Entrails of a Natural Man': A Conceptual Analysis of Warlords." *Review of African Political Economy* 34 (112):313–31.

Wang, Jianwei. 1996. Managing arms in peace processes: Cambodia. Geneva: United Nations Institute for Disarmament Research (UNIDIR).

Widyono, Benny. 2008. *Dancing in the Shadows: Sihanouk, the Khmer Rouge, and the United Nations in Cambodia.* New York: Rowman & Littlefield.

Willemyns, Alex, and Reaksmey Hul. 2014. "Once Pol Pot's Aide, Now a Capitalist Crusader." *The Cambodia Daily*, October, 28, 2014.

Williams, Timothy, and Rhiannon Neilsen. 2016. "'They Will Rot the Society, Rot the Party, and Rot the Army.' Toxification as an Ideology and Motivation for Perpetrating Violence in the Khmer Rouge Genocide?" *Terrorism and Political Violence*:1–22.

Willibald, Sigrid. 2006. "Does money work?" *Disasters* 30 (3):316–339.

Winslow, Donna. 1998. "Misplaced Loyalties: The Role of Military Culture in the Breakdown of Discipline in Peace Operations." *The Canadian Review of Sociology and Anthropology* 35 (3):345–67.

Wittgenstein, Ludwig. 2001. *Philosophical Investigations*. Oxford: Blackwell Publishing.
Wood, Elisabeth Jean. 2008. "The Social Processes of Civil War: The Wartime Transformation of Social Networks." *Annual Review of Political Science* 11:539–61.
Ysa, Osman. 2006. *The Cham Rebellion: Survivors' Stories From the Villages*. Phnom Penh: Documentation Center of Cambodia.
Zukerman Daly, Sarah. 2016. *Organizing Violence after Civil War: The Geography of Recruitment in Latin America*. New York: Cambridge University Press.

INTERVIEWS CITED IN THE TEXT

ABC-FUNCINPEC. -1. "Interview with an Assistant of a Brigade Commander, FUNCINPEC. February 29, 2016. Original in English. Place: Lowell, USA."
BAC-FUNCINPEC. -1. "Interview with a Battalion Commander, FUNCINPEC. June 13, 2015. Original in Khmer. Place: Battambang."
BAC-FUNCINPEC. -2. "Interview with a Battalion Commander, FUNCINPEC. June 13, 2015. Original in Khmer. Place: Camp Village, Battambang."
BAC-KPNLF. -1. "Interview with a Battalion Commander, KPNLF. August 1, 2015. Original in Khmer. Place: Phnom Penh."
BAC-KPNLF. -2. "Interview with a Battalion Commander, KPNLF. July 24, 2015. Original in Khmer. Place: Phnom Penh."
BAC-KPNLF. -3. "Interview with a Battalion Commander, KPNLF. June 12, 2015. Original in Khmer. Place: Battambang."
BAC-KPNLF. -4. "Interview with a Battalion Commander, KPNLF. July 11, 2015. Original in Khmer. Place: Phnom Penh."
BAC-KPNLF. -5. "Interview with a Battalion Commander, KPNLF. March 18, 2012. Original in Khmer. Place: Kien Svay."
BAC-KPNLF. -6. "Interview with a Battalion Commander, FUNCINPEC. June 15, 2015. Original in Khmer. Place: Banteay Meanchey."
BAC-KPNLF. -7. "Interview with a Battalion Commander, KPNLF. July 24, 2015. Original in Khmer. Place: Phnom Penh."
BAC-KPNLF. -8. "Interview with a Military Instructor and Battalion Commander, KPNLF. June 12, 2015. Original in Khmer. Place: Battambang."
BAC-NADK. -1. "Interview with a Battalion Commander, NADK. August 9, 2015. Original in Khmer. Place: Samlaut."
BAC-NADK. -2. "Interview with a Battalion Commander, NADK. March 14, 2012. Original in Khmer. Place: Pailin."
BAC-NADK. -3. "Interview with a Battalion Commander, NADK. June 10, 2015. Original in Khmer. Place: Veal Veng."
BAC-NADK. -4. "Interview with a Battalion Commander, NADK. July 27, 2017. Original in Khmer. Place: Pagoda, Battambang Province."
BC-FUNCINPEC. -1. "Interview with a Brigade Commander, FUNCINPEC. March 1, 2012. Original in Khmer. Place: Mongkul Borey."

BC-FUNCINPEC. -2. "Interview with a Brigade Commander, FUNCINPEC. July 19, 2015. Original in Khmer. Place: Phnom Penh."
BC-FUNCINPEC. -3. "Interview with a Brigade Commander. February 22, 2012. Original in Khmer. Place: Phnom Penh."
BC-FUNCINPEC. -4. "Interview with a Brigade Commander, FUNCINPEC. August 3, 2015. Original in Khmer. Place: Phnom Penh."
BC-KPNLF. -1. "Interview with a Brigade Commander, KPNLF. June 11, 2015. Original in Khmer. Place: Borvel."
BC-KPNLF. -2. "Interview with a Brigade Commander, KPNLF. March 3, 2012. Original in Khmer. Place: Borvel."
BC-KPNLF. -3. "Interview with a Brigade Commander, KPNLF. June 15, 2015. Original in Khmer. Place: Phnom Penh."
BC-KPNLF. -4. "Interview with a Brigade Commander, KPNLF. July 17, 2015. Original in Khmer. Place: Phnom Penh."
BC-KPNLF. -5. "Interview with a Brigade Commander, KPNLF. February 29, 2016. Original in English. Place: Lowell, USA."
BC-KPNLF. -6. "Interview with a Brigade Commander, KPNLF. May 24, 2011. Original in Khmer. Place: Phnom Penh."
BC-KPNLF. -7. "Interview with a Brigade Commander, KPNLF. June 13, 2011. Original in Khmer. Place: Svay Sisophon."
BC-KPNLF. -8. "Interview with a Brigade Commander, KPNLF. April 21, 2012. Original in Khmer. Place: Phnom Penh."
BC-KPNLF. -9. "Interview with a Brigade Commander, KPNLF. June 12, 2015. Original in Khmer. Place: Battambang."
BC-NADK. 2. "Interview with a Brigade Commander, NADK. March 13, 2012. Original in Khmer. Place: Anlong Veng."
BC-NADK. -1. "Interview with a Brigade Commander, NADK. July 13, 2015. Original in Khmer. Place: Samraong."
BC-NADK. -2. "Interview with a Brigade Commander, NADK. March 13, 2012. Original in Khmer. Place: Anlong Veng."
BI-CGDK. "Buddhist Instructor for CGDK factions. August 7, 2015. Original in Khmer. Place: Phnom Penh."
BI-KPNLF. "Buddhist Instructor, KPNLF. March 6 and 16, 2012. Original in Khmer. Place: Phnom Penh."
C-CPK. -1. "Interview with a Cadre, Communist Party of Kampuchea. July 12, 2017. Original in German. Place: Berlin, Germany."
CC-FUNCINPEC. -1. "Interview with a Company Commander, FUNCINPEC. August 9, 2015. Original in Khmer. Place: Battambang."
CC-FUNCINPEC. -2. "Interview with a Company Commander, FUNCINPEC. August 2, 2015. Original in Khmer. Place: Phnom Penh."
CC-FUNCINPEC. -3. "Interview with a Company Commander, FUNCINPEC. July 13, 2015. Original in Khmer. Place: Samraong, Oddar Meanchey."
CC-KPNLF. -1. "Interview with a Company Commander, KPNLF. August 2, 2015. Original in Khmer. Place: Phnom Penh."

CC-KPNLF. -2. "Interview with a Company Commander and Intelligence Officer, KPNLF. July 28, 2015. Original in Khmer. Place: Phnom Penh."

CC-KPNLF. -3. "Interview with a Company Commander and Spiritual Advisor, KPNLF. July 1, 2011. Original in Khmer. Place: Phnom Penh."

CC-NADK. -1. "Interview with a Company Commander, NADK. March 19, 2012. Original in Khmer. Place: Kirirom."

CC-NADK. -2. "Interview with a Company Commander, NADK. July 27, 2017. Original in Khmer. Place: Pagoda, Battambang Province."

DC-FUNCINPEC. -1. "Interview with a Division Commander, FUNCINPEC. March 20, 2012. Original in Khmer. Place: Phnom Penh."

DC-FUNCINPEC. -2. "Interview with a Division Commander, FUNCINPEC. June 1, 2011. Original in Khmer. Place: Phnom Penh."

DC-FUNCINPEC. -3. "Interview with a Division Commander, FUNCINPEC. May 20, 2011. Original in English. Place: Phnom Penh."

DC-FUNCINPEC. -4. "Interview with a Division Commander, FUNCINPEC. March 20, 2012. Original in Khmer. Place: Phnom Penh."

DC-KPNLF. -1. "Interview with a Division Commander, KPNLF. March 6, 2012. March 6, 2012. Original in Khmer. Place: Phnom Penh."

DC-KPNLF. -2. "Interview with a Division Commander, KPNLF. July 11, 2011. Original in Khmer. Place: Phnom Penh."

DC-KPNLF. -3. "Interview with a Division Commander, KPNLF. July 29, 2015. Original in Khmer. Place: Phnom Penh."

DC-NADK. -1. "Interview with a Division Commander, NADK. June 18, 2015. Original in Khmer. Place: Samraong."

DC-NADK. -2. "Interview with a Division Commander, NADK. November 15, 2017. Original in Khmer. Place: Sukhothai, Thailand."

DC-NADK. -3. "Interview with a Division Commander, NADK. August 9, 2015. Original in Khmer. Place: Samlaut."

E-US. -1. "Interview with a Cambodian Intermediary for the US embassy. May 20, 2011. Original in English. Place: Phnom Penh."

E-US. -2. "Interview with a Cambodian Intermediary for the US embassy. February 20, 2016. Original in English. Place: Washington."

FC-NADK. -1. "Interview with a Female Combatant, NADK. August 1, 2015. Original in Khmer. Place: Samlaut."

FC-NADK. -2. "First Interview with a Female Combatant, NADK. July 25, 2017. Original in Khmer. Place: Pailin."

FC-NADK. -3. "Second Interview with a Female Combatant. July 25, 2017. Original in Khmer. Place: Pailin."

FC-NADK. -4. "Interview with a Female Combatant, NADK. July 24, 2017. Original in Khmer. Place: Pailin."

GBC-KPNLF. -1. "Interview with a Guard of a Brigade Commander. June 13, 2011. Original in Khmer. Place: Svay Sisophon."

GC-KPNLF. -1. "Interview with a Group Commander, KPNLF. March 12, 2012. Original in Khmer. Place: Battambang, Camp Village."

GC-KPNLF. -2. "Interview with a Group Commander, KPNLF. June 16, 2015. Original in Khmer. Place: Banteay Meanchey."

GC-KPNLF. -3. "Interview with a Group Commander, KPNLF. July 1, 2011. Original in Khmer. Place: Phnom Penh."

GC-NADK. -1. "Interview with a Group Commander, NADK. March 14, 2012. Original in Khmer. Place: Pailin."

GS-FUNCINPEC. -1. "Interview with a Member of the General Staff, FUNCINPEC. Juni 24, 2017. Original in Khmer. Place: Paris, France."

GS-KPNLF. -1. "Email Interview with member of the General Staff, KPNLF. September 2012."

LN-C. -1. "Interview with a former Lon Nol commander, rank unknown. August 9, 2016. Original in English. Place. Fresno, CA."

LN-C. -2. "Interview with a former Lon Nol commander, rank unknown. March 1, 2016. Original in Khmer. Place: Lowell, MA."

LN-LG. -1. "First Interview with a Lieutenant General under Lon Nol. August 3, 2016. Original in English. Place: Long Beach, CA."

LN-LG. -2. "Second Interview with a Lieutenant General under Lon Nol. August 3, 2016. Original in English. Place: Long Beach, CA."

LN-LG. -3. "Third Interview with a Lieutenant General under Lon Nol. August 3, 2016. Original in English. Place: Long Beach, CA."

LN-LG. -4. "Fourth Interview with a Lieutenant General under Lon Nol. August 3, 2016. Original in English. Place: Long Beach, CA."

MC-NADK. -1. "Interview with a mid-range Commander, exact rank unknown. July 25, 2017. Original in Khmer. Place: Pailin."

Missionary. 2017. "Interview with a Christian Missionary, Presbyterian Church, Pailin. July 17, 2017. Original in English."

MPA-France. -1. "Interview with a Member of a Political Association close to FUNCINPEC. June 23, 2017. Original in Khmer. Place: Paris, France."

MPA-US. -1. "Interview with a Member of a Political Association within the USA. August 8, 2016. Original in English. Place: Fresno, USA."

MS-FUNCINPEC. -1. "Interview with a Medical Staff of the Military, FUNCINPEC. February 29, 2016. Original in English. Place: Lowell, USA."

PC-FUNCINPEC. -1. "Interview with a Platoon Commander, FUNCINPEC. June 14, 2015. Original in Khmer. Place: Phnom Penh."

PL-KPNLF. -1. "Interview with a Member of the Political Leadership, KPNLF. May 30, 2011. Original in English. Place: Phnom Penh."

RC-FUNCINPEC. -1. "Interview with a Regiment Commander, FUNCINPEC. March 3, 2012. Original in Khmer. Place: Battambang."

RC-FUNCINPEC. -2. "Interview with a Regiment Commander, FUNCINPEC. August 9, 2015. Original in Khmer. Place: Camp Village, Battambang."

RC-FUNCINPEC. -3. "Interview with a Deputy Regiment Commander, FUNCINPEC. June 6, 2011. Original in Khmer. Place: Pailin."

RC-KPNLF. -1. "Interview with a Regiment Commander, KPNLF. August 5, 2015. Original in English. Place: Phnom Penh."

RC-KPNLF. -2. "Interview with a Regiment Commander, KPNLF. June 2, 2011. Original in English. Place: Phnom Penh."

RC-KPNLF. -3. "Interview with a Regiment Commander, KPNLF. February 19, 2012. Original in Khmer. Place: Phnom Penh."

RC-KPNLF. -4. "Interview with a Regiment Commander, KPNLF. February 20, 2012. Original in Khmer. Place: Phnom Penh."

RC-KPNLF. -5. "Interview with a Regiment Commander, KPNLF. March 20, 2012. Original in Khmer. Place: Phnom Penh."

RC-NADK. -1. "Interview with a Regiment Commander, NADK. March 13, 2012. Original in Khmer. Place: Anlong Veng."

RC-NADK. -2. "Interview with a Regiment Commander, NADK. March 14, 2012. Original in Khmer. Place: Anlong Veng."

RF-KPNLF. -1. "Interview with a Rank-and-File Soldier, KPNLF. August 9, 2015. Original in Khmer. Place: Camp Village, Battambang."

RF-KPNLF. -2. "Interview with a Rank-and-File Soldier, KPNLF. August 9, 2015. Original in Khmer. Place: Battambang, Camp Village."

RF-KPNLF. -3. "Interview with a Rank-and-File Soldier, KPNLF. July 13, 2015. Original in Khmer. Place: Samraong."

RF-MF. -3. "Interview with a Rank-and-File Soldier, Multiple Factions. June 14, 2015. Original in Khmer. Place: Camp Village, Battambang."

RF-MF. -4. "Interview with a Rank-and-File Soldier. July 13, 2015. Original in Khmer. Place: Samraong, Oddar Meanchey."

RF-MF. -5. "Interview with a Rank-and-File Soldier, Multiple Factions. July 13, 2015. Original in Khmer. Place: Samraong."

RF-NADK. -1. "Interview with a Rank-and-File Soldier, NADK. August 9, 2015. Original in Khmer. Place: Samlaut."

RF-NADK. -2. "Interview with a Rank-and-File Soldier, NADK. March 2, 2012. Original in Khmer. Place: Pailin."

RF-NADK. -3. "Interview with a Rank-and-File Soldier, Khmer Rouge. July 13, 2015. Original in Khmer. Place: Samraong, Oddar Meanchey."

RF-NADK. -4. "First interview with a Rank-and-File Soldier, NADK. June 6, 2015. Original in Khmer. Place: Talo Commune."

RF-NADK. -5. "Second interview with a Rank-and-File Soldier. June 6, 2015. Original in Khmer. Place: Talo Commune."

RF-NADK. -6. "Interview with a Rank-and-File Soldier, NADK. February 25, 2016. Original in Khmer. Place: Lowell, MA."

SC-KPNLF. -1. "Interview with a Section Commander, KPNLF. June 16, 2015. Original in Khmer. Place: Banteay Meanchey."

SC-KPNLF. -2. "Interview with a Section Commander, KPNLF. June 11, 2015. Original in Khmer. Place: Battambang."

SC-KPNLF. -3. "Interview with a Section Commander, KPNLF. June 13, 2015. Original in Khmer. Place: Camp Village, Battambang."

SC-KPNLF. -4. "Interview with a Section Commander, KPNLF. March 11, 2012. Original in Khmer. Place: Battambang, Camp Village."

SC-NADK. -1. "Interview with a Section Commander, NADK. August 9, 2015. Original in Khmer. Place: Samlaut."

ARCHIVE MATERIAL

Anon. 1993a. "Conversation with Nhek Bunchhay." In *The John Sanderson Manuscript Collection*: Australian Defence Force Academy, UNSW Canberra.

Anon. 1993b. "Meeting with Khieu Samphan. President of the Party of Democratic Kampuchea (PDK) [Transcript of a Conversation with General John Sanderson]." In *The John Sanderson Manuscript Collection*: Australian Defence Force Academy, UNSW Canberra.

Anon. 1993c. "Talk with four NADK soldiers." In *The John Sanderson Manuscript Collection*: Australian Defence Force Academy, UNSW Canberra.

Bernander, Bernt. 1993. "Statistics on Demobilized Soldiers," Report by the Director for Rehabilitation to Mr. Y. Akashi. In *The John Sanderson Manuscript Collection*: Australian Defence Force Academy, UNSW Canberra.

Chan, Youran. 2009. "Written Record of Interview of Witness. Extraordinary Chambers in the Courts of Cambodia (ECCC), December 16, 2009. File: E3/46."

Im, Nguon. 1993. "Interview with Im Nguon, September 3, 1993." In *The John Sanderson Manuscript Collection*: Australian Defence Force Academy, UNSW Canberra.

Long, Dany. 2010. "Humanizing Perpetrators: Is It Possible?" The DC-CAM's Promoting Accountability Field Trip Report, Malai District. Documentation Center of Cambodia.

Military Information Branch. 1993. "Report." In *The John Sanderson Manuscript Collection*, edited by United Nations Transitional Authority: Australian Defence Force Academy, UNSW Canberra.

Roeurn. 1992. "Interviews with NADK Defectors from Divisions 95 and 909 at Banbatt Site 209 (Report)." In *The John Sanderson Manuscript Collection*: Australian Defence Force Academy, UNSW Canberra.

Saroeun, Tap. 1993. "Interview." In *The John Sanderson Manuscript Collection*: Australian Defence Force Academy, UNSW Canberra.

Siv, Nin. 1993.

Suoy, Lat. 2011. "Interview with Lat Suoy. Documentation Center of Cambodia, Interview Series, No. 3. Interviewer: Dany Long, Translator: Chy Therith."

Tun, Rochoem. 2010. "Interview with Rochoem Tun, alias Phi Phuon and Chiem. Date: December 19, 2010. Place: Malai district. Interviewer: Dany Long. Translated by Sok-Sreinith Ten. Phnom Penh: Documentation Center of Cambodia."

Index

About the Author

Daniel Bultmann is a researcher and teaching assistant at the Institute of Asian and African Studies at the Humboldt University of Berlin and a research fellow at the Department of Social Sciences at the University of Siegen, both in Germany. His research focuses on the sociology of peace and conflict, the social structure of armed groups, the study of collective violence, the analysis of social inequalities, the sociology of the body and its relation to different torture regimes, and the history and society of modern Southeast Asia, Cambodia in particular. He is currently a Visiting Fellow at the MacMillan Center at Yale University, where he is working on a collaborative project on body knowledge and torture practices under the Khmer Rouge.